J. Cushing Daniel

REAL MONEY

versus

FALSE MONEY—BANK CREDITS

The Most Important Factor in Civilization and
Least Understood by the People

BY

T. CUSHING DANIEL

Fredonia Books
Amsterdam, The Netherlands

Real Money versus False Money — Bank Credits:
The Most Important Factor in Civilization and Least
Understood by the People

by
T. Cushing Daniel

ISBN: 1-4101-0472-9

Reprinted from the 1924 edition

Fredonia Books
Amsterdam, The Netherlands
http://www.fredoniabooks.com

Maxim of the Money Lenders of the Old World:

"Let us control the money of a country
and we care not who makes its laws."

PREFACE

The greatest burdens that the people have to bear are interest and dividends on debts.

In 1911 we published "Daniel on Real Money." In this book the "false gold standard" of money is proven to be an economic fallacy of the most ruinous character to the people of the world, yet taught by the professors of Political Economy in the leading Universities.

The old Sophistries of "Intrinsic value of Gold," "the ratio and parity of gold and silver," fiat money, etc., are absolutely annihilated for all time.

In 1912 we published by the same author "High Cost of Living, Cause—Remedy." Giving the history of the infamous legislation by Congress that established the false gold standard in the United States, resulting in billions of dollars of interest and dividend bearing debts being put upon the resources and people of the United States, now amounting to over one hundred billion dollars. Upon a 5 per cent. basis of interest and dividends it makes an annual charge or tax upon the people of $5,000,000,000, which is now being added to the price of the things the people buy and use and in the "High Cost of Living" is absorbing all the earnings of the people.

In 1916 we published by the same author "The Betrayal of the People," an exposure of The Federal Reserve Banking Scheme enlarging the powers and privileges of the money trust, showing that the prosperity of banks under this scheme is built upon the ruin of the people.

In 1917 we published "The Real Issue, Democracy Against Plutocracy."

In 1919 we published by the same author "No Plutocratic Peace But A Democratic Victory."

We now publish a new edition of "Daniel On Real Money," condensing the most valuable parts of the foregoing publications in one volume and bringing this most vital question down to date as a text book for the people.

Mr. Daniel demonstrates that present conditions have been brought about by a dishonest money system, and the establishment of an honest money system in the interest of the people is the only cure.

In this book the author explains the remedy. He strips the whole subject of all its damnable sophistries, and states eternal verities directly to the people in order that they may, by their votes in the coming elections, protect themselves, their families, and save this Republic.

THE MONETARY EDUCATIONAL BUREAU,
WASHINGTON. D. C.

FOREWORD

In publishing this book after Mr. Daniel's death, which occurred Dec. 21, 1923, I would like to tell a few facts about his work for monetary reform.

So many have asked what personal profit or what preferment did he expect that I want them and all readers of this book to know his motive in taking up this work for the financial independence of the people, was the conviction, after many years of earnest thought and investigation, that a correct solution of the money problem would do most in solving the economic evils of our time, bringing relief to the people.

Shortly after the Civil War, as a young man, Mr. Daniel started a store in Fredericksburg, Va. On market days the farmers would come to town from the surrounding country and stop at his store to buy. They had so little to spend after their produce had been sold, that he began to wonder why the farmers received such a small return for their hard labor. He would go over to the "Wagon Yard" to talk to them, endeavoring to find the cause of their meager pay.

This was the beginning of his investigations, which extended over forty years in this country and in Europe. This book, which is a condensation and bringing to date of his other works, is the result. He was working on it up to a few days of his death. In preparing it for publication I have carried out his idea as nearly as possible.

I trust that those who realize the great financial fraud exposed in this book will not rest until they have done their part in educating others and bringing their influence to bear on their representatives in Congress to free the country from this economic curse, and to establish an honest money system in the interest of all the people of these United States.

JULIA R. W. DANIEL.

CONTENTS

REAL MONEY
versus
FALSE MONEY—BANK CREDITS

THE TRUE DEFINITION OF MONEY

The economic principles stated in this book are fundamental and of universal application. A dishonest money system is the underlying cause of present conditions, and the establishment of an honest money system is the only remedy.

I will first state the correct conclusions reached by the great disinterested authorities, giving the true Definition of Money and what constitutes the standard of value in a money system.

The great Aristotle, whose complete neglect of artistic forms and his adherence to "essential naked truths" induced Dante to speak of him as "the master of those that know" and placed him as the center and head of the philosophic family, speaking of the function of money, says, in "Ethics":

"Intercourse takes place between people having different objects of desire. In order that they may be exchanged with each other it is necessary that they should be compared, for which purpose money came forward and is as it were a medium, for it measures everything, both the excess and the defect; as, for instance, how many pairs of shoes will be equal to a house or to food; for if this is not done there will be no exchange or intercourse. All things, therefore, must be measured; but it is, in truth, want which holds all things together, for if persons wanted nothing from each other, or not equally, there would be

1

no exchange. Money, then, has been made, by agreement as it were, a substitute for demand, and is so called because it exists not by nature, but by law, and it is in our power to change it and make it useless for the purpose. If it were not possible to exchange there would be no commerce. If a man requires nothing at the present time money is, as it were, a surety to him for a future exchange that it shall be made when he wants it. But money itself is not always of the same value, but yet it has more tendency to remain fixed, wherefore everything ought to be appraised, for so there will be exchange. Money, 'like a measure, makes things equal'; for if there were no exchange there would be no intercourse, nor any exchange if there were no equality, nor any equality if there were no common measure. In truth, it is impossible that things differing so much should be commensurate, but for practical use it is sufficiently possible. Money makes all things commensurable, 'for all things are measured by money.' "

Hobbes in his "Nutrition of a Commonwealth" speaks of money as a measure—

"By means of which measure all commodities, movable and immovable, are made to accompany a man to all places of resort, within and without the place of his ordinary residence, and the same passeth from man to man within the commonwealth, and goes round about, nourishing as it passes every part thereof, insomuch as this concoction is as it were the sanguinification of the commonwealth. . . . By concoction I understand the reduction of all commodities which are not presently consumed, but reserved for nourishment in time to come, to something of equal value."

"When we speak of the value of either gold or silver we mean the 'power it has to purchase other commodities,' including the one element of money besides itself. Economists have been wont to make this distinction between value and price: 'Value is purchasing power—power in exchange'; price is the power to purchase money—it is the money value of commodities. Money itself, then, while it has value (the value of a given amount of money 'being measured by the quantity of commodities it will purchase') has not price.'' (Prof. Francis A. Walker, "Money," pages 229 and 230.)

"The value of money is, to appearance, an expression as precise, as free from possibility of misunderstanding as any in science. The value of a thing is 'what it will exchange for'; the value of money is what money will exchange for—'the purchasing power of money.' If prices are low, money will buy much of other things, and is of high value; if prices are high, it will buy little of other things, and is of low value. The value of money is inversely as general prices, falling as they rise, and rising as they fall.'' (John Stuart Mill, "Political Economy," Book III, Chapter 8.)

Professor Fawcett, professor of political economy, University of Cambridge, speaking of the term "value" when applied to money, says:

"When, therefore, in political economy the precious metals or the value of money is spoken of, 'the purchasing power' of money is referred to; or in other words the 'power of money to obtain other commodities in exchange for it.'

"It must, therefore, be distinctly borne in mind that although men of business consider the value of money to be represented by the rate of interest, yet the signification which is here attached to the money is such as to describe the value of money to be great when prices are low, and to be small when prices are high.'' ("Political Economy," page 364.)

No Such Thing as Intrinsic Value

What the Leading Authorities Say

"There is no such thing as intrinsic value.'' (Prof. Jevons, "Essay on Value of Gold.")

"There cannot, in short, be 'intrinsically' a more insignificant thing in the economy of society than money.'' (John Stuart Mill, "Principles of Political Economy," volume ii, page 23.)

"This author is led astray by the worse than useless

adjective 'intrinsic,' having never yet learned that there is only one kind of value in economics, namely, purchasing power.'' (Prof. Perry, ''Principles of Political Economy,'' page 341.)

Mr. MacLeod, speaking of the expression ''intrinsic value,'' says:

''This unhappy phrase meets us at every turn in economics, and yet the slightest reflection will show that to define value to be something 'external,' and then to be constantly speaking of 'intrinsic' value are utterly self-contradictory and inconsistent ideas. Thus over and over again it is repeated in economical treatises that money has intrinsic value, but that a bill of exchange or bank note is only the representative of value.

''Money no doubt is the produce of labor, but, as Adam Smith observed, if it would exchange for nothing it would have no value; so, M. Say says, that the value of gold and silver consists only in what they will buy. How then can its value be intrinsic? How can anything have intrinsic value unless it has the thing it will exchange for 'inside itself'? 'Money has intrinsic value!' Has a piece of money got the merchandise, and all the other things it will purchase inside itself? Money will exchange for anything—corn, houses, horses, carriages, books, etc., and each of these is the value of the money with respect to that commodity. But which of these is its intrinsic value? The incongruity of these ideas is so glaring that it is only necessary to call attention to it for it to be perceived at once. 'Yet from the very beginning of the science this phrase has infested it.'

''Moreover, we see on considering the term 'value' that it is nonsense to speak of the 'representative' of value. Value is a 'ratio'—an external relation. What can be the 'representative of a ratio,' or of an external relation? To say that money, because it is material and the product of labor, has intrinsic value, and that a bank-note is only the representative of value, is just as absurd as to say that a wooden yard measure is 'intrinsic' distance, and that the space of thirty-six inches between two points is 'representative' distance. It is of the first importance to economic science to exterminate this unhappy phrase 'intrinsic value,' which is clearly shown to be a contradiction in terms." (MacLeod, "Theory and Practice of Banking," 1, 50.)

Ricardo, one of the highest authorities, speaking of paper money says—

"By 'limiting its quantity' its value in exchange is as great as an equal denomination of coin, or of bullion in that coin.

"Money is to be known by its doing a certain work. Money is not gold, though gold may be money; sometimes gold is money and sometimes it is not. Money is no one thing, no group of many things having any material property in common. On the contrary, 'anything may be money'; and anything, in a given time and place, is money, which then and there performs a certain function. 'Always and everywhere, that which does the money work is the money thing.'"

"The claim that legal tender paper money is not money in the fullest sense of that term; that it cannot do all in the way of measuring values, so called, which gold or silver may do, is untenable, and it can be of no advantage to any really sound cause to seek to maintain it." (General Francis A. Walker, "Money, in Its Relations to Trade and Industry," Chapter 1, and Preface.)

INFLUENCE OF COST OF PRODUCTION ON THE VALUE OF MONEY

"In consequence of the great durability of gold, together with the fact that 'nearly all the gold used as money is practically in the market at any given time,' any change in the cost of production is likely to take a long time to produce its full effect on value. Hence the effects of all changes in the conditions of production of the precious metals are at first, and continue to be for many years, 'questions of quantity only, with little reference to cost of production.'" (Henry Sidgwick, "Principles of Political Economy," page 250.)

Again, it is said, it is the cost of production which determines value. "But it is always and everywhere the relation of the supply to demand that determines value.

Cost of production only affects value by affecting the actual or potential supply.'' (Prof. Francis A. Walker, "Money," page 245.)

"Labor once spent has no influence on the future value of an article." (Prof. Jevons, "Theory of Political Economy," page 159.)

"The great principal of cost and production fails us, because in the case of such durable commodities as gold and silver the accumulated stock on hand is immensely greater than the annual production or consumption." (Prof. Jevons, "Contemporary Review," May, 1881.)

"From their durability, the total quantity in existence is at all times so great in proportion to the annual supply that the effect on value even of a change in the cost of production is not sudden, a very long time being required to diminish materially the quantity in existence, and even to increase it very greatly not being a rapid process." (Stuart Mill, "Political Economy," Book 3, Chapter 7.)

"Alterations, therefore, in the cost of production of the precious metals do not act upon the value of money except just in proportion as they increase or diminish its quantity." (John Stuart Mill, "Political Economy," Chapter 9, Book 3.)

"Cost of production, so important and decisive as to the value of commodities bought with money, is, in the case of money itself, of no account whatever. For, any particular commodity we can do without; and so if it costs too much to produce no one will buy it, 'but money must be had at all costs, for without it no commodities can be procured at all.' And be it observed, money is comparatively permanent. It is not, like commodities in general, consumed in the use. Consequently there is a great and even enormous difference between it and things produced to be consumed. It is, as a rule, the rapidly perishing commodity whose value depends mainly on its cost of production. Each time it is wanted it must be made again. But money, once made, is there for almost any length of time, for though it wastes a little, yet not much; its value, therefore, can be hardly, if at all, appreciably dependent on its cost of production." (F. W. Bain, M.A., "The Principle of Wealth-Creation," page 101.)

It Is the Money Use That Gives Value to Gold

"The fundamental cause of value in the precious metals is 'their use as currency.' This conclusion is not so obvious as it might appear. Up to recently ordinary political economists have been accustomed to accept Mr. Senior's dictum, that the measure of value in the precious metals is their use in the arts. It is very possible that this view is still accepted, notwithstanding the experience of the last fifteen years, during which events have occurred which would, one might think, induce these people to reconsider their conclusion." (Thorold Rogers, Prof. P. E., Oxford University, "Industrial and Commercial History of England," page 324.)

"Gold and silver owe almost the whole of their value to the fact that they can be converted into and used as money. If gold and silver were absolutely excluded from the currency of the world their value would be greatly reduced, if it did not almost entirely cease to exist; and if either gold or silver were largely excluded from the currency of the world the value of the metal so excluded would experience a very great fall.

"The value of gold and silver is almost entirely due to their use as money and consequently the relative value of gold and silver depends upon the extent to which the different nations of the world use these metals as currency. If one nation after another decided to demonetize silver and to sell the silver contained in its currency, the value of silver relatively to commodities and still more so in comparison to gold, could be made to fall to a very small fraction of its present value.

"On the other hand, if the nations of the world demonetized 'gold,' and sold their gold, the value of gold in relation to silver would experience a very great fall.

"In short, we see that the demand for gold or silver is due mainly to the extent to which the legislatures of the different countries decide to use these metals as money, and, therefore, their relative value is and must continue to be regulated by legislation." (David Barbour, "Metallic Money," Chapter 2, page 34.)

"Gold and silver have real and artificial values—real and natural, as for gilding, for use in surgical appliances, forks, spoons, and other things; artificial for money for circulating mediums.

"This artificial value is much greater than the real (value). If some substitute for gold and silver were found which could be used more advantageously as money and displace them, their exchangeable values would be vastly less than at present. That is, if an ounce of gold exchanges for two quarters of wheat now anywhere, it would, if it ceased to be used as money, exchange for much less—how much is beyond speculation." (Lord Bramwell.)

"In so far as it (gold) has 'legal exchangeable value' its worth as a commodity is increased. We want no gold in the form of dust or crystal; but we seek for it 'coined,' because in that form it will pay baker and butcher. And this worth in exchange not only absorbs a large quantity in that use, but greatly increases the effect on the imagination of quantity used in the arts." (John Ruskin, "Munera Pulveris," page 83.)

"No doubt, if gold and silver were demonetized in every country, metallic money would lose the greatest part of its value. We must not deceive ourselves as to this matter, and the present fall in silver, caused by its demonetization in some countries, only too fully proves the fact. Yet many authors do harbor this illusion, or at any rate do not put their readers on their guard against it. Most of them seem to say that the government seal stamped upon gold and silver coins merely states their actual value, just as the tickets tradesmen put on their goods. But the declaration that the six gramme gold piece is worth twenty francs is not only 'declaratory,' but it is also determinative of value. It is because the will of the legislator, or, if it is preferred, the agreement of men, has chosen gold and silver as money, that these metals have acquired the larger part of their value, and they would lose it as soon as this agreement or this law happened to cease to exist. Aristotle, too, had perceived this very clearly. Says he in the 'Ethics,' Book V: 'It was through a voluntary agreement that money became the instrument of exchange. It is called 'nomisma' (from 'nomos,' law) because money is not a natural product, but exists only through law, and it lies with us to change it and rob it of its utility as we will.' " (Prof. Gide, "Political Economy," page 216.)

KEY TO THE MONETARY PROBLEMS

"The origin of buying and selling," says Paulus, "goes back to barter. Primitively, there was no money. One thing was not called 'merchandise' and the other 'price,' but every one, according to his needs, and according to his circumstances, bartered things useless to him for those which would be useful to him; for it often happens that what one has too much of, another lacks. But, as it would not always or easily happen that you had what I should have wished for, and that, conversely, I had what you wished to obtain, choice was made of a material which, being declared 'forever legal value,' would obviate the difficulties of barter 'by means of a quantitative equation.' And this material, stamped in the corner by the State, circulates with a power which it derives 'not from the substance but from the quantity.' Since that time, of the things thus exchanged, one is called merchandise, and the other is called price." (Paulus, "The Roman Jurisconsult."—Incorporated in Pandects of Justinian.)

"Money, while the same quantity of it is passing up and down the kingdom of trade, is really a standing measure of the falling and rising value of other things in reference to one another, and the alteration in price is truly in them only. But if you increase or lessen the quantity of money current in traffic in any place, 'then the alteration of value is in the money.'

"The value of money in any one country is the present quantity of the current money in that country in proportion to present trade." (Locke.)

"It is not difficult to perceive that it is the total quantity of the money in circulation in any country which determines what portion of that quantity shall exchange for a certain portion of the goods or commodities of that country. It is the proportion between the circulating money and the commodities in the market which determines the price." (David Hume.)

"If the quantity of purchasable articles increases while the quantity of money remains the same, the value of the money increases in the same ratio; if the quantity of money increases while the quantity of purchasable articles remains the same, the value of the money decreases in the same ratio." (Fichte.)

"And again, in whatever degree, therefore, the quantity of money is increased or diminished, other things remaining the same, in that same proportion the value of the whole and of every part is reciprocally diminished or increased." (John Stuart Mill, "Political Economy.")

"The value of money, other things being the same, varies inversely as its quantity; every increase of quantity lowering the value, and every diminution raising it in a ratio exactly equivalent." (John Stuart Mill, "Political Economy.")

"Alterations in the cost of the production of the precious metals do not act upon the value of money, except just in proportion as they increase or diminish its quantity." (John Stuart Mill.)

"The value of money in any country is determined by the amount existing. That commodities would rise or fall in price in proportion to the increase or diminution of money I assume as a fact that is incontrovertible.

"We have seen, however, that even in the case of metallic currency the immediate agency in determining its value is its quantity." (John Stuart Mill, "Principles of Political Economy," Volume 2, page 89.)

"If the quantity of gold in a country whose currency consists of gold should be increased in any given proportion, the quantity of other articles and the demand for them remaining the same, the value of any given commodity measured in the coin of that country would be increased in the same proportion." (William Huskisson.)

"The value of money is in the inverse ratio of its quantity; the supply of commodities remaining the same." (Sir James Graham.)

"If the value of all other commodities, in relation to gold, rises and falls as their quantities diminish or increase, the value of gold in relation to commodities must rise and fall as its quantity is diminished or increased." (Torrens, "Political Economy.")

"The rate at which money exchanges for other things is determined by its quantity. . . . Supposing the amount of trade and mode of circulation to remain stationary, if the quantity of money be increased its value will fall and the price of other commodities will proportionately rise, as the latter will then exchange against a greater amount of money; if, on the other hand, the quantity of money be reduced, its value will be raised, and prices in corresponding degree diminished, as commodities will then have to be exchanged for a less amount of money. . . . In whatever degree, therefore, the quantity of money is increased or diminished, other things remaining the same, in that same proportion the value of the whole and of every part is reciprocally diminished or increased." (Prof. DeColange.)

"The exchange value of any particular coin will vary in exactly inverse ratio to the variations in quantity of the aggregate." (Prof. Sidgwick, "Principles of Political Economy," page 251.)

"There is plenty of evidence to prove that an inconvertible paper money, if carefully limited in quantity, can retain its full value. Such was the case with the Bank of England notes for several years after the suspension of specie payments in 1797, and such is the case with the present notes of the Bank of France." (Prof. Stanley Jevons.)

"A well regulated paper currency is so great an improvement in commerce that I should greatly regret if prejudice should induce us to return to a system of less utility. The introduction of the precious metals for the purposes of money may with truth be considered as one of the most important steps toward the improvement of commerce and the arts of the civilized life; but it is no less true, that with the 'advancement of knowledge and science,' we discover that it would be 'another improvement to banish them again from the employment to which, during a less enlightened period, they had been so advantageously applied.' (Ricardo.)

"He (Ricardo) examined the circumstances which determine the value of money, . . . and he showed that its value will depend on 'The extent to which it may be issued' compared with the demand. This is a principle of great importance, for it shows that 'intrinsic worth is not necessary to a currency,' and that, provided the supply of paper notes declared to be a legal tender 'be sufficiently limited,' their value may be maintained on a par with the value of gold, or raised to any higher level. If, therefore, it were practicable to devise a plan for preserving the value of paper on a level with that of gold, without making it convertible into coin at the pleasure of the holder, the heavy expense of metallic currency would be saved.

"It appears, therefore, that if there were security that the power of issuing paper money would not be abused; that is, if there were perfect security for its being issued in such quantities as to preserve its value relatively to the mass of circulating commodities nearly equal, the precious metals might be entirely dispensed with, not only as a circulating medium, but also as a standard to which to refer the value of paper." (Mr. J. R. McCulloch "on Ricardo.")

"In adopting a paper circulation we must unavoidably depend for a maintenance of its due value upon the adoption of a strict and judicious rule for the regulation of its amount."—Lord Overstone.

"The reduction of paper would produce all those effects which arise from the reduction in the amount of the money in any country."—Alexander Baring.

"By limiting its quantity its value in exchange is as great as an equal denomination of coin, or of bullion in that coin.

"There is no point more important in issuing paper money than to be fully impressed with the effects which follow from the principle of limitation of quantity."—Ricardo.

"In discussing the laws of price, the principle was established that general prices depend upon the quantity of money in circulation compared with the wealth which is bought and sold before it is consumed. If more wealth is produced and an increased quantity of wealth is bought and sold for money, general prices must decline unless a larger quantity of money is brought into circulation."

The amount of money required to be kept in circulation depends upon the amount of wealth which is exchanged for money. Hence, "cæteris paribus, the amount of money ought to increase as the population and wealth of a country advance."—Prof. Fawcett, "Political Economy," page 371.

CORRECT DEFINITION OF A STANDARD

Gold, the false basis of credit money, annihilated by the logic of common sense.

When James Watt, the celebrated Scottish civil engineer, the inventor of condensing steam, tried to ascertain what could be properly called the dimension of an ounce, he found that as many as fifty different ounces were in common use. There was no standard in weights or measures—no universal ounce nor yardstick.

There was at one time more than twenty different measures of length—practically an unknown variety of foot-rules, so that twelve inches in one country might not be twelve inches in another. This condition and confusion made it absolutely necessary for the world to have a worldwide set of standards in order to carry on business and the people be able to buy and sell to one another.

This being the case, the representatives of the United States, Great Britain, Russia, Italy, Austria, Turkey, and Spain convened in Paris in 1870, but no definite action was taken. In 1872 men of scientific knowledge from thirty nations met in Paris and decided that new meters and new kilograms should be made to constitute the standard of the countries concerned. This was to fix international measure for these countries of length and mass. In 1875 a permanent international bureau of weights and measures was created. Thirty meters and forty kilograms were constructed among the different countries represented.

Two meters and two kilograms were numbered and sent to the United States and they are now locked up in the vault of the building of Standards of Weights and

Measures at Washington and they are the standards from which we make our yard and pound terms, simply translated from French into English.

In like manner the troy pound to regulate the coinage of metal into money, was obtained from England in 1827. It is made of brass and now kept in the mint of Philadelphia and constitutes the Standard Weight by which our coinage is governed. Albert Gallatin, American Minister to Great Britain, sent it to the United States.

On the arrival of this standard troy pound from England John Quincy Adams, President of the United States, went to Philadelphia and, breaking the seal, declared the weight to be a copy of the imperial troy pound of Great Britain.

I desire to make plain and rivet in the mind of the reader that this troy pound is simply a standard by which the metal gold is weighed when it is coined into a dollar, or measures how many grains of gold will be equivalent to a dollar according to law. It measures this gold just as it would measure the pound of any other material substance, and just as the yardstick would measure thirty-six inches of cloth or anything else. The metal gold in the dollar does not measure the value of the dollar, the purchasing power of the dollar is measured by the dollar and by the price of the thing it will buy.

And the value of the dollar when compared to other things depends upon the quantity of dollars out. Therefore the quantity of dollars constitutes the standard, affecting general prices, and not the gold in or out of the dollar.

If the dollars in a currency system are few in number the "standard" will be high and prices of other things low.

If the dollars be many the "standard" of value will be low, and the prices of other things high. It is only necessary to state this to prove it.

It would be just as logical to say that a yardstick made of gold would make the gold in the yardstick a standard of length instead of the thirty-six inches in the yard being the standard of the yard, as applied to length, or that if you destroy the gold yardstick and only had yardsticks left made of steel, the "standard" of length, thirty-six inches, would be destroyed. It would be just as reasonable to contend that the clock made of gold would constitute gold the "standard" of time. Or that the bushel measure made of gold would constitute gold the "standard" of its cubical contents.

The yardstick in the Bureau of Standards at Washington is declared by law to be the model for all other yardsticks, is made of bronze, but bronze is not a "standard of length."

Stripped of all sophistry, the gold dollar truly means that when gold the metal is coined into an American dollar, the said dollar shall contain in weight so many grains of the metal gold. It is simply a standard for this purpose.

A dollar does not change—50 cents cannot be one dollar, or 200 cents be one dollar, any more than eighteen inches could ever measure a yard, or seventy-two inches be less than two yards.

The law thus fixed the quantity of the metal gold going into the dollar, or how much gold is worth a dollar, but the gold does not fix the value or purchasing power of the dollar. An economic law far more universal fixes the value or purchasing power of the dollar, that of demand and supply.

Confounding the idea of money with measures of other things, such as pounds in weight and yards in measurement, it was attempted to establish a universal money unit such as the universal yardstick. It was taken up and discussed at the International Monetary Conferences, but finally abandoned as an absurdity, as the value of money depends upon its quantity and what is back of it for its redemption, and for that reason there can be no universal standard, such as a yardstick or pound, applied to money.

It was discussed and a resolution passed Congress in 1856 on the subject, discussed again in the International Conference of 1867. In the International Conference of 1878 at Paris it was shown that the United States Government cared nothing for the international unit of money.

Confounding the idea of money, the creation of a sovereign power, with the standard weight, a material substance, used as a standard by which gold and silver should be weighed, has up to the present time constituted the absolutely false basis called a gold standard upon which a most indefensible money system has been established.

The premises being false the whole system or super-structure is like a house built upon shifting sands, and this is demonstrated by the feverish conditions of the money market, never at rest, constantly changing the value of the dollar and the rate of interest on same, eternally varying, and the whole system breaking down in panics, the inevitable result of a narrow and false foundation, upon which an inverted pyramid of credit money or prom-ises to pay have been emitted by banks of issue.

The first essential of a correct monetary system as far as possible is a dollar unfluctuating in its purchasing and debt paying power and a low and unchanging rate of in-terest upon loans.

We have just the reverse under the present so-called "gold standard" system.

THE BANK OF ENGLAND

Reply of the governor of the Bank of England to our National Monetary Commission, 1910.

A. *"The Bank of England regulates the conditions under which the trade of the country is carried on, and imposes a charge on the trade of the country for legitimate accommodations."*

In order to show the relation of gold from an economic standpoint I will first trace it in England, recognized to be its stronghold. For England is more responsible for maintaining the so-called gold standard than all other countries. She opposed any departure from it in all the international conferences held in Europe. McLeod in his work on "History of Banking in England," page 18, states: "The Directors of the banks of England took alarm, and, as the Minister was in want of supply, they took advantage of the necessities to obtain a prolongation of their monopoly. The charter had still twelve years to run, but upon their advancing £3,000,000 ($15,000,000) without interest for six years Mr. Pitt agreed to renew it for twenty-one years from 1812. In 1800 an act to effect this was passed.

Statements of the Governor and Directors of the Bank of England in answer to questions of the American Monetary Commission, page 12, 1910.

A. "The Government debt of £11,015,100, which appears as an asset in the issue department, is the balance which was outstanding in 1884 of amounts which had been advanced to the Government and which, by the act of that year, the bank is empowered to include in the securities against which notes are issued."

Page 7. "The bank's exclusive privileges of banking continue subject to one year's notice and to repayment by the Government of the debt of £11,015,100—and all other public debt held by the bank at the time."

The original proprietor's capital in 1694 was £1,200,-

000 ($6,000,000), and has been increased at various times between 1694 and 1816, bringing the total up to £14,553,-000 ($72,765,000), at which figures it still remains. "The increases in capital have mostly been for the purpose of advancing money to the Government. In 1816, when the last increase in the bank's capital took place, the Government debt due to the bank was more than the entire capital of the bank, £14,686,800" ($73,434,000).

Thus the money lenders placed in bondage the English Government and its people, and the greatest act of sovereignty, the right to issue money, passed into the absolute control of a private corporation known as "The Bank of England."

Q. "Has the Government any voice in the management of the bank or any interest in it through the ownership of shares?

A. "The Government has no voice in the management of the bank nor does it own any stock."

The Government cannot revoke the charter of this corporation until it pays all its obligations to the bank. The record will show that the debt due by the Government has increased from £11,015,100 to £14,686,800 and is now going ahead of the increased capitalization of the bank. Therefore, the right of the Government to issue money has gone, so long as the Government is in debt to the Bank of England, and this will be the case indefinitely, as the national debt of the British Empire is $7,875,347,645 (Statesman's Year Book, 1910) and the bank can increase its holdings at any time. She can, therefore, never expect to rid herself of the Bank of England, short of repudiation of her debt.

There is nothing in the money systems of the old world worthy of our imitation. It is only necessary to state that not one of them was established upon a correct basis or in the interest of the people. As the English money system of Banks of Issue was imposed upon this Republic, we have only to trace the present money system of the United States from its Parent, the Bank of England. The name of "Bank of England," adopted like that of the National Bank of the United States, was a deception and fraud upon the people in the very start. It is a private banking cor-

poration trading under the prestige and fictitious credit
given it by the use of the name of the Government; improperly given and used by the bank with great profit
in carrying on the purely money making scheme to exploit the people.

The charter of this corporation, known as the Bank of
England, was granted July 27, 1694. The charter provided
that they shall "be capable in law to purchase, enjoy,
and retain to them and their successors, any moneys, lands,
rents, tenements, and possessions whatsoever; and to purchase and acquire all sorts of goods and chattels whatsoever, wherein they are not restrained by act of Parliament,
and to grant, demise, and dispose of same."

"The corporation is prohibited from engaging in any
sort of commercial undertaking other than dealing in bills
of exchange, and in gold and silver. It is authorized to
advance *money* upon the security of goods or merchandise
pledged to it, and to sell by public auction such goods as
are not redeemed within a specified time."

The charter gave this private banking corporation *no
authority* to *issue bank notes as money.*

But it is the same old story, the greed, avarice and
cupidity of man, working and operating through the in-
strumentality of a corporation, well described as an entity
with "No back side to be kicked and no soul to be
damned."

The temptation to the managers of this bank was too
great to resist when, in the course of business, the opportunity presented itself, whereby they could use their non-
interest-bearing notes to discount the borrower's note and
draw interest on same.

A reliable historian thus describes its operation:

"Upon such considerations, the bank decided to issue
notes payable to bearer on demand, in exchange for individual paper payable at a future day. The bank thus
undertook to do an impossibility, in the hope that it would
not be called upon to redeem the promise or make the
attempt. The bank had not the money and could not,
therefore, purchase the paper offered; the notes offered
by the bank were not money, though a much better substitute for money than the notes of individuals, which

could only circulate to a very limited extent as a medium
of payment. The bank issued notes payable to bearer,
without endorsement, which added to their facility in passing rapidly from hand to hand as currency. It departed
still further from *sound principles,* when it made these
notes payable on demand in *gold* and *silver*; for it must
be contrary to sound principles to undertake to do what
cannot be done. The bank notes were nothing more than
the *promissory notes* of the bank to circulate among those
who chose to take them, *not as money,* but a *promise* to
pay money. And the promise should have been only such
as the bank could perform; but it could never have been
imagined for one moment that by this process between the
bank and its customers they manufactured money."

"This process was supplemented by the bank depositing
the proceeds of notes discounted to the credit of the party,
as so much money deposited. It mingled a process of cash
and credit as absurd in theory as it was dangerous in
practice." Thus the apparently small beginning of issuing their notes non-interest-bearing for those of their
borrowers bearing interest, is the pernicious beginning of
the great credit money system of Bank of Issue in England, and engrafted upon this Republic by the same influences under the misleading title of "National Banks of
the United States." All of which has been paid for since
by the people of England and the United States by panics,
business depressions, causing untold loss and injury to the
people of both countries.

All this was inflicted upon the people upon the same
old theory of credit money or bank notes payable on demand, without the money in hand to do it. Upon the
presumption, of course, that the bank would not be asked
to pay for many of them at any one time.

This financial fraud of the Bank of England is the
parent of the evils for which banks in more modern times
are answerable.

The Bank of England had made its demand notes payable in specie, and the bank found it impossible to make
specie redemptions, and the directors in alarm appealed
to the Privy Council, and that body determined on the
27th of February, 1797, "that it is indispensably necessary

for the public service that the Directors of the Bank of England should suspend cash payments until Parliament can act for *its protection.*" Parliament sanctioned and continued this suspension from 1797 to 1820, or a period of 23 years. I would call the attention of those who oppose full legal tender money being issued, as the money of the United States, to the fact that the people of Great Britain carried on their business affairs for 23 years with non-legal tender paper currency, and during this term, notwithstanding the great expense of war, and consequent burdens of taxation, Great Britain increased in wealth and prosperity more than at any other time in her history.

A reliable historian describes the conditions as follows: "During this period, notwithstanding the vast expenditures of war and the burdens of taxation, Great Britain increased in wealth and prosperity more rapidly than at any other period in her history.

"During this time 3,000,000 acres of unimproved land was brought under cultivation, and the exportation of manufactured Cotton goods increased in amount from £7,000,000 in 1801 to £27,000,000 in 1822.

"All classes of society participated in the general prosperity which prevailed and during the entire period the nation never once suffered from commercial crash or money panic."

Resumption of Specie Payments in 1823.

At this date the money lenders forced specie resumption on the people of England and the reader should retentively remember the contrast—The same historian states: "Specie payments were accordingly resumed in 1823, and the resumption was accompanied by the most disastrous commercial crash and money panic that ever visited any nation. The era of general prosperity departed to return no more. Real Estate depreciated largely in value and the real estate owners of the kingdom decreased in number from over 150,000 to less than 40,000; business men, merchants, manufacturers, etc., were ruined by the thousand; wages were reduced and laborers thrown out of employment by the tens of thousands; and the public revenue fell off to such an extent that payments on the public debts ceased and have never practically been resumed.'' Alison, in his history of Europe, says: ''The effects of this extraordinary piece of legislation were soon apparent. The industry of the nation was speedily congealed, as a flowing stream is by the severity of an Arctic winter. The alarm became as universal and widespread as confidence and activity had recently been. The country bankers, who had advanced largely on the stocks of goods imported, refused to continue their support to their customers, and they were forced to bring their stocks into the market. Prices in consequence fell rapidly; that of cotton, in particular, sank in three months to half its former level. The country bankers' association was contracted by no less than five millions sterling ($25,000,000); and the entire circulation of England fell from $235,545,000 in 1818 to $174,385,000 in 1820, and in the succeeding year it sank as low as $142,757,000. The effects of this sudden and prodigious contraction of the currency were soon apparent, and they rendered the next three years a period of ceaseless distress and suffering in the British Islands. The accommodation granted by bankers diminished so much in consequence of the obligation laid upon them to pay in specie, which was not to be got, that the paper under discount at the Bank of England, which in 1810 had been $115,000,000 and in 1815 not less than $103,000,000, sank in 1820 to $23,360,000, and in 1821 to $13,610,000. The effect upon prices was not less immediate or appalling. They declined in general, within six months, to half their former amount, and remained at that low level for the next three years. Distress was universal in the latter months of 1819, and that distrust and discouragement were felt in all branches of industry which are at once the forerunner and cause of disaster.'' From Mr. Doubleday's history I also quote as follows: ''We have already seen the fall in prices produced by the immense narrowing of the paper circulation. The distress, ruin and bankruptcy which now took place were universal, affecting the great interests both of land and trade; but especially among land owners, whose estates were burthened by mortgages, settlements, legacies, etc., the effects were most marked and out of the ordinary course. In hundreds of cases, from the tremendous reduction which now took place, the estates barely sold for as much as would pay off the mortgages; and hence the owners were stripped of all and made beggars." Before the close of the year 1819 the distress became insufferable. Great meetings were held throughout England and Scotland during the summer. In August 60,000 people, men, women and children, assembled near Manchester. A collision occurred between the people and the troops, in which a number were killed and many wounded. This created intense excitement, and the meetings of the people held in Liverpool, York, Leeds, and various other cities, were attended by vast multitudes of suffering people, demanding vengeance. Serious riots occurred, which were only quelled by military force. In 1820 a conspiracy was discovered, which had for its object the murder of all the King's Ministers, and which was only frustrated through the cowardice of one of the conspirators, who betrayed his associates. Military training went on amongst the people, and the government was obliged to provide a large military force to prevent an outbreak. "On Sunday morning, the 2nd of April," says Alison, "a treasonable proclamation was found placarded all over the streets of Glasgow, Paisley, Stirling, and the neighboring towns and villages, in the name of a provisional government, calling on the people to desist from labor; on all manufacturers to close their workshops; and on all the friends of their country to come forward and effect a revolution by force, with a view to the establishment of an entire equality of civil rights. Strange to say, this proclamation, unsigned and proceeding from an unknown authority, was widely obeyed. Work immediately ceased; the manufactories were closed from the desertion of workmen; the streets were filled with anxious crowds eagerly expecting news from the south; the sounds of industry were no longer heard, and two hundred thousand persons in the busiest districts of the country were thrown into a state of compulsory idleness by the mandates of an unseen and unknown power." Five thousand troops were immediately assembled at Glasgow, and the insurgents were overawed. Before the end of the year the government had increased its volunteer force to 35,000 men. "Without doubt," says Alison, "this pow-

erful volunteer force, organized especially in the manufacturing districts at this period, and the decisive demonstration it afforded of moral and physical strength on the
part of the government, was the chief cause through which
Great Britain escaped an alarming convulsion.''

But the ruin, suffering and misery which had attended
the attempt to force specie payments could not be undone,
nor could the broken fortunes be restored. By a return to
specie payments finally, the specie basis banking and credit
system, *the whole tendency of which is to concentrate
wealth in the hands of the few,* was reëstablished; and
the industrial classes, especially the agricultural class, have
never since been able to recover from the blow they received.[1]

In 1822 the land owners of England numbered 165,000.
According to the census of 1861, the number was about
30,000, and one-half of the whole kingdom is now owned
by not more than twelve persons.

In 1837 another crash and money panic occurred in
England which also involved this country. When the
bank of England took gold from the United States to
supply the wants of England, the banks of the United
States were obliged to suspend; ''business in the United
States was brought to a complete stand and for three years
the American people were left without any gold and were
consequently obliged to use shinplasters.''

In England the losses were so enormous and the distress
so great that it required another act of parliament to alle-
viate the suffering. The same historian continues—''From
September 7th, 1844, when the bank was reorganized, to
February 4th, 1858, it altered its rate of interest fifty-six
times, raising it from time to time from two to ten per
cent., in an effort to retain its specie in its vault. This, in
the meantime, led to great financial embarrassment and a
panic was only averted by the bank suspending specie
payments (October 23, 1847) and affording relief by issuing irredeemable paper. In 1857, having ruined the merchants and business of England, it was again obliged to
suspend. Eleven changes in the rate of interest were

[1] Deflation is the same operation trying to get back to the false
gold basis.

made between April, 1857, and January, 1858. The bank
again drew upon the United States for gold, causing the
banks to suspend, involving thousands of people in ruin
and bankruptcies.

"In 1866 the Bank of England suffered another suspension in consequence of the war on the Continent of Europe;
but this time the United States escaped. Greenbacks were
the medium of exchange, and the nation was no longer at
the mercy of foreign banks. Gold was shipped abroad to
the amount of $45,000,000 and sold as a commodity at a
high price for the use of the Bank of England without
occasioning the slightest ripple in the business affairs of
the country."

In 1844 the poverty and distress so often brought upon
the people by the Bank of England made necessary an act
of the government limiting the notes that the bank could
issue to the amount of government securities and gold held
for their redemption; the bank kept on with its money
making scheme in another way. The discount of commercial paper, entered on its books, took the place of the
inflated note issues, but these discounts called largely for
gold, therefore, when there was the least drain on the
bank, gold discounts were shut off, interest was raised and
quadrupled and property of all kinds was dumped on the
market to pay the bank in money for the discounted paper.
This put the bank in a position to increase its possessions
out of the losses of the people. No intelligent man can
fail to recognize in the above a perfect picture of the
present National banking system of the United States.[1]
To complete the picture I will quote from Mr. Seley, of
London.

"The commerce of the country is now in the power of
the Bank of England, as it was before in the legislature.
For legislative enactment we have the decision of the
Bank Parlor; for a responsible government we have substituted an irresponsible body composed of twenty-four
directors, and a governor and deputy governor. To these
we have confided the commerce of this mighty empire.
Instead of a mercantile system supported by merchants
and manufacturers and agricultural interests, we have now

[1] The gold basis Federal Reserve System.

the monetary system endangering the welfare of merchants, manufacturers, and agricultural interests—for the benefit of the fund-holding classes.''

A Bank of Issue, in the final analysis, is a mere scheme devised by the avarice and cupidity of man to reap where he has not sown. The men organizing the Bank of England thought out the plan of issuing their non-interest-bearing notes for the time notes of their borrowers bearing interest in order to make something out of nothing.

The whole plan being based upon the theory that but a small percentage either of their non-interest-bearing notes outstanding or the credits allowed the borrower on their books would require the banks to pay out at any one time a large amount in cash or real money.

Realizing that such a profitable scheme would not long be tolerated by the people if it was made plain to them, that a corporation was making large sums of money out of them by loaning a substitute for money, or in other words, making money out of a creation of their own for which they had given no valuable consideration; yet knowing what a great money making scheme they had devised, their next thought was how they could perpetuate it.

The issuing of their own non-interest-bearing notes in large quantities made them feel their personal risks and liabilities for what might happen, as they knew they were trying to accomplish an impossibility. Like all men doing that which is illegal, or morally wrong, they naturally thought of self-preservation, and in order to accomplish this and still keep up the scheme, they offered to redeem their notes in specie, thereby making the responsibility impersonal. Realizing they could never redeem them on a specie basis, they shifted the responsibility to the English Government by getting the government to sanction it; knowing that if the government had sanctioned their doing an impossible thing the government would have to come to their assistance. This being the case the bank frequently suspended specie payments, subjecting the people many times to tremendous losses. While the ruin was going on among the people, the Bankers were able to take advantage of the great fall in prices, and again increased their possessions of property and securities that were forced upon the market.

When the government authorized the issue of non-legal tender paper money to supply the wants of trade, business at once improved.

When prosperity was restored by the use of this non-legal tender paper money, the bank would use its unfailing influence to resume specie payments, which meant contraction of the currency, a fall in prices, business depression and panics, and again widespread ruin among the people, and another harvest for the Banks.

This operation has been repeated upon the people of Europe until the great substrata of society there have been reduced to hopeless poverty.

Kind reader and voter, just keep these basic facts in your mind. This is the fraudulent basis of "Specie Redemption" which has developed into the gold brick swindle of the so-called gold standard, which will be shown to be the greatest fraud ever perpetrated on mankind. Nothing describes it but this: *A Gigantic Confidence Game* worked upon the people.

ESTABLISHING THE SO-CALLED BANK OF THE UNITED STATES

It is useless to consider Continental currency as at all relevant to a National Money System. Judge Story describes the situation after the Revolution as follows: "In the first place, there was an utter want of coercive authority to carry into effect its own constitutional measures. It may be called a Government which possessed no one solid attribute of power. In truth Congress possessed only the power of recommendation; it depended altogether upon the goodwill of the States whether a measure should be carried into effect or not."

It was therefore impossible to create a full legal tender dollar, as there was no power of sovereignty to bind all the people to its acceptance, hence it was impossible to establish a universal money system for the United States at that time.

In order to understand what real money is, the people of the whole world should expel from their minds that there is any such thing as a money of the world, or international money.

Money is the creation of an act of sovereignty and is real money, legal tender money, only within the jurisdiction of the country issuing it.

Hamilton has been given great credit by superficial students on the subject of money for the part that he performed in establishing a National Banking System in the United States, but to any one familiar with the subject it is well known that Hamilton originated nothing in this banking plan of his, *but bodily* adopted the *English Banking System* and *inflicted* it upon *our republican form of Government.* The whole mental process of the man was undemocratic, unrepublican and his National Banking Scheme was a part of his system for a strong centralized government and the rule of the few, the rich and well-born. Hamilton's whole theory of government

28

was absolutely wrong. Its foundation being that of money and aristocracy, two absolutely discordant elements in a Republic. In such a combination money dominates and the inevitable result is a plutocracy, the worst form of government. If Hamilton had been the student statesman of history that he claimed to be, he should have known the poverty, suffering and ruin this same credit money system had inflicted upon the great mass of the English people, and recognized at once that it was foreign and antagonistic to every principle of our republican form of government.

The British Parliament declared all colonial acts for the issue of paper currency to be void.

The British Board of Trade also strongly objected as early as 1764 to the use of legal tender money in the colonies, both realizing it would render the colonies independent of the power of Great Britain. The false basis of their objection being "every medium of exchange should have an intrinsic value, which paper has not." Such has always been the attitude of England on money.

In 1780 the American conflict had resolved itself chiefly into a rivalry in financial ability and resources between the Mother Country and the Colonies. This was the time that Hamilton, evidently inspired by international bankers, began to set forth his financial scheme. As early as this he wrote an anonymous letter proposing the establishment of a bank to be called the Bank of the United States. Where did he get this idea?

Now mark the basis of its establishment as outlined by Hamilton, and you have the answer. It provided "The basis of this institution was to be a *foreign loan* of $200,-000,000 as a portion of the bank stock; a subscription for $200,000,000 more guaranteed by $10,000,000 of specie or by a bona fide equivalent currency."

"The bank notes were to be made payable to the bearer in three months at 10 per cent."

In addition to this, an annual loan of $10,000,000 was to be furnished to Congress by the bank at 4 per cent. This plan starts out with the outrageous assumption that the United States was not to exercise its right of sovereignty and create its own money system, but at once

become a borrower and debtor to England and establish a
money system founded upon debt.

In April, 1781, in a letter to Robert Morris, Superin-
tendent of Finance, Hamilton boldly asserted the principle
"that it is in a National Bank alone we can find the
ingredients to constitute a wholesome, solid and beneficial
paper credit." To show that Hamilton was interested in
this kind of bank he wrote the Constitution of the Bank
of New York. Half a million dollars was subscribed at
a single meeting, and Hamilton was chosen one of its
directors.

Hamilton was also chairman of the committee on peace
arrangements between the States and the Mother Country,
and in this position reported regarding the department of
foreign affairs. The report provided that the secretary of
that department should occupy the position of chief of the
Diplomatic Corps, and that it should be his duty to lay
before Congress such plans for conducting the political
and commercial intercourse of the United States with foreign powers as might appear to him to be best adapted to
promote their interest.

The subsequent acts of Hamilton show he was in sym-
pathy with the financial group of England.

In 1787, when the Union was formed and the Constitution adopted, all the States agreed to surrender, and did
surrender, control over the issue of money in order that
this sovereign power might be vested in the Congress of
the United States representing the people of every State
in the Union, in order to establish a "National Currency
in the interest of all the people, as provided in the Constitution, wherein the Congress was given the exclusive
sovereign power to create and regulate the (quantity)
value of money.

Thus, if Congress authorized the issue of full legal
tender money, every dollar becomes a universal order for
all things on sale, all service for hire, and the ultimate
of payment for all debts within the jurisdiction of the
United States. By this means every money unit or legal
tender dollar would have squarely back of it the entire
resources, national wealth and services of all the people
as the basis of its continuous redemption.

I will now show how the entire system was perverted and set aside by the pernicious influence of those who established the so-called "National Banks" of issue in the United States. It was simply imposing, under a different name, the European money system upon our people. A reliable historian described the political conditions in the United States at that time as follows: "At the time the Federal Constitution was framed there was a large and formidable party with aristocratic notions and tendencies under the leadership of Alexander Hamilton, which was in favor of 'a strong Government.' This policy grew out of a want of faith in the people, and the belief that they were incapable of self-government."

Hamilton expressed his conclusions of Government as follows:

"I believe the British Government forms the best model the world ever produced, and such has been its progress in the minds of many that this truth gradually gains ground. All communities divide themselves into the few and the many. The first are rich and well born; the other, the mass of the people."

He then states that the rich and well-born should govern.

The money power of the world has never been slow to single out such men for their service.

England and her money lenders saw the opportunity for money lending and money making in the matchless and boundless resources of this continent and determined to make a debtor country of the United States. To those who know the direct influence they did exert in establishing their money system here, it was not at all surprising that Hamilton was made the first Secretary of the Treasury—and at once strongly recommended the *English System of Banks of Issue.*

On the 13th of December, 1790, Hamilton submitted to Congress his views in reference to the establishment of a National Bank, and from the moment of its incorporation, and the formation of the so-called Bank of the United States, the irrepressible conflict was on between the money power represented by Hamilton and the Tories, who advocated a strong centralized Government and a Bank of Issue, and the people, represented by Thomas Jefferson, who believed in a Government of the people, by the people and for the people, and that Congress should create money and regulate the value thereof in the interest of the people. This is the beginning from which the issues of to-day have sprung. Up to the present time the organized money power has won over unorganized democracy, and its greed and oppression have forced the *money question again* upon the people for a correct solution.

Alexander Hamilton in 1790 recommended a National Bank, involving not merely the power of incorporation, but the grant of exclusive privileges for twenty years, independent of the control of future Congresses. This was in direct violation of the Constitution of the United States. At this early date such conclusive evidence shows that Alexander Hamilton was representing the British banking interests and aiding international bankers to gain control of the money system of the United States.

President Washington doubted the constitutionality of Hamilton's recommendation and got Madison to draw up a veto for it, which he was induced to waive only at the last hour.

The record shows that on the money question Alexander Hamilton betrayed the people of the United States.

Through Hamilton's influence Congress chartered the first so-called Bank of the United States in February, 1791, with a capital of $10,000,000 for a period of twenty years. This bank started by stealing the name of the government of the United States to deceive the people, who, after achieving their liberties in the War of the Revolution, would enter into debt slavery by the incorporation of the dishonest British Banking and Currency System in the United States.

William Pitt, Chancellor of the Exchequer, said of the inauguration of the first National Bank of the United States under Hamilton: "Let the American people go into their debt-funding schemes and banking systems, and from that hour their boasted independence will be a mere phantom."

Thomas Jefferson as Secretary of State gave a strong written opinion denying the power of Congress to incorporate a *Bank of Issue*. Madison opposed it in Congress and made a powerful speech denouncing it as a violation of the Constitution.

In 1811 this Bank applied to Congress for a renewal of its charter.

The Virginia Assembly at the session of 1810-1811, instructed, by a vote of 125 to 35, its Senators in Congress to vote against the re-charter of this Bank as unconstitutional, and a direct and fatal violation of States rights. Henry Clay and other leading statesmen defeated its re-charter on the grounds that it was unconstitutional, anti-American, and strictly a British institution.

The second so-called Bank of the United States began business the first of January, 1817. In 1818 the people had become alarmed at its encroachments upon their rights, as well as the evils it inflicted on the public. As a result, the legislative committee of the State of New York made the following report in 1818:

"Of all aristocracies, none more completely enslave a people than that of money; and, in the opinion of your committee, no system was ever better devised so perfectly to enslave a community as that of the present mode of conducting banking establishments. Like the siren of the fable, they entice to destroy. They hold the purse-strings of society, and by monopolizing the whole of the circulating medium of the country, they form a precarious standard by which all the property in the country—homes, lands, debts and credits, personal and real estate of all description—are valued, thus rendering the whole community dependent upon them; proscribing every man who dares to expose their unlawful practices."

From the opinion of the Supreme Court of the United States, delivered by Chief-Justice Marshall in the case of McCulloch v. State of Maryland—improperly termed the case of the Bank of the United States—the constitutionality of the power and privileges granted by Congress in the charter of this so-called Bank of the United States, which was really a banking corporation, organized for private gain, was not on trial in this case. It was confined to the question—could Congress charter a bank or corporation if it was a "necessary and proper" fiscal agency of the Government in the interest of the people.

I quote the following extracts, vital to a correct understanding of this case, from the opinion and decision of the Court delivered by Chief-Justice Marshall.

1819.   McCulloch v. State of Maryland.   Wheaton's Reports. Vol. 4, page 415. "The subject is the execution of those great powers on which the welfare of a nation essentially depends. It must have been the intention of those who gave these powers to insure, as far as human prudence could insure, their beneficial execution."

Page 419. "That any means adopted to the end, any means that tended *directly* to the execution of the constitutional powers of the Government were in themselves constitutional."

Page 421. "But we think the sound construction of the constitution must allow to the national legislature that discretion, with respect to the means by which the powers it confers are to be carried into execution, which will enable that body to perform the high duties assigned to it, in the manner *most beneficial* to all the people, which are not prohibited, but *consist* with the *letter* and *spirit* of the constitution, are constitutional."

Page 422. "But being considered merely as a means, to be *employed only* for the purpose of carrying into execution the given powers, there could be no motive for particularly mentioning it (a bank in the constitution)."

Page 423. "But where the law is not prohibitive, and is really calculated to effect any of the objects entrusted to the Government, to undertake here to inquire into the degree of its necessity, would be to pass the line which circumscribes the judicial department, and to tread on legislative ground. This court disclaims all pretentions to such a power."

Page 431. "The legislature of the Union alone, therefore, can be trusted by the people with the power of controlling measures which concern all, in the confidence that it will not be abused."

In this case the Court simply decided that the legislature of Maryland could not tax a branch of this bank already charted by Congress.

Page 436. "But this is a tax on the operation of the bank, and is, consequently, a tax on the operation of an instrument employed by the Government of the Union to carry its powers into execution. Such a tax must be unconstitutional.''

Judgment. "On consideration whereof, it is the opinion of this Court that the act of the Legislature of Maryland is contrary to the Constitution of the United States and void.''

CHIEF-JUSTICE MARSHALL IN THE CASE OF THE BANK OF THE UNITED STATES, 1819

Chief-Justice Marshall and the associate Justices of this great Court never decided that the sinister and infamous provisions incorporated in the charter of this so-called Bank of the United States were constitutional, or that it was a "necessary and proper" fiscal agency of the Government. Chief-Justice Marshall in rendering the decision of the Court simply decided that Congress had a right to charter this bank if it was "necessary and proper" as a fiscal agent of the Government, but left this responsibility where it properly belonged, with the Representatives of the people in Congress, they having the power to amend or repeal the charter of the bank, if it proved not to be a "necessary and proper" fiscal agency of the Government. This so-called Bank of the United States closed its doors October 9, 1839.

That it was not a necessary and proper fiscal agency of the Government was conclusively demonstrated by the following disclosures, to say nothing of the dishonest, unconstitutional, and democracy wrecking powers and privileges granted by Congress to this Banking Corporation organized for private gain.

Benton, in his history, "Thirty Years in Congress," states:

"An hundred millions of dollars was the lowest at which the destruction was estimated; and how such ruin could be worked, and such confidence kept up for so long a time, is the instructive lesson for history; and that lesson the report of the stockholders' committee enables history to give. From this authentic report, it appears from the years 1830 to 1836—the period of its struggle for a re-charter—the loans and discounts of the bank were about doubled—its expenses trebled. Near thirty millions of these loans were not of a mercantile character—neither made to persons in trade or business. To whom were they made? To members of Congress, to editors of newspapers, to traveling politicians, to brokers and jobbers, to favorites and connections; and all with a view to purchase a re-charter.''

It is shown at this time that the members of Congress were not only improperly interested in this bank, but some of the ablest of them even then apprehended the great danger to the Government in chartering or allowing a banking corporation to issue a substitute for money— Daniel Webster had declared his hostility to bank currency repeatedly, as "one of the greatest of political evils," and "a contrivance for cheating the laboring classes of mankind."

Henry Clay said in 1811:

"I conceive the establishment of this bank (National Bank) as dangerous to the safety and welfare of this republic."

John Randolph, Senator from Virginia, as a warning, said:

"Charter a bank with thirty-five millions of capital; let it be established and learn its power, and then find, if you can, means to bell the cat. It will be beyond your power, it will overawe your Congress and laugh at your laws."

Such is the present condition of the Congress of the United States, and it should be reorganized on this issue to protect the people from financial ruin.

Counsel for the so-called Bank of the United States in his argument made the statement: "A legislative construction in a doubtful case persevered in for a course of years, ought to be binding upon the court." Chief-Justice Marshall in replying to this statement said:

"It will not be denied that a bold and daring usurpation might be resisted after an acquiescence still longer and more complete than this."

This has a direct application to the present fraudulent gold basis banking and currency system, inflicted upon

the people of the United States by International Bankers.
In this connection, I call especial attention to the fundamental explanation of our form of Government by Chief-
Justice Marshall, for the present and future guidance of
the people of the United States, laid down in this opinion:
"To the formation of a league, such as was the Confederation, the state sovereignties were certainly competent,
but when in order to form a more perfect union, it was
deemed necessary to change this alliance into an effective
government, possessing great and sovereign powers, and
acting directly on the people, the necessity of referring
it to the people, and deriving its powers directly from
them, was felt and acknowledged by all
"The Government of the Union then is emphatically
and truly a Government of the people. In form and in
substance it emanates from them, and is being exercised
directly on them and for their benefit.
"It is the government of all: its powers are delegated
by all; it represents all, and acts for all."
This means that in this Republic ultimate power rests
nowhere, but comes back to the people whose power is
supreme over their Government. And no "Divine right
of kings," or "Judicial Court" can ever deprive them
of this power under the provisions of the Constitution of
the United States.
This divine right of the people to govern themselves
shall live forever and, save by annihilation, can never die.
International bankers have purposely and persistently
misrepresented the decision rendered by Chief-Justice
Marshall in the "Bank Case" to conceal the flagrant violation of the constitution in the provision of the act itself,
incorporating this so-called Bank of the United States.
To say that Chief-Justice John Marshall of Virginia knew
anything about the false currency principle incorporated
in the charter of the first so-called Bank of the United
States, allowing banks the power to create debts upon the
people without loaning lawful money, or what was in the
minds of international bankers and Alexander Hamilton when they incorporated this false, dishonest and
economically unsound currency principle in the charter
of this bank, has no justification and is, in fact, directly

in conflict with the opinion of the court, as delivered by Chief-Justice Marshall in what is known as the Bank Case.

The crux of the decision of the Supreme Court of the United States in the Bank Case was this: If the so-called Bank of the United States was a proper and necessary fiscal agency of the Government it was constitutional for Congress to charter the bank. And the reverse, that if it was not a proper and necessary fiscal agency, it was unconstitutional and Congress should repeal its charter.

The Constitution of the United States is a written agreement between the people and their Government, for the benefit and protection of the people.

With the powers given to it the chartering of banking corporations, organized for private gain, by Congress is not only a vital violation of the Constitution, but absolutely destructive of the fundamental principle upon which this Government is established.

These banking corporations were organized, starting with the so-called Bank of the United States, for the purpose of controlling the money and credit of the United States and creating debts upon its resources and people. Congress in persistent violation of the Constitution subsequently incorporated the same false gold basis banking and currency principle in the National Bank Act, Federal Reserve Act, National Land Bank Act, Joint Stock Land Bank Act, and Rural Credits, all resting upon the false gold basis, which means that the Representatives of the people in Congress in violation of the Constitution, have granted these corporations, organized for private gain, the nation-wrecking privilege of creating debts upon the resources and people of the United States by the loaning of a fictitious money, thus acquiring the property and earnings of the people, without paying for same in money or anything of equivalent value.

Chief-Justice Marshall in his decision in this celebrated Bank case put the responsibility squarely up to the Representatives of the people in Congress, not only for granting the charter, but for its continuance; plainly stating that the Supreme Court had no intention of passing upon the bank being a proper fiscal agent of the Government.

In view of the legislative record made in the development of this system, culminating in the fraudulent gold basis Federal Reserve Act, it has become a subject of everlasting disgrace to every Congress and every Democratic and Republican Administration since that of Andrew Jackson, that this corporation system of legalized robbery of the people should have been allowed to operate under charters granted by the Representatives of the people of the United States.

VETO BY PRESIDENT TYLER OF THE BANK BILL OF 1841

In 1834 John Tyler of Virginia said:

"I believe the bank to be the original sin against the Constitution, which in the progress of our history, has called into existence a numerous progeny of usurpation. Shall I permit this serpent, however bright its scales or erect its mien, to exist by and through my vote?"

Madison opposed the first bank. In 1811 the bank tried and failed to get a re-charter from Congress. In 1815 the charter of a bank located in Philadelphia passed Congress, President Madison vetoing it.

President Jackson, in his message, charged the Bank of the United States with converting itself into a monstrous electioneering machine, which it was the duty of the President to suppress at all hazards.

President Tyler's objections to the bank were enduring, since its existence was a standing violation of the Constitution. "Let the Constitution be once looked upon as a mere system of convenient rules—as the by-laws of a corporation, alterable at pleasure—and good-by to the rights of the South and the integrity of the Union. We may boast of our laws, but they will be impotent and feeble; we may sing of liberty, but it will be the song of the bird in the cage."

The bill passed the Senate by twenty-seven to twenty-two. Henry A. Wise wrote to Tucker: "The Fiscal Corporation has gone to Tyler. He is firm and will give it a quietus forever."

The climax of the session had at last arrived. The Whigs had laid their mines in all directions under the executive, and they now, at a given signal, applied the

match. "The war upon Mr. Tyler became appalling."
The papers burst out into a tirade of vituperation and
invective, the fires of a thousand effigies lighted the streets
of the various cities. Whig orators and politicians vied
with one another in casting at him the filth and garbage
of falsehood and defamation; hundreds of letters were
received and opened by the President's private secretary,
threatening him with certain assassination; threats and
adjurations were addressed to him by numberless Whig
deputations to approve the Fiscal Corporation; the
terrors of being left alone in the administration of the
Government, and of being gibbeted by public disclosures
from his cabinet advisors, were proclaimed to drive him
into submission or resignation. All in vain. The President, with nerves apparently of laminated steel, and
courage of twisted and corded strength, signed his name
on the 9th of September, 1841, to his second veto message.
"This proved," cried Wise, "that his was no nose of wax,
but a firm, immovable lover of the Constitution, a fearless
patriot, a wise and sagacious statesman, and an honest
man."

1862—WAR MEASURES TO RAISE MONEY

The wars of the world and their demoralizing effects have done most to foist upon the people a false money system. The money lenders and those who live on interest have utilized the national debts of the world to their profit. The international banking institutions when buying Government bonds have always posed as public benefactors, and have it appear in the public press that they are the saviors of the credit of the country in its times of need, yet an investigation of the history of the sale of Government bonds will show that these dealers in the misfortunes of the country have in every instance driven the hardest bargain and exacted the highest rate of interest.

The celebrated Englishman, John Ruskin, made the following statement:

"National debts paying interest are simply the purchase by the rich of the power to tax the poor.

"The real thieves of Europe, the real sources of deadly war in it, are the capitalists, that is to say, the people who live by percentages on the labor of others instead of fair wages for their own."

As to the condition of the United States at the beginning of the war between the States, 1861, the crops had been unusually good and the people of the United States were enjoying prosperous conditions. The state of the banks and the currency in 1861 was as follows:

Currency in circulation	$ 202,000,000
Deposited in banks	257,200,000
Loans	696,700,000
Specie	87,600,000
National wealth	16,159,616,000

WAR MEASURES TO RAISE MONEY

At this time, and during an extra session of Congress, July 17th, 1861, a loan act was passed authorizing the

Secretary of the Treasury to borrow $250,000,000 and to issue coupon bonds or registered bonds or Treasury Notes as he might deem advisable.

The bonds were to bear interest not exceeding seven per cent. per annum and they were to run for twenty years. The Treasury Notes were to bear interest at seven and three-tenths per cent. and exchangeable at any time for twenty-year six per cent. bonds.

By an act of August the 5th, 1861, supplementary to the act of July 17th, 1861, the Secretary of the Treasury was authorized to issue bonds bearing interest at six per cent. per annum, payable after twenty years from date of issue, which might be exchanged for Treasury Notes bearing seven and three-tenths per cent. interest. I desire to call special attention to these acts of Congress, for in them is contained conclusive evidence that International Bankers were laying their plans to forestall the Congress of the United States from exercising its right of sovereignty to create full legal tender money in the interest of the people and establish an American Money System. The Treasury Notes, described in this Act of Congress, were handicapped, if not destroyed, as a circulating medium, by being turned into a seven and three-tenths per cent. investment for money, and in the subsequent Act of Congress made convertible into a six per cent United States Bond, which would eventually retire them as a circulating medium, making way for the issue of Bank Notes—the English money system. The subsequent acts of the money power in depreciating the value of the non-legal-tender-notes (greenbacks so called), and converting them into bonds is conclusive evidence of the fact.

This form of Treasury Note, bearing interest and not a legal tender, is really only an evidence of indebtedness and differs only in form from a bond. No private person or corporation is obliged to accept it at its face value in payment for debt, services or property; it therefore lacks the essential qualities of money as a circulating medium.

The fact that it bears interest and is payable for specific dues or taxes to the Government does not help it in its use as money, but offers a premium to those who have

obligations to pay to depreciate its value in order to purchase them at a low price.

. Just as was done by the bullionists when they discredited
and depreciated the greenbacks—non-legal tender notes
—as they had cornered the gold, it was to their interest to
buy greenbacks, with gold, as cheap as they could, and
then exchange them at their face value for United States
six per cent. bonds. This was the beginning of their plan
to establish banks of issue to emit credit money based on
debts under the title of "National Banks of the United
States" which has developed into the present money trust.
As additional evidence, I will submit the legislation in the
interest of the people, which they subsequently defeated
in Congress, to issue legal tender money.

LEGAL TENDER ACT

Introduced in the House of Representatives December
30, 1861. Duly considered by the "Committee on Ways
and Means" and on January 7, 1862, reported from the
Committee to the House.

The bill authorizing the Secretary of the Treasury to
issue on the credit of the United States $100,000,000 Treas-
ury Notes *full legal tender for all debts public and private.*

Thaddeus Stevens, Chairman of the Ways and Means
Committee, in charge of the Legal Tender Bill, concluded
his speech as follows:

"We believe that the credit of the country will be
sustained by it, that under it all classes will be paid in
money which they can use, and that it will confer no
advantages on the capitalist over the poor laboring man.
If this bill shall pass, I shall hail it as the most auspicious
measure of this Congress; if it should fail, the result will
be more deplorable than any disaster which could befall
us."

This was an honest attempt to establish an American
Money System, as provided in the Constitution, and issue
full legal tender dollars as the currency of the people of
the United States. This bill was no sooner made public
than an organized effort was made by the moneyed interests, represented by the Bankers of New York, Boston

and Philadelphia, to kill it. They at once said that, if a full legal tender American dollar was authorized and issued by the sovereign power of the Congress of the United States, it would be the beginning of a *permanent money system in the interest of the people of the United States,* and not in the sole interest of bankers and bullionists. They saw, if this *Bill became a Law, it would deprive them of the power to shave either the Government or the people.* These bankers organized themselves into a delegation, hurried to Washington, organized their forces in a formal manner and invited the ''Finance Committee of the Senate'' and the ''Committee of Ways and Means of the House'' to meet them in the office of the Secretary of the Treasury of the United States, January 11th, 1862. The meeting was held and they entered their vigorous protest against this bill and submitted their own plans as a substitute from which I quote the following sections:

1. ''A tax bill to raise 125,000,000 dollars over and above duties on imports by taxation.''

2. ''Not to issue any demand Treasury notes, except those authorized at the extra session of July last.''

3. ''A suspension of the sub-treasury act, so as to allow the banks to become depositories of the Government of all loans, and to check on the banks from time to time as the Government may want money.''

4. ''Issue six per cent. twenty-year bonds, to be negotiated by the Secretary of the Treasury, and *without any limitation as to the price he may obtain for them in the market.*''

5. ''That the Secretary of the Treasury be empowered to make temporary loans to the extent of any portion of the funded stock authorized by Congress, with power to hypothecate such stock, and, if such loans are not paid *at maturity, to sell the stock hypothecated for the best market price that can be obtained.*''

The following statement in regard to this proposition was printed in the New York *Tribune* of January 13th, 1862:

''The Sub-Committee of Ways and Means objected to any and every form of 'shinning' by the Government through Wall or State streets and the knocking down of

Government Stocks to 75 or 60 cents on the dollar, the inevitable results of throwing a new and large loan on the market *without limitation as to price,* and finished by firmly refusing to assent to any scheme that should *permit a speculation* by brokers, and *bankers and others,* in the *Government securities* and particularly any scheme which *should double the public debt of the country,* and double the expenses by *damaging the credit of the Government."*

This bankers' delegation remained in Washington several days and went into further consultation with Secretary Chase, which resulted in an agreement with him that Congress should be urged to pass the National Bank Bill and that the amount of the demand notes already issued by the Secretary of the Treasury should not be increased beyond the 50,000,000 dollars authorized by the Act of July, 1861, and also that Congress should be urged to extend the provisions of the existing loan act so as to enable the Secretary of the Treasury to exchange *interest bearing Treasury Notes* for the demand notes, *not bearing interest* and get them out of the way.

INFLUENCES OF BANK OF ENGLAND AND THE ROTHSCHILDS

An able writer on this legislation comments as follows: "Here begins one of the darkest chapters in American history. It will be found that every step taken by Congress from this on, in matters pertaining to the finances of the nation, has been dictated by the money power. Foreign capitalists, such as the Rothschilds, became deeply interested in the scheme of robbery inaugurated by the passage of this Act, and through their agents, such as August Belmont, banker and whilom chairman of the Democratic National Committee, have aided the money power here materially in *controlling the policy of both* of the *great political parties.* The amount stolen from the people during the Civil War by the financial policy then adopted, and which now encumbers the nation in the shape of a bonded debt, payable principal and interest in gold, is estimated by such writers upon the subject of finance as J. S. Gibbons (contributor to Johnson's Universal Cyclopedia) at *over one thousand million dollars,* to say nothing of the thousands of millions of which the people have been robbed indirectly, by means of the pernicious monetary system then foisted upon the country."

It is a well-known fact that the Rothschilds were back of the drain on American gold and silver from 1851 to 1863—when nearly $480,000,000 went out of this country. And again from 1864 to 1876, when nearly $770,000,000 followed.

This Bill passed the House February 6, 1862, by a vote of 93 to 59. On February 14, 1862, the bill passed the Senate with the following *amendments:*

1. That the legal tender notes should be receivable for all claims and demands against the United States of every kind whatever, *"except for interest on bonds and notes, which shall be paid in coin."*

2. That the Secretary might dispose of United States bonds *"at the market value thereof, for coin or Treasury Notes."*

3. An additional section, No. 5, "that duties on imported goods and proceeds of the sale of public lands," etc., should be set apart to pay *coin interest on the debt of the United States;* and one per cent. for a sinking fund, etc.

On the 18th of February, 1862, Mr. Stevens reported the legal tender bill, as amended by the Senate, from the Committee of Ways and Means to the House, and said:

"I hope the gentlemen of the House will read the amendments. *They are very important, and, in my judgment, very pernicious,* but I hope the House will examine them."

On Wednesday, the 19th, Mr. Spaulding opened the debate. I quote as follows:

"Mr. Chairman, I desire especially to oppose the amendment of the Senate which requires the interest on bonds and notes to be paid *in coin* semi-annually, and which authorizes the Secretary of the Treasury to sell six per cent. bonds at the market prices for coin to pay the interest.

"The passage of the measure, the Legal Tender Bill, in this House was hailed with satisfaction by the great mass of the people all over the country. It received the hearty endorsement of such bodies as the Chambers of Commerce of New York, Cincinnati, St. Louis, Chicago, Buffalo, Milwaukee and other places. I have never known any measure to receive a more hearty approval from the people.

"I regret to say that some of the amendments of the Senate render the bill incongruous, and tend to defeat its great object, namely to prevent all forcing of the Government to sell its bonds in the market to the highest bidder for coin. It might be very pleasant for the holders of the seven and three-tenths Treasury Notes and six per cent. bonds, to receive their interest in coin semi-annually, but very disastrous to the Government to be compelled to sell its bonds, at ruinous rates of discount, every six months to pay them gold and silver, while it would pay only Treasury Notes to the soldier, sailor and all other creditors of the Government.

"I am opposed to all those amendments of the Senate which *discriminate* in *favor* of the *holders* of *bonds* and *notes by compelling the Government to go into the streets every six months to sell bonds at the 'market price,' to purchase gold and silver in order to pay the interest 'in coin' to the capitalists who now hold United States stocks and Treasury Notes heretofore issued, or that may hold bonds and notes hereafter to be issued;* while all persons in the United States (including the Army and Navy and all who supply them with food and clothing) are compelled to receive non-legal tender Treasury Notes in payment of the demands due them from the Government.

"Why make this discrimination? Who asks to have one class of creditors placed on a better footing than another class? Do the people of New England, the Middle States, or the people of the West and the Northwest, or anywhere else in the rural districts, ask to have such discrimination made in their favor? Does the soldier, the farmer, the mechanic, or the merchant ask to have any such discrimination made in his favor? No, sir; no such unjust preference is asked for by this class of men. They ask for a legal tender note bill pure and simple. They ask for a national currency which shall be of equal value in all parts of the country. They want a currency that shall pass hand to hand among all the people in every State, County, City, Town and Village in the United States.

"Who then, are they that ask to have a preference given

to them over other creditors of the Government? Sir, it is a very respectable class of gentlemen, but a *class of men* who are *very sharp in all money transactions*. They are *not generally* among the *producing classes;* not *among those who, by their labor and skill,* make the *wealth* of the *Country;* but a *class of men* that have accumulated wealth, men who are willing to lend money to the Government if you will make the security beyond all question, give them a high rate of interest, and make it payable in coin. Yes, sir; the men who are asking these extravagant terms, who want to be preferred creditors, are perfectly willing to lend money to the Government in her present embarrassment, if you will only make them perfectly secure, give them extra interest, and put your bonds on the market at the 'market price' to purchase gold and silver to pay them interest every six months. Yes, sir; entirely willing to loan money on these terms! Safe, no hazard, secure, and the interest payable 'in coin'! Who would not be willing to loan money on such terms? Sir, the *legal tender* Treasury note bill was intended to avoid all such financiering and protect the *Government, and people who pay the taxes,* from all such hard bargains. It was *intended as a shield in the hands of the patriotic people of the Country against all forced sales of bonds, and all extravagant rates of interest.*

"The very discrimination proposed carries on its face notice to everybody, that although the notes are declared to be 'lawful money and a partial legal tender in payment of debts,' yet there is something of higher value, that must be sought after at a sacrifice to the Government to pay a peculiar class of creditors to whom it owes money, a kind of absurdity and self-stultification which does not appear well on the face of the bill. It is an unjust discrimination *which does not appear well now,* and will not *look well in history.* You will, if the Senate's amendment is adopted, depreciate, by your own acts, your own bonds and notes, and effectually destroy the symmetry and harmonious workings of the whole plan."

Mr. Stevens closed the debate. I quote from his speech as follows:

"Mr. Speaker, I have a very few words to say. I ap-

proach the subject with more depression of spirits than I
ever before approached any question. No personal motive
or feeling influences me. I hope not, at least. I have a
melancholy foreboding that we are about to consummate a
cunningly devised scheme, which will carry great injury
and great loss to all classes of the people throughout this
Union, except one. With my colleague, I believe that no
act of legislation of this Government was ever hailed with
as much delight throughout the whole length and breadth
of the Union, by every class of people, without any excep-
tion, as the Legal Tender Bill we passed and sent to the
Senate. Congratulations from all classes: merchants,
traders, manufacturers, mechanics, and laborers poured
in upon us from all quarters. The Board of Trade from
Boston, New York, Philadelphia, Cincinnati, Louisville,
St. Louis, Chicago and Milwaukee approved its provisions
and urged its passage as it was.

"It is true there was a doleful sound came up from the
caverns of bullion brokers, and from the *saloons of the
associated banks. Their cashiers and agents were soon on
the ground, and persuaded the Senate,* with but little de-
liberation, to mangle and destroy what it had cost the
House months to digest, consider, and pass. They fell
upon the bill in hot haste, and so disfigured and deformed
it, that its very father would not know it. Instead of being
a beneficent and invigorating measure, it is now positively
mischievous. It has all the bad qualities which its enemies
charged on the original bill, and none of its benefits. It
now creates money, and by its *very terms declares* it a
depreciated currency. It makes two classes of money—
one for the banks and brokers, and another for the people.
It discriminates between the rights of different classes of
creditors, allowing the rich capitalists to demand gold, and
compelling the ordinary lender of money on individual
security to receive notes *which the Government had purposely discredited*."

In a speech at Philadelphia, January 15, 1876, Judge
Kelly says: "I remember the grand 'Old Commoner'
(Thaddeus Stevens) with his hat in his hand and his cane
under his arm when he returned to the House after the
final conference, and shedding bitter tears over the result.

'Yes,' said he, 'we had to yield; the Senate was stubborn. We did not yield until we found *that the country must be lost or the banks be gratified,* and we have sought to save the country in spite of the cupidity of its wealthier citizens.' ''

FULL LEGAL TENDER ACT DEFEATED AND NON-LEGAL TENDER "GREENBACKS" AUTHORIZED

He who reads the history of the fate of this Bill to create a full legal tender dollar and the amendments to this bill, that substituted the non-legal tender "Greenback" for the full legal tender dollar; yet characterizes the full legal tender money herein advocated, as a revival of the "greenback theory," or as a "recrudescence of greenbackism," is either a fool or a knave.

Thus in 1862 was the legal tender bill defeated and the Government prevented from exercising its highest act of sovereignty to create money and regulate the value thereof —and the International bankers and money lenders prevented the United States from establishing an American money system in accord with its constitution and forced upon this republic the British money system, banks of issue and specie redemption.

It should be borne in mind at this date that the Rothschilds and their correspondents in the United States had cornered all the gold in sight, leaving in the currency system in the United States only $25,000,000 of gold, most of which was in the control of the banking interest. They immediately began to make it abnormally valuable by creating extraordinary demands for it, consequently they used every effort to depreciate the non-legal tender notes of the Government and bought them for gold, which they controlled, at less than fifty cents on the dollar, exchanging them at par for United States bonds bearing the highest rate of interest.

Secretary of the Treasury McCulloch, in touch with the foreign bankers and their representatives in the United States, in his first annual report, December 4th, 1865, to Congress, made the following recommendations which were embodied in the act of Congress April 12th, 1866, authorizing the Secretary of the Treasury to sell 5-20 bonds, and with the proceeds to retire 6 per cent compound interest, notes and greenbacks, and other evidences of indebtedness of the Government. This act gave Secretary McCulloch unlimited control over the monetary system of the United States. The dealers in these war debts in Europe and the United States held hundreds of millions of these securities which they had bought at prices ranging from 35 cents on the dollar, up. While these securities were being issued during the war the money power depreciated their value, in order that they might be bought in at the lowest possible price. With this in view they made the interest on bonds and duties on imports payable in gold only, to discredit the Government currency. In order to confuse the people hopelessly on the subject of money they succeeded in having the Treasury Department issue fifteen different forms of its obligations. Therefore, it was impossible for the people at that time to understand all these intermixed and various forms of indebtedness and currency. Issuing the securities of the Government in these peculiar forms gave the banks a golden opportunity to prey upon the people.

GOVERNMENT FORESTALLED IN EXERCISING ITS HIGHEST ACT OF SOVEREIGNTY BY BANKS BEING GIVEN THE POWER TO ISSUE A SUBSTITUTE FOR MONEY

In the autumn of 1862 a "confidential circular" was issued by an agent of European capitalists to American bankers, known as "The Hazard Circular." It reads as follows:

"Slavery is likely to be abolished by the war power, and chattel slavery destroyed. This, I and my European friends are in favor of, for slavery is but the owning of labor, and carries with it the care of the laborer; while *the European plan, led on by England,* IS CAPITAL'S CONTROL OF LABOR, BY CONTROLLING WAGES. THIS CAN BE DONE BY CONTROLLING THE MONEY. *The great debt that capitalists will see to it is made out of the war, must be used as a measure to control the volume of money. To accomplish this the bonds must be used as a banking basis.* We are now waiting to get the Secretary of the Treasury to make this recommendation to Congress."

NATIONAL BANKERS' CIRCULAR

"Dear Sir:—It is advisable to do all in your power to sustain such daily and weekly newspapers, especially the agricultural and religious press, as will oppose the issuing of greenback paper money, and that you also withhold patronage or favors from all who will not oppose the Government-issue of money. Let the Government issue the coin, and the banks issue the paper money of the country; for then we can better protect each other. To repeal the law creating National Banks, or to restore to circulation the Government-issue of money, will be to provide the people with money, and will, therefore, seriously affect your individual profit as bankers and lenders. See your member of Congress at once, and engage him to support our interest that we may control legislation.''

This circular was signed by the official representative of the National Bankers' Association, James Buell.

The original copy of the circular was obtained personally by the Hon. Isaac Sharp, Acting Governor of Kansas (who had been, when very young, a favorite law student of Thaddeus Stevens, hence his interest in the question), from Mr. J. W. Simcock, the cashier of the First National Bank of Council Grove, Kansas. Mr. Sharp at the time was attorney for that bank—Mr. Simcock at the same time gave him the circular of the American Bankers' Association signed by Buell. Mr. Sharp states that when in London he traced up Mr. Hazard and found him to be the Solicitor of an English Bankers' Association in touch with bankers throughout Europe and was financially connected with the Rothschilds.

"State of Colorado,   ⎫ ss.
  County of Arapahoe, ⎰

"Frederick A. Luckenbach, being first duly sworn on oath, deposes and says: I am 62 years of age. I was born in Bucks County, Pennsylvania. I removed to the City of Philadelphia in the year 1846, and continued to reside there until 1866, when I removed to the City of New York. In Philadelphia I was in the furniture business; in New York I branched into machinery and inventions and am the patentee of Luckenbach's Pneumatic Pulverizer, which machines are now in use generally in the eastern part of the United States and in Europe. I now reside in Denver, having removed there from New York two years ago. I am well known in New York. I have been a member of the Produce Exchange and am well acquainted with many members of that body. I am well known by Erastus Wyman.

"In the year 1865 I visited London, England, for the purpose of placing there Pennsylvania oil properties in which I was interested. I took with me letters of introduction to many gentlemen in London—among them, one to Mr. Ernest Seyd from Robert M. Foust, ex-Treasurer of Philadelphia. I became well acquainted with Mr. Seyd and with his brother, Richard Seyd, who I understand is yet living. I visited London thereafter every year and at each visit renewed my acquaintance with Mr. Seyd, and upon each occasion became his guest one or more times—joining his family at dinner or other meals.

"In February, 1874, while on one of these visits and while his guest for dinner, I, among other things, alluded to rumors afloat of Parliamentary corruption and expressed astonishment that such corruption should exist. In reply to this, he told me he could relate facts about the corruption of the American Congress that would place it far ahead of the English Parliament in that line, so far the conversation was at the dinner table between us. His brother Richard and others were there also, but this was table-talk between Mr. Ernest Seyd and myself. After the dinner ended, he invited me to another room where he resumed the conversation about legislative corruption. He said: 'If you will pledge me your honor as a gentleman not to divulge what I am about to tell while I live, I will convince you that what I said about the corruption of the American Congress is true.' I gave him the promise, and he then continued: 'I went to America in the winter of 1872-73 authorized to secure, if I could, the passage of a bill demonetizing silver as it was to the interest of those I represented—the Governors of the Bank of England—to have it done. I took with me £100,000 Sterling, with instructions that if that was not sufficient to accomplish the object, to draw for another £100,000 or as much more as was necessary.' He told me German bankers were also interested in having it accomplished. He said he was the financial advisor of the bank. He said, 'I saw the Committees of the House and Senate and paid the money and stayed in America until I knew the measure was safe.' I asked him if he would give me the names of the members to whom he paid the money—but this he declined to do. He said: '*Your people will not now comprehend the far-reaching extent of that measure—but they will in after years.* Whatever you may think of corruption in the English Parliament, I assure you I would not have dared to make such an attempt here as I did in your country.' I expressed my shame to him for my countrymen in our

Legislative Bodies. The conversation drifted into other subjects, and after that—though I met him many times—the matter was never referred to again.

"(Signed)   FREDERICK A. LUCKENBACH.

"Subscribed and sworn to before me at Denver, this 9th day of May, 1892.

"(Signed) JAMES A. MILLER,
"Clerk, Supreme Court,
"State of Colorado."

(Seal)

The *Bankers' Magazine*, August, 1873, says:

"In 1872, silver being demonetized in France, England and Holland, a capital of $500,000 was raised and Ernest Seyd, of London, was sent to this country with this fund, as the agent of foreign bondholders and capitalists, to effect the same object here, which was accomplished."

The Congressional Record of April, 1872, page 2032, says:

"Ernest Seyd, of London, a distinguished writer and bullionist, *who is now here*, has given great attention to the subject of mint and coinage. After having *examined* the *first draft of the bill*, he made sensible suggestions which the Committee adopted and embodied in the bill."

It should be borne in mind that in 1866-67 the people of the United States were generally occupied in the great losses and demoralization as the result of the Civil War. Few people, at this time, knew anything about money apart from trying to get hold of dollars to meet their daily needs. There was one man in the United States who was then making a study of it as a means of amassing a private fortune and was coöperating with the leading foreign money-lenders and bullionists. John Sherman in 1868 was chairman of the Finance Committee of the United States Senate. At this time, when hundreds of millions of United States bonds were held in Europe, and when speculation in the debts growing out of our Civil War concentrated in London, Senator John Sherman, fortified with the great prestige of Chairman of the Finance Committee of the United States Senate, visited London in 1867 in his

own interest. At this time no one in the United States
was asking or advocating any movement that would affect
the use of silver as money. After conferring with these
dealers in bonds, in London, Sherman went over to Paris
to attend the International Conference of 1867. Mr. Samuel B. Ruggles, a member of the New York Chamber of
Commerce, in contact with the banking interest of New
York, secured the appointment as delegate from the United
States to that Conference. Mr. Sherman at once got in
contact with Mr. Ruggles in Paris and both of them became strong advocates of the so-called Gold Standard.
On the 17th day of May, 1867, Mr. Ruggles addressed a
letter to Mr. Sherman in which he stated that the International Conference was then in session "to agree, if possible, on a common unit of money." The next day, May
18th, Mr. Sherman answered Mr. Ruggles. In this letter
he stated that he favored the proposition, saying: "If this
is done, France will surely abandon the impossible effort
of making two standards of value. Gold coins will answer
all the purposes of Europe." This letter was read in full
to the Conference as the views and opinions of the Chairman of the Finance Committee of the United States Senate.
Any one reading this letter in full will see that it was a
carefully prepared product resulting from the conference
held in London by John Sherman and those representing
the European money power, with whom he had made his
business connections on a gold basis. On the 6th of January, 1868, John Sherman introduced in the Senate—"A
Bill in Relation to the Coinage of Gold and Silver," which
was referred to his Committee on Finance, he called this
bill up in the Senate on the 9th of June, 1868, and strongly
urged its passage, using, as his main argument, the reports
of Samuel Ruggles of the proceedings of the Paris Conference. Fortunately, there was on the Senate Finance
Committee an honest man of ability who knew something
about the money question and exposed the scheme. Senator E. D. Morgan, of New York, submitted a minority report in which he opposed any international regulation of
money, as something that would fetter the United States
and said, "that it would be well for the government to
increase, rather than discontinue, the coinage of silver and

that it should be poured in the current of commerce in full volume.'' Mr. Morgan then said: ''The war gave us self-assertion of character and removed many impediments to progress. Its expensive lesson will be measurably lost if it fails to impress upon us the fact that we have a distinctive American policy to work out—one sufficiently free from the traditions of Europe to be suited to our peculiar situation and the genius of our enterprising countrymen.'' Senator Morgan's opposition killed this bill to demonetize silver. The reading of Mr. Morgan's report settled its fate and it would not have received a single vote in the Senate. Senator Morgan put such a prompt quietus on this bill that its villainous motive was not discovered by the leading men in Congress. Those back of it realized at once that they could not afford to have it discussed in the open—John Sherman used that stealth and diplomacy which characterized his whole life in the United States Senate, and succeeded in doing that, by stealth and chicanery which he and his backers knew was impossible of accomplishment by fair and honest methods. They knew it was a matter of the first importance that their personality and interest in the bill should be concealed from the public. In order to do this they had a long and technical bill framed by Boutwell through John Jay Knox in 1870 at a time when the subject was not before the people and little or no interest was taken in it as it was thought to be a scientific Mint bill drawn up by specialists in the U. S. Mint and Treasury.

This bill was entitled ''An act revising and amending the laws relative to the Mints, assay offices and coinage of the United States,'' and was always represented to Congress as a measure for the sole convenience of the specialists in the Mint and Treasury. It should be borne in mind that at this time the United States needed all the money that it could possibly get through the operations of the Mint to carry on the tremendous task of developing the resources of the country and paying off its bonded indebtedness that had been forced upon the people by the money power back of this bill. Yet the above methods were resorted to by the money powers to prevent the United States from adding to the money supply, their object being to convert silver money into debts, thereby contracting the currency and at the same time making the hundreds of millions of United States bonds that they held, payable in gold. This was done without the knowledge of the voters or tax-payers of the country, who had to meet these obligations, and suffer the loss and fearful consequences of this treasonable act. The record will show that the leading men in the Congress of the United States were absolutely ignorant of this infamous conspiracy. I give the testimony of the representatives of the people in Congress, including the President of the United States at that time as to the passage of this bill.

U. S. Grant stated: "I did not know that the act of 1873 demonetized silver. I was *deceived* in the matter."

Senator Morgan, December 12th, 1877:

"Did the people demonetize silver? Never! It cannot even be fairly said that Congress did it. It was done in a corner darkly. It was done at the instigation of the bond-holders and other money kings, who now, with upturned eyes, deplore the wickedness we exhibit in asking the question, even, who did this great wrong against the toiling millions of our people?"

Judge Kelly, in the House, May 10th, 1879:

"Never having heard until a long time after its enactment into law of the substitution in the Senate of the section which dropped the Standard dollar, I profess to know nothing of its history; but I am prepared to say that in all the legislation of this country there is no mystery like the demonetization of the standard silver dollar of the United States."

Senator Voorhees, January 15th, 1878:

"No man has ever dared to whisper of a contemplated assault upon it (the Standard silver dollar) and when the twelfth day of February, 1873, approached, the day of doom to this American dollar, the dollar of our fathers, how silent was the work of the enemy! *Not a sound, not a word, no note of warning to the American people that their favorite coin was about to be destroyed; that the greatest financial revolution of modern times was in contemplation and about to be accomplished against their dearest rights!* Never since the foundation of the government has a law of such vital and tremendous import, or indeed of any importance at all, crawled into our statute books so furtively or noiselessly as this. Its enactment there was so completely unknown to the people, and indeed to four-fifths of Congress itself, *as the presence of a burglar in a house at midnight to its sleeping inmates.* This was rendered possible partly because the clandestine movement was so utterly unexpected and partly from the nature of the bill in which it occurred. The silver dollar of American history was demonetized in an act entitled ''An act revising and amending the laws relative to the mints, assay offices and coinage of the United States.''

Senator Howe, February 5th, 1878:

''The act of 1873, I charge it with guilt compared with which the robbery of $200,000,000 is venial.''

Senator Beck, January 10th, 1878:

''It (the bill demonetizing silver) never was understood by either House of Congress. I say that with full knowledge of the facts—No newspaper reporter—and they are the most vigilant men I ever saw in obtaining information —discovered that it had been done.''

Senator Beck, ''I know that the bondholders and the monopolists of this country are seeking to destroy all the industries of this people, in their greed to enhance the value of their gold. I know that the act of 1873 did more than all else to accomplish that result, and the demonetization act of the Revised Statutes was an illegal and unconstitutional consummation of the fraud.''

This law struck down the silver money of the government in 1873 which, by construction, became debts payable in gold. It should be remembered at this time that the money power back of the demonetization of silver had previously succeeded in stopping the government from issuing its full legal tender money and had established National Banks of Issue in the United States—therefore the destruction of the legal tender silver money of the government left the National Banks completely in control of the currency based upon the fraudulent foundation of gold which these International bankers could manipulate and control.

NATIONAL BANKS

Alexander Hamilton made the following admission: "Money is with propriety considered as the vital principle of the body politic: as that which sustains life and motion and enables it to perform its most essential functions." (Federalist No. 29.)

Nevertheless, he was willing to transfer the control of this *vital principle* over to this so-called Bank of the United States, a corporation similar to the so-called Bank of England, both being banking corporations organized for private gain, with the power and privilege to create debts upon the people with a "bank created currency," and "bank credit," false and fictitious money represented by credit and debit figures on the books of banks.

While Alexander Hamilton was acting in the interest of European bankers in establishing the British Banking system in this country, these International Bankers were increasing their hold *on gold*—the *controlling basis* of the corporation being established, and to be known as the Bank of the United States.

THE NATIONAL BANK ACT IN 1863

This law creates banks similar to the "Bank of the United States" fathered by Alexander Hamilton.

The International Bankers who put this charter through Congress used the name "National Bank" to conceal their sinister and far-reaching purpose in establishing these corporations, organized for private gain, to control the money system of the people of the United States, which in its operation would destroy this Republic.

Lincoln, about the close of the Civil War, in a letter to Mr. Elkins of Illinois, said:

"Yes, we may congratulate ourselves that this cruel war is nearing the close, but I see in the future a crisis approaching that unnerves me and causes me to tremble for the safety of my country. As a result of the war corporations have been enthroned, and an era of corruption in high places will follow and the money power of the country will endeavor to prolong its reign by working upon the prejudices of the people until wealth is aggregated in a few hands and the republic is destroyed. I feel at this moment more anxiety for the safety of my country than ever before in the midst of war."

Salmon P. Chase, Secretary of the United States Treasury, and subsequently Associate Justice of the Supreme Court of the United States, was deceived by International Bankers, whom he considered his friends, and authorities on the subject of money; but unlike Hamilton, when he realized that he had been deceived, and that the act was unconstitutional, he denounced this "National Bank Act," as follows: "My agency in procuring the passage of the National Banking Act was the mistake of my life. It has built up a monopoly that effects every interest in the country. It should be repealed. But before this can be accomplished the people will be arrayed on one side and the banks on the other in a contest such as we have never seen in this country."

I would call especial attention to the fact that John Sherman was in charge of the bill and made a favorable report upon same from the Finance Committee of the Senate on February 2, 1863. It was taken up in the Senate on February the ninth and passed on February twelfth by a vote of 22 to 21. It was then sent to the House on the thirteenth of February and never referred to the Committee on Ways and Means, which should have been its regular order; was taken up on the nineteenth and passed the House on the twentieth of this same month by a vote of 78 to 64. It was approved by the President and became a law February 25th, 1863.

Thus this bill changed the whole currency system of this country and transferred the sovereign right of the Government "to *issue money*" to Banking Corporations organized for private gain. Thus we see the vicious principles of the two so-called United States Banks perpetuated in the hydra-headed so-called National Banks of the United States.

At this time, when the attention of the people was entirely diverted from this subject, and oblivious of the real nature and character of the bill, being absorbed in all the excitement and exigencies of a civil war, John Sherman, the agent of international bankers, takes advantage of this opportunity to inflict upon the United States the pernicious English System of gold-basis *banks of issue* and passed this bill through both Houses of Congress in the short space of ten days.

The fifth section of the act incorporating National Banks provides as follows: ''No Association is authorized to commence business until it shall have deposited United States Bonds to the amount of $30,000 with the Treasurer of the United States. Sixth: Every such association is entitled to receive from the Comptroller of the Currency circulating notes to the amount of ninety per cent. of the Capital Stock, if it does not exceed $500,000; eighty per cent. if it exceeds $500,000 and does not exceed $1,000,000; seventy-five per cent. if it exceeds $1,000,000 but does not exceed $3,000,000, and sixty per cent. if it exceeds $3,000,000.'' It should be borne in mind that no national bank notes were issued until 1864 and that the $500,000,000—of 5–20 bonds were not sold until the latter part of 1863; therefore matters were not yet in good shape for the bankers and bullionists. But in 1864 their plans were perfected to run up gold to the highest premium. Mr. Fessenden, who was then Secretary of the Treasury, pronounced the action very unpatriotic. United States Bonds bearing 6 per cent. interest were bought at this time as low as 35 cents on the dollar, in gold.

Thus the *bankers* and *bullionists* by *depressing* the *value* of *United States Bonds* were *enabled to buy them at this low price to establish national banks in this Country.*

In order to show that National Banks were not instituted as a war measure for relief of the people, an examination will disclose that, on July 1, 1865, after the close of the war, there were only $146,366,030 bank notes issued. Thus these banks of issue were foisted upon the United States at a time when they were neither desired nor needed. *The whole purpose of those back of the Scheme was to prevent the Government from exercising its constitutional function to issue money in order that the banks might usurp that power.*

The question involved was one entirely as to the quantity of money to be issued. Will any one contend that the United States at that time could not have sustained the value of and redeemed all the full legal tender dollars necessary to meet the expenses of the war when the railroads alone in the United States have made themselves responsible for the payment, dollar for dollar, of about 9 billion dollars of bonds and 8 billion dollars of stock. The former would have been secured upon the entire wealth or assets of the United States, and the latter simply on the railroad properties and their earning powers. The development of the United States after the war is the conclusive answer.

In 1865—total money in circulation in the United States was $770,129,755, and only reached as high as $774,445,610 in 1873—or a per capita circulation of $18.04.

In 1865—National Wealth—$22,067,472,000.

Population—34,748,000.

Will any one contend that, with a national wealth of over 22 billion dollars, with a population of over thirty-four million in a country producing everything the human family requires, the United States was not justified in issuing an increase of full legal tender money to meet the needs of the Government, when it is shown that the National wealth increased to over $32,000,000,000 by 1873 and its population to 41,677,000?

Instead of the United States issuing its full legal tender money redeemable in its entire National wealth, which was increasing faster than that of any other country, and the services of more than thirty-four million people working in the most productive country in the world, Congress authorized Banking Corporations to issue, indirectly, a spurious National Currency, yet based upon the National wealth, in the form of a United States Bond, payable by the people in gold, with interest—and thus allowed the money lenders to control the Money System of the United States.

Zach Chandler, a high Republican authority, made this statement on April 29th, 1869; see Congressional Globe, page 1850.

"I move to strike out, after United States, 'elsewhere.' I am opposed to contracting a foreign loan under any circumstances. We have gone through the war without borrowing one dollar from abroad. If our bonds have gone abroad it is because the money was sent here to buy them and take them, but I am opposed now to applying to the English stock exchange or any foreign stock exchange, hat in hand, begging that they will now, that we do not need it, loan to us a little money. We have shown our ability to carry this debt, and I am opposed to contracting a loan anywhere."

F. J. Scott, in the *North American Review* of September, 1885, set forth in graphic language the power of this banking institution against which the masses are protesting. He said: *"The unity of the national banking interest threatens the corruption and control of the machinery of political parties. Its power is omnipresent. It is subtle and strong to maintain laws for its own private profit.*

"Behold our banking association changed in the twinkling of an eye from one having one hundred thousand dollars of its own money to invest, to one with that amount securely invested, and ninety thousand dollars more in hand to lend. Was ever ninety thousand dollars more deftly taken in? Were this pretty subsidy the only objection to the system, it might be let alone; . . . but the principle upon which the system is founded is dangerous to the stability of business and steadiness of values.

"In Congress, where alone this power may be modified or destroyed, a large number of members of both Houses are officers and stockholders of the National Banks, and have not yet been known from any delicate appreciation of their public duties to refrain from voting on questions concerning the banks on account of having private interests therein."

MOVE OF THE MONEY POWER TO MAKE THE PRINCIPAL AS WELL AS THE INTEREST ON UNITED STATES BONDS PAYABLE IN GOLD

The money power having possession of all of the outstanding obligations of the Government, immediately began to use their unfailing influence upon Congress and the

Treasury to increase their value by making them payable in gold. A living historian at the time describes it as follows:

"The first move made by the bullionists and bondholders was to educate the public sentiment, through the press, in regard to the 'sacredness of the public faith.' The leading newspapers of the principal cities took up the song, and before a great while the gentlemen of the country press, who are not quick to learn which way the wind blows, were heard, together with the demagogues of both parties, joining in the chorus."

"The Hon. Thaddeus Stevens expressly asked the Chairman of the Ways and Means Committee and was plainly answered by him, *that only the interest* was payable in coin. Mr. Stevens then continued, 'If I knew that any party in this country would go for paying in coin that which is payable in money, thus enhancing it one-half; if I knew there was such a platform and such determination on the part of any party, I would vote on the other side. I would vote for no such swindle upon the tax-payers of this country; I would vote for no such speculation in favor of the large bondholders, the millionaires who took advantage of our folly in granting the coin payments of interest.'"

Senator Morton declared that "we should do foul injustice to the Government and the people of the United States after having sold these bonds on an average for not more than sixty cents on the dollar, now to propose to make a new contract for the benefit of the bondholders." This historian goes on to state that "the presidential campaign of 1868 was impending and it became necessary for the money power to resort to extraordinary efforts to obtain the direction of political affairs. The Rothschilds were in possession of several hundred millions of 5–20 bonds, purchased at about sixty cents on the dollar, or less, and were particularly interested. Their agent, August Belmont, of August Belmont & Co., International Bankers, who had secured the position of Chairman of the Democratic National Committee, was instructed by Baron James Rothschild, as early as March 13, 1868, that unless the Democratic party went for paying the 5–20 bonds in gold, it must be defeated. Belmont and his satellites were unable to control the making of the platform. The platform read, 'Resolved, "Third: When the obligations of the Government do not expressly state upon their face, or the law under which they were issued does not provide, that they shall be paid in coin, they ought in right to be paid in the lawful money of the United States." ' " This doomed the party to defeat. The money power was more successful with the Republican party at that time and through their aid Grant was triumphantly elected President.

In his inaugural address he alluded to "the sacredness of the public faith," and "let it be understood that no repudiator of one farthing of our public debt will be trusted in place."

In due time such a bill passed Congress and was the first act of Congress receiving Grant's official sanction.

This Act of Congress was in direct violation of the contract under which these bonds had been issued, and it could have been repealed. Therefore, the Rothschilds and the money power lost no time in getting the Secretary of the Treasury to pay off these bonds in gold or its equivalent.

An able financial writer familiar with this legislation and the influences controlling the then Secretary of the Treasury, discussed it as follows:

"This signal act of robbery, for it is only one of the many acts of robbery which have been perpetrated by the money power during the past few years under the guise of law," will foot up about as follows:

Amount of 5–20 6% bonds	$500,000,000.00
Interest in gold at 6% compounded semi-annually for ten years	403,096,132.71
	$903,096,132.71
Cost of $500,000,000 bonds at, say, sixty cents on the dollar	300,000,000.00
Net profit in ten years in gold	$603,096,132.71

The next move of the money power was to have the public debt refunded, in order to place its payment in coin beyond all question. This was done by the Act of Congress, July 14, 1870.

It is clearly shown that the money power had complete control of Congress during all this time and put laws through Congress to suit themselves, the people occupying the position of the forgotten men.

Hon. Moses W. Field of Michigan, a member of this, the 43rd Congress, describes its make-up as follows: "Six lumbermen, thirteen manufacturers, seven doctors, fourteen merchants, thirteen farmers, three millers, one land surveyor, one priest, one professor of Latin, one doctor of laws, one barber, one mechanic, ninety-nine lawyers, and one hundred and eighty-nine bankers, which included stockholders in national banks," a clean majority of them being bankers or interested in national banks.

The amount of paper emissions of the Government, including debts, doing the work of money in 1865 and 1866 was about $1,800,000,000. The condition of the people in the United States at this time is described as follows:

"In 1865-66, after the termination of the war, industry, by reason of the abundance of money in circulation, was rife throughout the country, and production went on as it had never done before. The Secretary of the Treasury, McCulloch, himself has since admitted the people were individually out of debt."

Under such conditions, what reason or justification could there be found for the resumption of specie payments, for the purpose of contracting the circulating medium of the country. It was plainly brought about by the International bankers, or money power, as their next move to permanently establish the *gold basis and banks of issue money system,* in order to exploit the people of the United States.

DESTRUCTION AND DESOLATION CAUSED BY THE RESUMPTION OF SPECIE PAYMENTS IN THE UNITED STATES

Resumption, 1875, of Specie Payments. At which time Congress *was a packed Jury in the Interest of the Money Power.*

In 1875 they put into operation the English scheme of robbing the people, "specie resumption," and passed a law decreeing resumption to take place January 1st, 1879.

In December, 1866, we had $1,906,687,770 in circulation.

Col. B. S. Heath, author of "Finance Revolution," says:

"During this year there were but 520 business failures in the whole country, involving a loss of but $17,625,000. Labor was well paid and fully employed.

"1873. This year the storm reached its climax. The people became panic-stricken, and 5,183 business firms were precipitated, with a loss of $228,499,000. Five hundred thousand men are thrown out of employment; wages cut down all over the country, and strikes are of frequent occurrence.

"Who wonders times were hard, and men idle? Still, with all this array of wreck and ruin, with the finger-board of contraction, at the close of each year, pointing to the cause, the people were asleep, or on their knees praying for some interposition of Providence in their behalf, while John Sherman went marching on with the torch of death, to burn the remaining $300,000,000 of the people's money.

"Three million men are out of employment.

"Bankruptcies multiplying with great rapidity.

"The tramp nuisance culminates.

"Wages are cut down to starvation prices.

"Strikes, riots and general consternation seize the people, and the circulation is cut down to $600,000,000.

"In 1873 came the crash, and all the languages of the world cannot describe the agonies suffered by the American people from 1873 to 1879. Thousands and thousands supposed they had enough; enough for their declining years, enough for wife and children, and suddenly found themselves paupers and vagrants. Business stood still. The men stopped digging ore; they stopped felling the forest. The fires died out in the furnaces. The men who had stood in the glare of the forge were in the gloom of despondency. There was no employment for them. The employer could not sell his product. The great factories were closed, the workmen were demoralized, and the roads of the United States were filled with tramps."

THE AMERICAN BANKERS' ASSOCIATION

PANIC CIRCULAR

In order to show that the people were deceived in the Presidential Campaign of 1892 and that the money power was the controlling force back of this campaign and that their purpose was to stop the Government from adding to the currency system by the coining, or use of any more silver as currency, and by doing this increase the hold of the money power and banking interest over the money system of the United States, in the Campaign of 1892 the people were kept excited and their attention centered on the Tariff, the Nominal Issue, while the real issue was being kept from them. They talked Tariff while the real issue was money. A valuable witness is at hand from the inner money circle to prove that this was the case. Mr. Solomon, a partner of Speyer & Co., International Bankers, made the following statement in the *Forum* for July, 1895, entitled "Sound Currency and the Dominant Issue."

"It was well understood that a reform of the tariff was to be the nominal issue of the campaign of 1892, and that all the changes were to be rung upon that theme, but enthusiasm for a reform of the tariff would not have produced for the anti-snapper movement the sinews of war. What did produce them was the conviction that the triumph of the Democratic party, with Mr. Cleveland at its head, would mean a repeal of the purchasing clause of the Sherman Act. A large number of the men who joined actively in the work of organization, though also tariff reformers, could not have afforded to make the numerous self-sacrifices necessary to taking an active part in a canvass on any but such a vital issue as that of the maintenance of the integrity of the currency."

This article was written by Mr. Solomon, who was in a position to know the facts, and he put himself on record as above, three years after the people thought they had elected Cleveland upon the Tariff Issue. In this connection, I desire to call the attention of the people of this country to what is known as the American Bankers' Association. This Association is made up of local clearing house associations numbering 140, throughout the United States. In other words, the American Bankers' Association is a combination of the various Local Clearing House Associations throughout the United States, composed of the individual banks in the different communities throughout the United States.

The Clearing House Associations are autocratic bodies organized upon the plan of the Clearing House Association of New York, which, in fact, is the parent organization, was formed in 1853, and is one of the important factors of the money power. It is a voluntary organization, has no charter from the state, is not amenable to legislative or judicial control. It absolutely controls its membership, which at present embraces every large bank and trust company in the City of New York. After a Bank has once become a member of any of these "Clearing House Associations" and uses its machinery to clear for them, the fate of such a bank is absolutely at the mercy of the Association, for the reason that, if the Association declines or stops clearing for them, a run is immediately made upon the bank and it has to close its doors. Bearing in mind the power of the American Bankers' Association, which through its Clearing House Association membership reaches every Bank of any importance in the United States, it is obvious that none of them would be willing to antagonize its influence and power.

It is important to bear in mind that, at the time of Cleveland's Inauguration, business conditions throughout the United States were in a prosperous state, crops were good and the mercantile agencies reported conditions "very satisfactory and unusually strong." At this time the Government was purchasing and putting into circulation 4,500,-000 ounces of silver a month, represented by United States silver certificates. This the Banks determined to stop, and, as soon as Cleveland had taken the oath of office as President of the United States, the American Bankers' Association, realizing that there was a large majority in Congress against the repeal of this act whereby the Government was issuing additional currency, determined to force its repeal by creating a panic in order to do so. Just eight days after Cleveland was sworn into office, on March 12, 1893, the American Bankers' Association, representing the Incorporated National Banks of the United States, through their all-powerful influence and control of the currency of this country, deliberately planned to destroy the prosperity and business welfare of over 80,-000,000 people in order to increase their stranglehold on the Monetary System of the United States, their plan being to drive the people into misery and poverty, hiding their intentions by loudly proclaiming that it was due to the Government adding to the currency by issuing silver certificates, charging that the panic was brought on by the Government using silver bullion and issuing silver certificates to increase the currency. Fortunately, the Panic Circular sent out on the 12th of March, 1893, by this organization, the American Bankers' Association, is at hand and can be correctly designated as the panic circular of the organized money power of the United States, as it was the immediate and only cause of the panic of 1893. It reads as follows:

"Dear Sir:—The interests of national bankers require immediate financial legislation by Congress. Silver, silver certificates and treasury notes must be retired and the national bank notes, upon a gold basis, made the only money. This requires the authorization of $500,000,000 to $1,000,000,000 of new bonds as a basis of circulation. *You will at once retire one-third of your circulation and call in one-half of your loans.* Be careful to make a money stringency felt among your patrons, especially among influential business men. Advocate an extra session of Congress for the repeal of the purchase clause of the Sherman law; and act with other banks of your city in securing a large petition to Congress for its unconditional repeal, as per accompanying form. Use personal influence with congressmen; and particularly, let your wishes be known to your senators. The future life of national banks as fixed and safe investments depends upon immediate action, as there is an increasing sentiment in favor of governmental legal tender notes and silver coinage.''

The testimony of Cleveland verifies the condition of prosperity at this time. He states:

''Our unfortunate financial plight is not the result of untoward events, or of conditions related to our national resources; nor is it traceable to any of the afflictions which frequently check national growth and prosperity. With plenteous crops, with abundant promise of remunerative production and manufacture, with unusual invitation to safe investment, and with satisfactory assurance of business enterprise, suddenly financial distrust and fear have sprung up on every side.''

That of Senator Hill of New York as to the action of the Bankers in following the directions given them by the American Bankers' Association.

Senator Hill, in a speech in the Senate, on August 25, 1893, said:

''They (the bankers) inaugurated the policy of refusing loans to the people, even upon the best of security, and attempted in every way to spread disaster throughout the land. These disturbers—these promoters of the public peril —represent largely the creditor class, the men who desire to appreciate the gold dollar in order to subserve their own selfish interests; men who revel in hard times; men who drive harsh bargains with their fellow-men regardless of financial distress, and men wholly unfamiliar with the principles of monetary science.''

CARLISLE DECISION TURNED DOLLARS INTO DEBTS

From 1862 to 1893 the control of the government was in the hands of the Republican party. During all this time all legislation on money had been dominated by the banking interest, but at this time the money interest realized that there was a large majority in Congress which was opposed to discontinuing entirely the further use of silver, by the government, as money; so they determined to make the Democratic party their scapegoat and tool in order to put over the next financial conspiracy upon the people of the United States and still further strengthen the hold and control of banks of issue over the circulating medium of the country. There never was a more comprehensive plan put in operation by the banking associations to coerce Congress to pass this bill. The writer was in contact with senators and the representatives of the people in Washington; appeals were being made to them from their constituents all over the United States to withdraw their objections to the passage of this bill, as their banks had notified them that they could not give them banking accommodations unless this bill was passed. So great was the pressure upon a certain senator whom I knew intimately, and who so clearly understood the fraud that was about to be perpetrated upon the people, that he said: "It was the greatest trial of my life to refuse to comply with their request, yet I would have lost my self-respect and would have surrendered my honest convictions upon a question I knew would be of greatest injury to the people." Holding these convictions, he tendered his resignation to the legislature of his state, which was declined.

In this fight for the unconditional repeal of the silver act the organized banking interests made a direct attack on the silver and silver certificates in order to discredit them, the object of the bankers being to stop any further addition of money issued by the government in order that banks of issue might substitute their notes and strengthen their monopoly over the money system of the United States. Space will not permit me to describe the loss and suffering brought upon the people, which covered a period of about six years.

I will now come to the next step taken by this association of the banking interests to absolutely discredit and convert into debts, $350,000,000 of money, that had already been issued by the government. In order to do this I would call attention to the law of 1890, which provides, Section 1, "That the Secretary of the Treasury is hereby directed to purchase, from time to time, silver bullion to the aggregate amount of 4,500,000 ounces, at the market price thereof . . . and to issue, *in payment for such purchases of silver bullion, Treasury notes of the United States.*"

Section 2. "That the Treasury notes issued in accordance with the provisions of this act shall be redeemable on demand, in coin, at the Treasury of the United States, and when so redeemed may be reissued.''

After forcing through Congress the act stopping the coinage of silver, they put into operation what has been aptly termed "the endless chain process."

John G. Carlisle, who had been speaker of the House of Representatives and a lifelong opponent of the so-called gold standard, had stated (I quote him): "According to my views of the subject, the conspiracy which seems to have been formed here and in Europe to destroy by legislation and otherwise from three-sevenths to one-half the metallic money of the world is the most gigantic crime of this or any other age. The consummation of such a scheme would ultimately entail more misery upon the human race than all the wars, pestilences and famines that ever occurred in the history of the world.''

Cleveland appointed Carlisle Secretary of the Treasury, and the administration, through influence brought to bear by the money interest, determined to increase the public debt by the issue of bonds, and simultaneously to discredit and turn into debts $350,000,000 of United States Treasury notes and silver certificates, and use them to force a bond issue for the benefit of the banks as a basis for the increased issue of national bank notes. The writer has in his possession conclusive evidence of the following statement: Although the law provided that Treasury notes should be redeemed in coin at the discretion of the Secretary of the Treasury, the whole object of the law being that the Secretary should use the option in the interest of the people and redeem the Treasury notes in either gold or silver, using that which was most convenient at the time, the Bank of France without exception has so exercised this option. President Cleveland used his influence over Carlisle to get him to construe the law so that he should redeem these United States Treasury notes in gold. Carlisle was an able lawyer and familiar with all the statutes bearing on the subject of money, was also aware of the motives of those who were demanding such an illegal construction of this law; he was so much exercised and concerned in the importance of such action that he requested two United States Senators, his closest friends, to confer with him.

One was Senator Blackburn of Kentucky, the other Senator Daniel of Virginia. The conference was held at Secretary Carlisle's K Street residence, he having an appointment to see President Cleveland at the White House that night. These two senators urged Carlisle to adhere to the law that plainly stated that the Treasury notes issued in payment for silver bullion should be redeemed in coin, either silver or gold, at the option of the Secretary of the Treasury, and that for him to do otherwise would leave the United States Treasury, the fiduciary department intrusted with the people's money, at the mercy of the moneyed interest. Carlisle left the house saying that he would not relinquish the option to redeem these Treasury notes as provided in the law and allow the holder of these notes to demand gold in payment for them, which would leave the Treasury of the United States in an absolutely defenseless condition, and enable the holder of these notes to raid the gold reserve of the Treasury. Senators Blackburn and Daniel waited for him to return from his interview with Cleveland at the White House. He had evidently had a long and trying conference, and it was midnight before he returned. He met his friends, evidencing the greatest humiliation, and said that Cleveland had induced him against his own convictions to redeem these Treasury notes in gold. Carlisle looked as if he had sold his birthright.

The unthinking cannot realize the far-reaching significance of this decision. It was the first time in the history of the money of the world that a dollar was decided to be a debt redeemable in another dollar. The direct result was the conversion of 350,000,000 Treasury notes, or dollars, into debts redeemable in gold. It opened the door of the United States Treasury to the planned attack on its gold reserve and forced an issue of 262,000,000 of bonds on the taxpayers in a time of profound peace. I would impress upon the voters of this country the vital importance to them of this action, as it is the absolutely false and indefensible premise upon which the banking interest of this country proposes to build their so-called National Reserve Association of the United States, viz., the baseless and fraudulent assumption that it is necessary, in order to maintain the equality, or, as they term it, the parity of our dollars, that we should construe all other dollars in our currency system to be debts redeemable in gold, and, in order to deceive the people, they have created a gold reserve of $150,000,000 in the Treasury to be used in maintaining, as they claim, the equality or parity of our dollars.

Is there a sane, honest man who will contend for one moment that the integrity of our currency system and the equality, parity or purchasing power of the American dollar are maintained in their value by $150,000,000 of gold (ostensibly held as a reserve, yet which can be raided and withdrawn by the money interest at any time), and not by the $134,000,000,000 of national wealth and the services of 94,000,000 people in the United States pledged for its redemption?   (1912.)

THE GOLD BASIS BANKING SYSTEM

Let us sum up the experience of the United States, and show the cost of our public debt to the tax-payers, and the profit made on it by the national banks and foreign investors in the bonds of the United States, all paid by the taxes of the people, and, as a rule, received by non-producers. The account of the United States Treasury alone shows the following:

PAGE 113. ANNUAL REPORT OF THE SECRETARY OF THE TREASURY, 1909.

Paid interest on the public debt from 1860 to 1909	$2,612,144,531.10
Paid on principal public debt from 1865 to September 30, 1910	1,377,831,931.01
	$3,989,976,462.11
Balance of this debt unpaid about	$1,000,000,000.00

Let the banking system established in the United States after the Civil War, as managed by bankers for the last forty-five years, be the test of the merit of these men and the system, and see if they are worthy to be trusted with the control of the money of this great country, upon which depends the business and welfare of one hundred and ten million people. You can judge the future only by the past, and what man has done from self-interest in the past he will do again in the future if the opportunity is given him.

Out of these losses of the war the burden of a great debt fell upon the people of the United States. Who, or what class of men, made money out of this misfortune of the people of this country?

In the light of our present-day intelligence, a remarkable transaction took place at this time. The representatives of the American people in Congress assembled chartered national banks, virtually telling them (for the result demonstrated it), ''We will issue to you millions of first mortgage bonds upon the property of the people of the United

States and pledge the services and assets of all the people to redeem them at par with interest, and in order that you may pay for them without inconvenience will allow you to deposit them in the United States Treasury, still draw your interest on them, and the Government will allow you to issue 90 per cent. of the money it will require you to pay for them, and we will make your national bank notes absolutely good, by agreeing to redeem them at par." Many of these bonds were bought as low as $65.00 and sold as high as $120.00. These bond issues bore interest rates ranging as high as 7.3 per cent.

Such is the origin of the bank note in this country and the beginning of the false premises upon which it is now proposed to establish a permanent money system. Money issued by banks and based on debt! Yet there is no man who can successfully contend that a promise to pay money is better than money itself, or that any credit contrivance is as good as real money to do business on.

As a matter of fact, when you say that a bank note, a silver certificate, or any kind of promise to pay, has to be redeemed in something else—for instance, gold—before it becomes a legal tender to pay a debt, it simply means that debts are issued as a circulating medium instead of real money. I would ask a careful examination of the following:

FROM "WEALTH, DEBT, AND TAXATION"—PAGE 43, CENSUS REPORT. ALSO REPORT COMPTROLLER CURRENCY—PAGE 59, REPORT, 1909.

	1860	1870	1880
National wealth..	$16,159,616,068	$24,054,814,806	$43,642,000,000
Population	31,443,321	38,558,371	50,155,783
Amount of money	442,102,477	722,868,461	1,185,550,327
	1890	1900	1904
National wealth..	$61,203,755,972	$82,304,517,845	$107,104,192,410
Population	62,622,250	76,295,220	81,867,000
Amount of money	1,685,123,429	2,339,705,673	2,803,504,135
	1909		
National wealth..	$117,000,000,000		
Population	88,926,000		
Amount of money	3,406,328,354		

The total money in circulation is less than shown in the figures here given, and the percentage of increase should therefore be less. See "Comptroller of the Currency," for 1909, page 59,—Amount of money in 1909, $3,124,679,057.

It is here clearly shown that this country at any time in its history could have used its full legal tender dollars for all the money in its currency system, having more real value back of them for their redemption than all the gold in the world. If this had been done it would have saved the tax-payers of the country up to 1910 $5,000,000,000.

Lord Goschen, the English authority on foreign exchange, practically admitted this could have been done as far back as 1865. I quote, "What, it may be asked, will be the value of gold to them—the people of the United States—if they neither require it for internal circulation, which they may think can be managed as well by paper, nor for payment of foreign liabilities, from which, under our hypotheses, they will be comparatively free."

"If that mischievous financial policy which has had its origin in the North American Republic during the late war in that country should become indurated down to a fixture there that Government will furnish its money without cost. It will pay off its debts and be without a debt. It will have all the money necessary to carry on its commerce. It will become prosperous beyond precedent in the History of Civilized Governments of the World. The brains and wealth of all countries will go to North America. That Government must be destroyed, or it will destroy every monarchy on this globe."—*London Times*, 1865.

This country has accumulated more national wealth in two generations than the rest of the world in centuries, and it is the height of folly for the Government to be paying interest on money guaranteed by itself and secured upon bonds.

The effect of the burdens of debt and interest charges is telling upon the nerves and vitality of the Americans. You can see it depicted in the faces of 90 per cent. of the business men you meet on the streets of our large cities. The eager, anxious and necessitous hunt for the illusive dollar, to meet their debts and expenses, is shutting out all contentment and real joys from their lives, and has brought about artificial conditions, breeding disease and hurrying many of them to premature graves.

To my mind it is a very remarkable thing that this old fallacy, fastened after the war upon the American money system by the foreign and American money lenders, without the knowledge or suspicion of the American citizen as to its full meaning, should have so long escaped his intelligent investigation. It is true, the subject has been clouded and concealed by the discussion of the relative merits of bimetallism and monometallism since 1868 to the recent establishment of the so-called gold standard—the last subterfuge of the advocates of a credit currency. Money predicated on debts, to be issued and controlled by banks!

It is an utterly indefensible system, and its birth and history absolutely discredit it and should condemn it for all time. A simple statement of the case should annihilate it, for in its final analysis it becomes a *reductio ad absurdum* and is a standing reflection upon the good sense of the American people.

With this privilege of issuing money with the endorsement of the Government, the money lenders of any country could become millionaires, and would desire to make the system permanent, thus constituting them the dominant class. This is the case in the United States at present.

It was in this way that a national bank note was created, and the insidious beginning of issuing promises to pay, or debts redeemable in gold, instead of money itself, the ultimate of payment. Our whole present money system is an utterly weak credit contrivance. The bankers would say to the American people of the twentieth century, "We know that you have accumulated $175,000,000,000 of national wealth, and you can at any time bankrupt the world by issuing bonds upon same and buying its gold, yet we shall contend you can't issue your own money without our assistance, therefore we must control a great bank of issue to supply and control the amount of money we think the American people ought to have, and in this way we can become their guardians and regulate their business for them, making business good or bad as it suits our interest.

"For this exclusive right to issue money we will allow the United States Treasury to hold our miscellaneous bonds and assets as security upon which we will continue to draw interest, and thus be enabled to lend out the millions of money the Government allows us to issue against them, yet we will require the Government to guarantee to redeem our notes for us and, to disarm suspicion, allow us to call them 'national currency.' We still consider this an equitable arrangement, as it simply segregates us from the great mass of American people, and allows us to 'eat our cake and have it too.' We, the money lenders, no longer accept the correct meaning of the old adage because we have demonstrated it can be done for the last forty-five years.

"Yet in order that our money may be accepted by the people at large we need the endorsement of the sovereign power of the people of the United States that they will redeem all our bank notes or promises to pay in gold, and if necessary issue bonds to buy the gold to redeem our notes, and then be taxed to pay the bonds, principal, and interest."—For what? In order that "Banks of Issue" may foist their notes upon the people and control these promises to pay in the place of money itself issued by the Government.

Under their operation there has grown up in this country the greatest speculative borrowing system the world has ever known; every condition is made conducive to borrowing or getting into debt and nothing favorable to getting out of debt.

There is no more reason or justification for a banking corporation being allowed to invest its money in miscellaneous securities, or lend it on the property of others, and then be allowed to use these securities or this property as securities to issue money on, to be loaned again, than it is for an individual to invest his money in real estate, or anything else and have the right to issue a like amount. To give banking corporations composed of individuals this privilege is to put them in position to manufacture debts indefinitely and draw interest from the people.

At this point I desire to call special attention of the reader to the following, according to the report of the Comptroller of the Currency, 1909, page 5.

"Of the $5,128,882,351 loans and discounts of national banks on September 1, 1909, one-fourth, or $1,398,879,624, consisted of demand paper, of which $957,349,934 was secured by stocks, bonds, etc."

National banks alone had loaned out money payable to them on demand with individual or firm names, $441,-

529,690 and secured by stocks and bonds $957,349,934, amounting to $1,398,879,624. Taking into consideration and deducting the legal reserves of banks and money impounded in the United States Treasury and held in trust, there is left only $1,652,300,000 for actual circulation to carry on the entire business of this country and sustain its enormous values. You can readily imagine the power of a money lending class holding a demand call for money sufficient to withdraw practically every dollar in actual circulation. A demand for 10 per cent. of it would cause a panic sufficient to destroy the value of untold millions of the people's holdings.

The following copied from the Report of the Comptroller of the Currency for 1909, page 5, is worthy of the most careful study, as it sets forth in a compact and comprehensive manner the unstable and precarious money situation of this country upon which all business depends:

SUMMARY OF THE SPECIAL REPORTS OBTAINED FOR AND COMPILED BY THE NATIONAL MONETARY COMMISSION FROM 22,491 BANKS OF THE UNITED STATES AND ISLAND POSSESSIONS (INCLUDING NATIONAL, STATE, SAVINGS, AND PRIVATE BANKS AND LOAN AND TRUST COMPANIES), SHOWING THEIR CONDITION AT THE CLOSE OF BUSINESS ON APRIL 28, 1909.

RESOURCES

1. Loans and discounts:

(a) On demand, unsecured by collateral...	$ 660,425,952.28
(b) On demand, secured by collateral.....	1,939,634,898.23
(c) On time, with two or more names, unsecured by collateral	2,539,965,833.06
(d) On time, single-name paper, unsecured by collateral	1,351,781,832.63
(e) On time, secured by collateral........	2,036,358,417.46
(f) Secured by real estate mortgages or liens on realty....................	1,127,276,405.37
(g) Not classified	269,373,194.28

Let the people be no longer misled by statements in official documents and the public press that we have a per capita "circulation" of $34.98 of money in our currency system. The fact is, as stated above, that we have only $1,652,300,000 for actual circulation after deducing the legal reserve of the banks as required by law, and amount held in United States Treasury. From the following Excerpt from Report of Comptroller of the Currency, 1909, page 58, the per capita "circulation" is shown to be but $18.54:

"By using the details of figures showing monetary stock on May 1, 1909, the per cent. of money in the Treasury will be 9.06, the amount not in the Treasury or banks 48.50, or $1,652,300,000 instead of $1,661,900,000, and the per capita of money not in the Treasury or banks $18.54 instead of $18.68."

Furthermore it will be seen from the Report of the National Monetary Commission, 1909, Special Report from the Banks of the United States, that they have loaned *on demand* $2,598,404,221.07, or $946,104,221.07 more money than is in actual existence for the circulation or available for use as real money.

It should be borne in mind that the banking institutions have it in their power to make demand on these so-called time loans secured by collateral at very short intervals, hence they lack duration and stability as to time of payment, and this greatly augments the danger.

This being the situation, the American people are brought face to face with the practical danger of there being $7,-044,206,902 of money loaned out by banking institutions every dollar of which has a string tied to it and only $1,652,300,000 of money in actual circulation to carry on the entire business of the United States, not taking into consideration the demands for money created by the other tremendous outstanding liabilities enumerated in this table and held by these banks alone. It is safe to say a 5 per cent. call by the banks on these loans secured by stock and bonds would bring on a panic, and a 20 per cent. call take every dollar out of actual circulation.

There is far more than enough of American securities in the hands of European banking establishments specifically payable in gold to exhaust the supply of gold held by the United States Treasury and the banks, at any time, and produce a panic.

In addition to this, it is now a regular thing for American holders of large blocks of stock, in order to conceal their identity, to sell them out abroad as if it were done by European holders, and also send them out of the country and borrow on them in the foreign market, thus reducing the apparent stock supply in the United States. This borrowing of money abroad to carry them eases the money conditions in New York, which has the effect to advance the price of these securities in New York, giving the owners a chance to unload them at home at the highest they can force the price to. On the other hand if they sell them abroad it depresses prices in New York, and they buy them in at the low price, working both ends of the line, and the money market, to swindle the buying and gambling public.

The favorite plan is for the large owners in conjunction with the banks and trust companies in which they are controlling factors to offer to loan up close to the market value of the securities, and thus push them up by stages —as was done by the National City Bank with Amalgamated Copper Stocks, etc., and then unload them on the public.

It is a very easy matter for these combinations to create a gold movement either way, and keep this see-saw arrangement going without end, exploiting investors, going and coming, and eternally demoralizing all legitimate business.

It would be more business-like and far wiser for us to allow the Europeans to keep their money, which would increase their purchasing power for the things we have for sale, and use our balance of trade against them in buying back American securities upon which our people are paying over $225,000,000 annually, according to the most reliable estimates to be had in the year 1911. On the other hand, by depleting their money supply we reduce prices in European countries and increase their exports by forcing them to undersell us.

With a balance of trade against Europe it is unjustifiable upon any theory based upon common sense that the people of the United States should be paying foreigners this interest instead of keeping these American securities at home.

Based upon the interest estimated the amount of American securities held abroad would amount to $5,000,000,000 in 1911.

As a demonstration of the great danger and loss that

may occur at any time to the American people from this state of things I would ask a careful examination of the following statement showing the difference between the market value of the stocks of railroads and industrial corporations between the panic year of 1907 and July 19, 1909.

	Closing Price July 19, '09.	Low 1907.	Gain.	Appreciation.
American Car & Foundry common....	62	24⅜	37⅝	$11,287,500
American Car & Foundry preferred...	*118¼	78	40¼	12,075,000
American Cotton Oil common........	74	21	53	10,725,663
American Cotton Oil preferred.......	*103½	70	33½	3,416,531
American Locomotive common	61¼	32¼	29	7,250,000
American Locomotive preferred.......	*119	83	36	9,000,000
American Smelting & Refining common	93⅞	58¼	35⅝	17,812,000
American Smelting & Refining preferred	112	81¾	30¼	15,125,000
American Sugar common	127	92¾	34¼	15,412,500
American Sugar preferred	*125	106	19	8,550,000
Corn Products common	23¼	8	15¼	7,587,561
Corn Products preferred	87	46	41	12,217,016
Mackay Cos. common	*80	40	40	16,552,160
Mackay Cos. preferred	*74	50	24	12,000,000
National Biscuit common	*106	58½	47½	13,887,100
National Biscuit preferred 125½		90	35½	8,805,597
North American	83¾	37	46¾	13,922,000
Peoples' Gas	116	70¼	45¾	15,986,055
Pressed Steel Car common	44⅛	15⅝	28½	3,562,500
Pressed Steel Car preferred	106	64	42	5,040,000
Pullman Company	*190	135¼	54¾	54,750,000
Railway Steel Spr. common	46½	21½	25	3,375,000
Railway Steel Spr. preferred	105¼	72	33¼	4,488,750
Republic Iron & Steel common	33	12	21	5,743,920
Republic Iron & Steel preferred	107	50½	56½	11,781,380
Sloss-Sheffield common	84¾	26	58¾	6,375,000
Sloss-Sheffield preferred	*116½	80	36½	2,445,500
United States Rubber common	39	13½	25½	6,034,830
United States Rubber 1st preferred ..	117	61¼	55¾	20,035,307
United States Rubber 2d preferred ...	83	39	44	4,384,600
United States Steel common	71⅝	21⅞	49¾	252,976,362
United States Steel preferred	127⅝	79⅛	48½	174,752,338

Total $835,188,948

* Last previous sale.

By a careful examination and comparison of the prices of stocks before the panic of 1907 and those of July 19, 1909, it will be seen that they have simply regained the loss brought on by the money contraction and panic of 1907. Few really appreciate the awful consequences of such a fall in the value of these stocks alone. It is well known that a great majority of the individual holders of these stocks had bought them on margins and that the stocks were in the hands of banking institutions as collateral for loans subject to a call for payment at any time. Imagine the havoc and loss among this army of small investors where a loss occurred in the market value of these securities amounting to over $3,206,702,000, a decline in value of twice the entire amount of gold money in the whole currency system of the United States. Add to this the fall in the value of all things in the United States owned and dealt in by the people, the absolute refusal of banking institutions to accommodate the legitimate demand of business, and some idea can be formed of the extent of this calamity. In addition to the incalculable loss, two million men were out of employment as the direct result. Under such conditions as now exist where every one is encouraged to become a speculator, and hence a borrower, the equity of the multitude in what they think they own is periodically wiped out, and the distinguishing quality of a people under a republican form of government, which endows them with greater energy, enterprise, and individual effort, becomes their curse, owing to an evil financial system—the effect of which is to cheat them when young and beggar them when old.

While the real workers and producers are bringing into existence everything needed by the human family for its comfort and happiness, and a kind providence has blessed them beyond the former children of the earth, by the selfish machinations of men called financiers, international bankers, etc., we are cursed with a money system which can only be properly designated as a monumental fraud perpetrated on an unsuspecting people.

Up to the present time all legislation on money has been to increase the debtor class. It is now high time owing to the tremendous wealth and productive force of the people of the United States that this process should be reversed, and debt paying instead of debt making be the object of all future legislation affecting the money system.

There is nothing embarrassing and hampering the future of our people more than paying the tremendous tribute to an interest account, that is indirectly carried by them, in addition to their individual obligation, and added to the cost of the things they buy.

To make its awful significance clear I will use a striking illustration, which will be familiar to all, although it is only one of a class of operations which practically cover every important industry in this country. I refer to the United States Steel Corporation.

The important base of the operations of this corporation was owned by Andrew Carnegie and a few competitors. The firm had developed the largest steel and iron manufacturing business in this country. Its profit and legitimate earnings were yielding a large income upon the money invested, after paying reasonable wages to all employed. The owners were getting rich in building up a large legitimate business, left open to competition, that friend of the consumer. These gentlemen, being in funds, would as a matter of business have no mortgage upon their plants to create a fixed charge of interest which would be a handicap in meeting competition. In meeting fair competition in legitimate business the first and most important use of money is to reduce fixed charges.

Upon this basis steel and iron in all its useful forms could be bought and used by the people at a reasonable price.

A radical change takes place, a notorious promoter and financier, and his associates in like business, conceive an idea, and the following proposition is made to Carnegie and a few competitors. If you, Mr. Carnegie, and others, who own these steel plants, will turn this whole outfit over to us, hereafter to be known as the United States Steel Corporation, we will have issued to you and associates $475,266,500 in first mortgage bonds, secured upon all the property you sell us and bearing 5 per cent. interest, in payment for same. Here is a fixed annual interest charge of $23,762,225 placed upon the cost of running the plants, and added permanently to the cost of steel rails and structural iron, etc., entering into all building operations of any size in this country. The financiers and promoters now take charge of the business in place of the real owners who ought to be working it, and the next step is to convert the imaginary equity of these plants into paper tokens of wealth. Thereupon they capitalize it as follows:

First mortgage bonds	$475,266,500
Second, Preferred 7 per cent. Cumulative Stock	400,000,000
Third, Common Stock	550,000,000
	$1,425,266,000

What is the direct result of this operation upon the price of the products of this business to the American people? 1. This steel and iron industry is loaded down with a mortgage of $475,266,500, bearing 5 per cent. interest, making a fixed charge upon the product (for no effort is made to pay it off and it will no doubt be funded later for a larger amount) of $23,762,500 a year. 2. Preferred 7 per cent. cumulative stock, $400,000,000, making a charge of $28,000,000 a year. 3. Common stock, $550,-000,000, upon which they are now paying 5 per cent., which amounts to another charge of $27,500,000 a year.

Here is the consummation of a deliberate plan to add a burden of cost to the price of steel and iron products to the consumers of $79,162,500 a year by this corporation, after deducting all the legitimate cost of running the business and paying large salaries to its officers and agents. This is the tax the consumers pay one corporation in the steel and iron business alone. Such is the economic result of the iron manufacturer being replaced by the manufacturers of debts in the shape of bonds and stocks to the amount of $1,425,266,000.

It is no longer the first object of this new management to turn out the best quality of products to meet possible competition and succeed on the merits of its business. The *modus operandi* of the promoting bankers is altogether a different process. It introduces the modern "get rich quick" scheme and, "let the people hold the bag" and posterity inherit the debts. They have so far worked this plan successfully upon most of the great productive resources of this country. The first move after securing the business is to control the output, put up the prices, and if necessary reduce wages in order to pay dividends upon these paper tokens of wealth.

The banking and financial institutions, largely controlled by these same financiers, stand ready to accept these manufactured debts as collateral for loans, and by such accept-

ance at once give them a money value, and, as their value
is increased on the market they likewise increase the
amount of money they will loan on them, which in turn
pushes up their market value again, and as the people
or the market will absorb or digest them they will feed
them out. So perfectly have they got this banking machinery working that Morgan & Co. simply allotted so
much of the stock of the United States Steel Corporation
to banks to be disposed of. Thus, these paper tokens of
wealth, manufactured for the purpose and amounting to
$950,000,000 above the $475,266,500 first mortgage bonds
upon the property, are pushed up in market value until
they can be unloaded on the people. Now we see the most
celebrated American bankers and financiers in their won-
derful feat of jugglery with the money of the country.
They have created from something that did not exist
paper tokens of wealth and then converted them into
nearly $950,000,000 of money, and, forsooth, they are the
same men who must have a sound dollar, an honest dollar,
a gold dollar, with strings tied to it in order that they
may jerk the foundation from under the American money
system at any time, and make the people stand the loss.

I ask in the name of the American people if this
legalized robbery has produced or added anything to the
material wealth of the country, or its physical or moral
well-being? On the contrary it has become as injurious
to the well-being of this country as the after-effect of war.
It is loading down the great industrial resources with the
burden of debts and interest charges. How can the consumers, producers, and workers hope to pay it and get
things they need in the upbuilding of this great country
at a reasonable price, or ever compete in the foreign market
on a fair business basis? High prices here will increase
imports and decrease exports, to the great injury of the
country.

This process will inevitably destroy our balance of trade
with foreign countries, for how can we ever expect to
compete with them, when our manufacturing establishments are handicapped by the burden of debts, bearing
interest, that have to be added as a fixed charge to the
cost of the goods manufactured, and the high wages paid

to the workmen which have to be maintained in order that they can live, owing to the high cost of everything they need? What chance of sale do the American products stand in competition with a foreign establishment out of debt, and paying lower wages to its workmen, who can live so much cheaper than those in this country? They are thus able to undersell us with ease, hence our great increase in imports of foreign goods.

The trust combinations gave us the main reason for their existence the lowering of the cost of doing business, in their greater economy of operating thereby enabling them to capture the foreign markets. The result shows they have put up the prices of the things they control so high in this country that the foreigner is capturing the American markets.

This is a total departure from all well-recognized principles. Heretofore, as soon as a prudent man accumulated any profit, he paid off any mortgage he might have on his business establishment, in order to reduce his fixed charges and reduce the cost of carrying on the business. In this way he was prepared to meet any competitor in turning out or selling the finished products, and so long as he was satisfied with a reasonable profit he need fear no fair competition. Under this condition the law of demand and supply would operate and the people buy at a reasonable price.

These manufacturers of debts, in conjunction with banking, have evolved a plan by which the present manufacturer can retire from business, and still draw his income. Their plan being to put a mortgage upon the entire business and add the interest upon same to the first cost of goods to be paid for by the consumer—it is an indirect charge or tax upon the buyer, but they have arranged it so that he will not see it that way. They then add another improvement in business methods, and although they have not received a patent on it by the United States Government, they find their plan accomplishes the same result, viz., monopoly. In effect, it is a contravention of the laws of nature; the laws of demand and supply no longer regulate the value of the things they handle. They thus stop all competition on the things they market and make the people pay their price.

It simply means, the manufacturers stop fighting each other, get together, and make the money out of the millions of consumers by advancing the price. They think that by doing a gigantic business the size of it will so daze the minds of the people that they will not realize how it has happened, and the people's Representatives in Congress will hide behind the sage remark, that consolidation is the new and approved order of business. They have everything their own way, for, with a protective tariff wall high enough to keep out foreign competition on the things they sell, they can exploit the people. And in addition to this they and their associates control the money supply, so the people cannot get away from them. Their competitors without money accommodation will have to go out of business.

The combination of the bankers, financiers, and promoters have found this scheme so successful and profitable that they have blanketed almost every important industry of the United States with bond and stock issues until the paper tokens of wealth dealt in on the stock exchanges of this country now amount to about seventy billion dollars, the dividends upon which can be paid in only two ways, by advance on the price of the things sold to the people, or by reducing the wages of the men who make them.

It has been said that "some men lie with such volubility that truth seems to be a fool." Far truer is it that these financial bandits get millions so easily that he who works honestly for his money seems to be a fool.

The whole system is rotten to the core, an ulcer upon the body politic. It would never have fastened itself with all its corrupting influence upon the American people without the coöperation of this Government with the present money lending system.

The indictment will hold as against the banking interests, for without their assistance and coöperation this fungus growth of stocks and bonds issued in absolute violation of all moral, legal, and economic laws, could never have been fastened upon the great industries of this country. And its future mortgaged by unscrupulous financiers and speculators!

When a country furnishes and encourages by its money system the creation of debts for its people to invest their money in, less money will go legitimately into productive enterprises affording employment to the workers who build up the real wealth of the country. The inevitable effect is, and will be, that nonproducers and parasites will increase, and producers decrease. Debts and interest will accumulate until the earning power of its debts is greater than the net profits of labor, which build up the real national wealth.

This is a reversal of natural and economic laws, which are and should be under normal conditions most favorable to the producer and the man who works. As a demonstration of the correctness of these laws, you might destroy money, loans, banks, financial institutions, courts and corporations, yet leave man the earth and his labor will re-create them all.

Manufacturing unnecessary debts upon the natural resources and material wealth of this country, with no idea of ever paying them off, has gone on long enough. They have already created a mountain of abnormal demands upon the American people who now indirectly pay interest on bonds and dividends on stocks without end, until it is crushing legitimate business and placing such a demand and burden upon the real money supply of this country that it can no longer sustain it.

No man or corporation can load down a business with a mortgage for all it is worth, bearing interest, and sell its output to the consumer at a fair price or survive legitimate competition.

No country or nation overloaded with interest and dividend earning debts can meet fair and legitimate competition.

THE BANKING SYSTEM AND STOCK
GAMBLING

Now let us look at the condition of stock gambling that has grown up under the present banking system of the United States. Few who indulge in it call it gambling, yet to those who know the inside of the game, the promoter of the combinations, syndicates in investments, "speculations," "fliers," and "business ventures," know it to be nothing more nor less than "a game to get something for nothing."

It is definitely stated by those in the business that, "the industries of the American people are now represented by $70,000,000,000 of paper tokens, in certificates of stocks, bonds, etc., which are 'dealt in' on the stock exchanges, and that the purchase and sale of these paper tokens each year represent the employment of more money than all the manufacturing, all the farming, all the transportation business of the American people." It is also stated that the amount of deposited money in banks and trust companies of America furnished those who subsist directly or indirectly on the business of stock gambling is far greater in amount than that employed in the real productive business of America.

Then again, it is stated that "the amount of money taken each year for the living expenses of those directly and indirectly engaged in the business of stock gambling, not a man of whom is a legitimate producer of anything of value to his fellow-man, is far greater than that taken by those engaged in managing any ten lines of legitimate business."

In the face of this condition of things what becomes of the test that any right-minded and honest man would apply to his life, asking, What have I returned to the great store-house of the world for all I have taken out of it? Any man who deliberately goes into any business where he tries to get something for nothing is a moral degenerate, call him financier, international banker, cambist, or what not.

The evil effect upon the American people of the accumulation of mammoth private fortunes, through the means of stock gambling and over-capitalization of trust corporations, can be charged directly to the banking system of our country. The moneys deposited in the larger banks, especially in the large cities, which also receive the money of the great life insurance companies, are under the control of a comparatively small number of men who are largely interested in, and control through stock operations, the great industrial corporations that have issued the majority of the stocks and bonds upon loans by the national banks and affiliated trust companies, etc., they taking and holding same as collateral to the amount of $7,754,493,769, as will be shown by an examination of the loans of these institutions, a large portion of which are loaned on demand (see Report of the Comptroller of the Currency, 1909, page 5).

The present loaning system of the banks encourages debt-making by the people, based upon speculative gambling, made respectable mainly by the bankers encouraging it.

Any one desiring to buy the favored stock or bonds in which the management of these banks are interested can borrow 90 per cent. of their ''stock exchange'' value from these banks. Thus a man having only $100 can go into debt $900, and having $1,000 can borrow $9,000.

In any legitimate business the same man would have to deny himself and accumulate $40,000 of property of the best character before any bank would loan him $20,000.

This being the case is there any wonder that men are induced to gamble by buying and selling stocks and bonds on margins?

Under the legitimate process as a producer of wealth it would take him half his life to get this bank accommodation, whereas, under the gambling process, he can commence business on $1,000 and at once become a debtor, paying interest to a bank on $9,000.

The bankers and promoters of these stock and bond issues, in order to float them on the market, use the money of the depositors in the banks, and, as a rule, the so-called millionaires are the largest borrowers.

Banks handling the circulating medium of exchange—money—should be run in the interest of the people and not as private snaps for bankers and promoters. This money does not belong to the bankers and promoters, but to the depositors in the banks; yet this money, within the reach and control of these banking financiers, is used by them in the control of large stock and bond operations, which swing the market value of the securities either way, subjecting the small investors to ultimate loss.

It's a well-known fact that no man can invest money in any legitimate useful or profitable undertaking for less than ninety days and expect to get any returns in the way of earnings upon it. Also that if a bank is not sufficiently in funds to loan it for ninety days it should not make the loan at all.

The system of call loans, demand loans, and thirty-day loans, instituted by banks to loan bank credit is destroying the time of our people by keeping them forever in attendance on banks. It not only takes the time of the people from useful and productive pursuits, but multiplies debts against every man in sight until to-day there is not a man to be found who is not paying tribute to, and dancing attendance on, banks and money lenders. The result of this system of lending is destroying the mental and physical energy of the American people and seriously affecting their usefulness in all legitimate business.

There is no more certain way of enslaving a people to a creditor class than by making debtors of them in a country where the population and demand for money is increasing without a corresponding increase in the supply of real money. This slavery is the most cruel known to the human race: it is not only the means by which the master enjoys the earnings of the man through ingenious instruments of credit, but it takes hold upon his mind and nervous system until life itself becomes a debtor's prison.

As before stated, there are now over $70,000,000,000 of these paper tokens of wealth, which are dealt in on the stock exchanges, the direct result of the present pernicious financial system as managed by the so-called bankers of to-day. It has had the demoralizing effect of turning most of the American people into gamblers. They all want to get rich quick and they think the only respectable short cut to quick and easy money is stock market gambling and promotion of stock issuing and consolidation schemes to fleece the people.

The actual value destroying effect of this gambling by the American people in the rise and fall in the prices of these $70,000,000,000 of paper tokens of wealth, is beyond calculation and is to-day the greatest evil of our moral and industrial being. The promotion of stock gambling by the banking associations and trust combinations has given them absolute control over the volume of money in circulation, thereby making business good or bad in order to make money on the rise and fall of prices or to weed out competition by withholding credit from competitors and strengthen thereby their monopolies.

The amount of money used to carry on the business of the country is shown to be $2,343,509,292. The amount loaned by the national banks alone is $5,128,882,351 (see Report of the Comptroller of the Currency for 1909, page 5). A call on outstanding loans of a payment of 5 per cent. or 10 per cent. would mean a demand of 250 to 500 million dollars and would bring on a panic sufficient to drive down prices several billions of dollars, and paralyze the business of the entire country, as happened in the panic of 1907. These banking associations and combinations being in possession of the money, what an opportunity, to be seized by them, to buy up the best things to be had, *e.g.*, the purchase of the Tennessee Iron and Coal Company by the United States Steel Trust.

We know that under recent consolidations and community of interests, the larger loans making up this total are controlled by the banking institutions of the larger cities, and they in turn are absolutely dominated by the financial promoters of the railroads and industrial trust combinations of the country, and as such are responsible for the issuing of more stocks and bonds of a questionable character than the world has ever before known, and on such issues have loaned these enormous sums from their deposit liabilities—the people's earnings.

This brings us to the plain and inevitable conclusion that a comparatively small body of men, for all practical purposes, now have control of the money and are able to make, and regulate at their pleasure, the value of the issues of stocks and bonds.

WALL STREET—GOLD MOVEMENT AND MONEY MARKET

"New York, November 7, 1907.—A fresh reminder, if any were needed, of the prevailing state of affairs in the international money markets was had to-day in an advance by the Bank of England of its minimum rate of discount from 6 to 7 per cent. This is the third advance in the bank's discount figures since last Thursday, and the rate fixed to-day is the highest recorded in just thirty-four years.

"It goes without saying that the local money market remained in a very unsettled condition. Renewal rates for standing loans were fixed at 20 to 25 per cent., but most of the borrowing on call was arranged under 20 per cent."

"SIX MONTHS' FAILURES

"Total Number for Period, 8709, and Liabilities $124,374,833

"New York, July 3, 1908.—Commercial failures in the United States during the first half of 1908, according to statistics compiled by Dun's Review, are 8,709 in number and $124,374,833 in amount of liabilities."

"New York, June 17, 1908.—Another matter to-day affecting the market adversely was a sudden jump in the volume of engagements of gold for export to the unexpectedly large quantity of $3,250,000, with indications that a sum equally great, if not greater, would be taken at the end of the week.

"The fact is indisputable that Germany and France are still in the world market for the yellow money, and while this continues and rates of money here remain as depressed as they now do, it is altogether probable that gold will go on moving out of the country."

"New York, March 14, 1908.—Former Comptroller of the Currency, A. B. Hepburn, now president of the Chase National Bank, after two months' sojourn in Europe gave out the following interview to-day: 'The one thing that most strongly impresses itself upon the mind of a careful observer in Europe, at the present time, is the fact that the continent of Europe does not like the United States. They regard us as bumptious people that ought to be spanked into some sort of decorum, and they would welcome and rejoice in any international complications, not involving themselves, that would bring us into difficulties. We are their commercial and financial rivals. They think, or affect to, that their present financial and commercial difficulties are chargeable to us—their depression is a reflex of ours, *accentuated* by the $100,000,000 of gold which we took during December and January. The balance of trade in favor of the United States, during November, December, and January, was over $300,000,000, and every dollar of gold we took was obtained by commodity bills, and yet they seem to think that Europe loaned it to us as a matter of favor.' "

"New York, July 17, 1909.—Great numbers of ambitious promotion schemes are coming to a head which will call for the investment of a vast aggregate sum. And then there must be taken into account the steady drain of gold for export. Just why gold should be going out of the country in anywhere near its present volume is one of the things not easily explained.

"The international trade balance continues to run strongly in our favor, and there is nothing to show that the old world has turned back upon this country any considerable quantities of American stocks and bonds. The reasonable explanation is that our financial institutions are strengthening their credits and increasing their balances abroad. By so doing, they can reduce the visible surplus in the money centers of the United States, thereby creating a deceptive appearance of diminished stocks and still keep available large funds to be drawn against in case of need.

"It is almost as easy these days for international bankers to draw on *foreign balances* as it is on *home deposits*."

"New York. October 21. 1909.—The financial event of

to-day and for the present month thus far was the advance in the Bank of England's discount rate, this morning, from 4 to 5 per cent. following upon an advance in the bank's rate last week from $3\frac{1}{2}$ to 4 per cent.

"The Bank of England only managed to maintain its 4 per cent. discount rate last week by large borrowing of funds in the open London market, and must presumably, in order to make its present high rate effective, again indulge in open market borrowing on an unusually heavy scale. Although the Bank of England to-day managed to issue 155,000 pounds of new gold in the open London market, it shipped 1,000,000 pounds to Turkey, Egypt, and Brazil. It goes without saying, however, that the rise in the English bank rate to-day caused an advance in money rates in every financial quarter, and also led to a further distinct pointing of exchange towards London."

"*New York, February* 8, 1910.—Direct charges are made by stock exchange experts to-day that the pronounced liquidation in the stock market is for the purpose of influencing the administration in Washington and the Supreme Court of the United States in dealing with the trusts cases now pending against the Standard Oil and the Tobacco Trust."

"Colossal Bond Sales Abroad Save Market

"But for This Lavish Buying, Gold Had Left Country in Volume to Create Money Panic

"*New York, Wall St., March* 18, 1910.—By Boersianer.
"An American house has sold to foreigners since January $50,000,000 of miscellaneous bonds. This experience is only one of many. Firms with European connection practically all report an unprecedented demand for cis-Atlantic coupon securities from Europeans. None of these bond sellers attempt to make even a random estimate of the total amount placed abroad in the last eleven weeks, but it is colossal.

"The inquiry is quite spontaneous—absolutely free of drumming on the part of American houses; in fact, the enormous sales have been made in spite of the warning attitude of one of finance's leading factors, the National City Bank. The several vice-presidents of that institution are sincerely adjuring caution at home. The president of this bank, who is abroad, is imparting his misgivings to the bank's numerous and powerful European connections."

"*New York, April* 26, 1910.—It is reported that the Bank of England has reduced its bid price for American eagles from 76s. 6d. to 76s. 5d. per ounce, and as this converged the foreign demand for gold for the moment upon gold bars rather than gold coin, it was perhaps significant that sterling exchange rose during the day nearly 20 points, bringing the price of sterling nearer to the point at which these bars could be taken for foreign shipment.

"It was also announced that $2,000,000 gold coin had actually been taken for export to London to-morrow."

"*New York, April* 28, 1910.—Pronounced liquidation seemed to mark the course of this morning's stock market and a tightening of call money added to the weakness as the market progressed from bad to worse.

"During the noon hour the market had an appearance of semi-demoralization. The calling of loans by the banks forced heavy liquidation, and the rapid decline in prices uncovered stop-loss orders and exhausted margins, throwing additional burden on the market."

"*New York, April*, 1910.—The shipment of more than $11,000,000 of gold from this center has helped the financial situation abroad."

"See Problem for Nation

"It may be said that in view of the drain of gold from the National Treasury, owing to enormous quantity of bank note redemption being conducted, there are not a few observers who maintain that certain problems of finance are maturing, and will have to be grappled with, that have not previously recurred for a long period."

"*May* 5, 1910.—Another new development of to-day was news that the Southern Railway is concluding terms for the sale of a block of general development bonds, probably about $10,000,000, in Germany. It was also re-

ported that the 'Big Four' is negotiating for a sale of
$30,000,000 debentures in Berlin, instead of $10,000,000
as stated yesterday. . . . William Rockefeller, one of the
directors of the St. Paul, said the negotiations for the
sale of $50,000,000 St. Paul debentures in Paris were con-
cluded except signing of the papers.

"The American securities either sold abroad or under
present negotiations comprise $60,000,000 St. Paul deben-
tures, $40,000,000 Baltimore and Ohio bonds, $10,000,000
New York City warrants $30,000,000 'Big Four' deben-
tures, $10,000,000 Missouri, Kansas, and Texas bonds of
a new issue, and approximately $10,000,000 Southern Rail-
way development bonds. It may be that others under
secret negotiations will bring the total up to $200,000,000."

"*New York, July* 9, 1910.—Special Correspondence of
The Star.

"Not until the market approached dangerously near a
state of utter demoralization did the flood of inside stock
stop pouring out, and not until then did the great money
combination in Wall Street come to the relief of an over-
strained situation. The rescue was effected Wednesday,
but even then the big interests made it clearly understood
that their heart was not in the movement, and that they
only gave the market support at the urgent demands of a
frightened stock exchange membership.

"Since the decline of the stock market commenced late
last autumn there has been a shrinkage in the market
price of railroad and industrial stocks and bonds amounting to between $3,000,000,000 and $4,000,000,000, according to the statisticians who have gone into the mathematics
of the case.

"Heavy Selling by Insiders

"The losses during the early stages of the down movement were due to the inability of the market to absorb
the heavy volume of stuff that was sold by insiders, but
for the last three or four months the shrinkage is traceable
to more definite and specific causes. The frank attitude
of the great banking interests became hostile to prices.
Leaders in the world of high finance assumed a pose of

angry disapproval of what was going on in politics and the courts of the land. They proclaimed from the house-tops that the attitude of the administration and of Congress and of the judiciary threatened the stability of property and was an injurious and baleful persecution of rail-roads and industrials.

"According to their accounts the politicians and the bench were engaged in relentless warfare upon national prosperity and they would have to take measures for self-protection. These measures took the form of relentless attack upon the value of the properties over which they exercised control. It seemed necessary for them to give the politicians and the country an object lesson. The stock exchange was the stage and the terrific break in values was the lesson."

"FINANCIAL POWERS LET MARKET SLIDE

"New York, July 26, 1910.—Stubborn but huge accounts were at last brought to the sacrificial block, the liquidation felled Missouri Pacific to 41 from 53¾, Rock Island Preferred to 60 from 70, Southern Railway Preferred from 50¼ to 43⅓. The principal figures in finance began liquidating in the latter part of 1909. Since that date when steel common was quoted at 94⅞ represents a shrinkage in market valuation of over $160,000,000, other front rank issues have shrunk proportionately. Leading interests remained coldly indifferent to the conflagration. New York banks emulated the stern passivity *of those higher up.*

"Heavy loans were called east and west early in the day. The stocks had been bought on credit and were perforce relinquished by the narrowing margin—Chicago sold heavily, followed by similar liquidation in New York and London."

"AVERT COPPER WAR

"J. P. Morgan in Charge

"July 23, 1910.—For a year or more the factions tried to get together, but some hitch always came up which

blocked the deal, and it was recognized that the whole scheme might fall down for lack of a leader in whom everybody could place confidence and who could command obedience in case of the stubborn and willful opposition of any individual or company.

"LOOK TO THE ROTHSCHILDS

"Some such arrangement has evidently been tentatively reached. From Paris comes word that the Rothschilds will be able to control the copper situation on the other side, and with 75 per cent. of production under one management here it would look as though war had been averted and that matters would gradually adjust themselves upon a healthy and permanent basis. It is upon this theory that the speculators have been buying copper stocks in this market for the last two days "

BANKERS OF NEW YORK, ANNUAL DINNER AT WALDORF-ASTORIA. TIME FOR PEOPLE TO MIND THEIR OWN BUSINESS AND LET MONEYED INTERESTS ALONE

New York, January 17, 1911.—"The hero who was present was J. P. Morgan. Mr. Aldrich and Speaker Cannon were absent. The financiers had things absolutely their own way and they worked the opportunity to the limit. It was frankly the sense of the gathering, as voiced by the speakers and uproariously applauded by the bankers, that the time had come for people to mind their own business and let bankers, corporations, and other moneyed interests alone.

"The Presidents, Vice-presidents, and directors of almost every banking institution in the City of New York were present. It was freely said among the bankers that at no dinner that has taken place in this city in years has so much real wealth been represented. The only discordant note was when former Governor Frank S. Black, without so much as cracking a smile, declared that twenty-five years ago half the men in the room were receiving smaller incomes than the bricklayer gets to-day."

Contrast this picture of the American money system, where the rate of interest and the supply of money changes almost daily with its demoralizing and ruinous effects upon business here, and the low and uniform rates of interest and a never-failing supply of money for commercial and legitimate business afforded the French people as shown in the statement made by the managers of the Bank of France and the Crédit Lyonnais to questions of the National Monetary Commission, 1910.

M. Pallain, Governor of the Bank of France

Q.—Is the rate of discount at all times the same at the central bank as at all the branches?

A.—Yes.

Q.—Is the rate the same at the bank and the branches for loans on securities?

A.—Yes.

Q.—Does the Bank of France make the same charge for the discount of bills and for loans upon collateral?

A.—The bank usually charges somewhat more for loans upon collateral than for the discount of bills. The rates at present are 3 per cent. and 4 per cent., respectively.

Q.—Do you think that it would perhaps be more advantageous for the Bank of France, considered simply as a bank, to impose different rates under different circumstances and at different places?

A.—As a banking establishment, if we thought it advisable to apply different rates, we could easily become the masters of the market. But in our position of Bank of France, organized to serve the interest of public credit in a democratic country, we do not believe ourselves justified to use this option.

Crédit Lyonnais

Answer to questions put by the National Monetary Commission, 1910, to Baron Brincard, administrateur délégué, and other officials of the Crédit Lyonnais.

Page 222. Q.—Is there any restriction under law or under your by-laws as to loans made to administrators or officers of the bank?

A.—So far as the law is concerned, there is none; but, as a matter of fact, no director or officer would ever apply for a loan.

Page 224. Q.—Will you describe the character of the items constituting your portfolio of bills discounted which amount to about $211,000,000?

Page 225. A.—The bills discounted are commercial or industrial bills, representing normal transactions and bearing satisfactory signatures as drawers, drawees, and endorsers.

Q.—With two names or more?

A.—Always at least two, often three or four signatures; but never only one.

Page 227. Q.—Let us take up the question of discount rates. Do your large banks follow the Bank of France rate?

A.—We have two discount rates in France—that of the Bank of France, which is the official one, and then the rate outside of the Bank of France. At the present moment our discount rate is 1 per cent., the official rate being about 3 per cent.

Q.—Does the Bank of France ever loan below its published rate?

A.—No; it never does.

Q.—What proportion of your portfolio is commercial paper?

A.—It is almost entirely commercial paper. The proportion varies, but it is always very largely commercial paper.

Page 229. Q.—Take a first-class bill and a first-class loan of the same maturity, what would be the difference in the rate?

A.—Generally, at the Bank of France, the rate for loans on collateral is one-half per cent. above the discount rate, but in the private banks there is no rule; they fix the rate according to the condition of the market.

Q.—But in practice it is customary to charge a little higher rate than on prime bills?

A.—Yes.

A.—*"In practice no one has ever complained that the*

Bank of France would not discount a normal bill presented by a proper person."

Rate of interest in Germany, 2¾ to 4 per cent. No interest paid on deposits.

Rate of interest in England 3½ to 4 per cent. No interest paid on deposits by Bank of England.

STATEMENTS BEFORE THE BANKING AND CURRENCY COMMITTEE OF THE SIXTIETH CONGRESS

On the Aldrich Bill, which as amended became a law entitled, "An Act to Amend the National Banking Laws." H.R.21871.

Mr. Glass. Mr. Forgan's objection to the Aldrich Bill and to your bill was that it accentuated the endless-chain system; in other words, that the Government is required to redeem the notes in gold.

Mr. Vreeland. It says "lawful money."

Mr. Glass. It means gold.

Mr. Vreeland. It means lawful money.

Mr. Glass. Does not that ultimately mean gold?

Mr. Vreeland. That is the theory upon which we are running our Government.

Mr. Glass. You say that the $750,000,000 provided for by your bill could be issued in three days?

Mr. Vreeland. I think $500,000,000 could be issued in three days.

Mr. Glass. Would that not facilitate any attempted raid on the gold in the Treasury?

EXTRACT FROM STATEMENT OF MR. C. C. GLOVER, PRESIDENT RIGGS NATIONAL BANK OF WASHINGTON, D. C.:

Mr. Glover. There is no question about it. I have been forty years a banker, and I have passed through all of the panics during that time. We went through a condition here in November, 1907, that you gentlemen could hardly appreciate, unless you were in the banking business. I saw the suspension of the entire business of the United States. The greatest banks in the country could not make the deposit to their 5 per cent. fund. The largest banks in Pittsburgh and elsewhere, with millions of capital and surplus, had to apply to people here in Washington to make the most ordinary deposits for them. The banks in New York refused to remit in currency any sum deposited with them. When I wrote to banks there to make deposits on account of the 5 per cent. fund for banks throughout the country, it was positively refused.

Mr. McMorran. Would there not be more necessity for the gold than in ordinary times? The currency would be issued only under an emergency call. Then, during an emergency, in all probability there would be a greater demand for the redemption of that currency in gold than at other times.

Mr. Vreeland. It has not been my observation, Mr. McMorran, that there is more demand for gold in times of panic than there is a demand for any kind of money. In the streets of New York last fall these bank notes sold for a higher premium than gold laid down side by side with them.

Mr. Vreeland. We can import gold from Europe, but that takes time. The effect of that is mostly on the imagination of the public. Crowds of people, as you may remember, would go down to the wharves in New York City and see the steamers that had $5,000,000 or $6,000,000 in gold coming in—$5,000,000 or $6,000,000 coming in and $13,000,000,000 of deposits in the country! Yet it was of great value, in that it acted on *the imaginations of the people.*

Mr. Forgan. They do not lend it at all. They do not *lend the gold out;* they keep the gold that is shipped to them as a reserve and on the basis of that they can *expand their credits,* of course, but they can not contract their credits.

Mr. Waldo. That is *just* what makes the *trouble,* is it not?

Mr. Forgan. I know.

Mr. Waldo. It may be, Mr. Forgan, that this whole trouble will be met when you get credit currency; but if we need any such reserve as the statute now provides, we certainly ought to have it and not have what is merely a pretense.

Mr. Forgan. Yes, but you know the *reserve is for*

sentimental effect. It is for creating an *impression on the public mind.* It is for demonstrating the strength of the banks. You have a certain amount of it and you ought to have that certain amount of it where it will be in sight, where the people of the country will see it, and the trouble with us now is this, that in the fall of the year our lawful money which is largely made up of Government notes and greenbacks, is all shipped out into the country and gets into active use and is taken out bodily; the actual reserve, you understand. We have now to ship the actual reserve and every shipment we make reduces our power *to lend by four* times.

Mr. A. B. Hepburn, President of the Chase National Bank, New York City. In his statement before the Banking and Currency Committee of the House of Representatives, April, 1908, Mr. Forgan stated that the banks of St. Louis and Chicago were so much stronger than New York because of their having a demand on New York in addition to their cash reserves. New York has the same credit abroad, and instead of this disappearing, it acts to the credit of the New York banks abroad, and they brought in $100,000,000 of gold and relieved the situation, but they could not bring it quick enough. *It does go down there and is loaned,* but it is loaned where it can be reached in the regular course of business, in season to answer any ordinary business demand.

Mr. Clarke. But in the banks of Europe it had a power there by which they issued currency against it. When it came to the United States and was put into the Treasury, what was its power here as compared to what it was there?

Mr. Hepburn. In Germany one dollar of gold would count for three dollars of currency which they could issue without limit.

APRIL 15, 1908.—MR. JAMES B. FORGAN OF CHICAGO, REPRESENTING THE AMERICAN BANKERS' ASSOCIATION, BEFORE THE COMMITTEE ON BANKING AND CURRENCY

Mr. Prince. We find in the Aldrich Bill the following language: "Such notes shall state upon their face that they will be redeemed by the *United States* in *lawful money* upon presentation at the Treasury. This legend shall be *certified* by the *written* or engraved *signature* of the Treasurer and Register and by the *imprint* of the *seal* of the *Treasury*.''

Assume that this bill is in operation and $500,000,000 of circulating notes are issued thereunder and the country is in a panicky condition, what would be the effect upon the Public Treasury if these five hundred millions were presented by banks other than banks of issue, or by the holder of the note not connected with the bank, for redemption in lawful money, which means gold. What would the Government have to do?

Mr. Forgan. The Government under such circumstances would probably go to the limit in disposing of their available funds and would likely not be in a position to meet the demand.

Mr. Prince. There is a way, is there not, Mr. Forgan? They could raise money the same as anybody else does, by issuing their obligations.

The Chairman. They would be driven to raise the money by *issuing of bonds*.

Mr. Prince. To maintain our present gold basis and to maintain our money at a parity.

Mr. Forgan. Yes.

STATEMENT OF HORACE WHITE

Mr. Prince. You now reside in New York, Mr. White?

Mr. White. Yes, sir; in New York City. I am a retired ex-editor of the New York *Evening Post,* and earlier than that of the Chicago *Tribune.*

Mr. Prince. Are you the author of any works on the money question?

Mr. White. Yes; I am the author of a work called "Money and Banking," published by Ginn & Co., and they have just sent me word that there is a great demand for the work and they want a new edition.

When proposals were made for currency reform some twenty years ago, one of the reasons advanced for it was that with the extinction of the national debt the bond security of the notes would be withdrawn and that the existing system would necessarily come to an end. At that time nobody had conceived the idea of extending a public debt already matured if the Government had the money with which to pay it and stop the interest. Nobody would have dared to propose it, for at that time the national finances were the leading issue in politics and the Democrats were keen to take advantage of every blunder committed by their adversaries. But new political issues arose. The Spanish war came, and following it we had Cuba, the Philippines, Porto Rico, and still later Panama and other things to engross our attention. The public mind was no longer centered on finance. So the men in authority, who ought to have foreseen the coming crisis and made plans for bank circulation on some other basis, extended a large part of the maturing public debt for thirty years, although they had the money in hand or in sight to pay it off and stop the interest.

In preparation for this step Congress passed an act, March 14, 1900, authorizing the Secretary of the Treasury to refund the outstanding debt maturing in 1904, 1907, and 1908 into new bonds to run thirty years, bearing interest at 2 per cent. per annum. From time immemorial prior to the passage of this act it had been the policy of the Government to pay its interest-bearing debts as soon as possible, in order to avoid unnecessary burdens upon the tax-payers. To this end bonds redeemable at pleasure of the Government after some short period were generally preferred. Thus the 5–20 bonds issued during the war were made redeemable at any time after five years, but payable at the end of twenty years. Under this system the Treasury could use its surplus revenues to pay off bonds at par instead of buying them in the market at a premium, and the money would be restored to the channels of business as promptly as though it were deposited in banks. But in the former case the Government would save the interest, and in the latter the banks would reap the benefit.

How this change of policy was carried into effect was shown in the Treasury report for 1904, in the following tabular statement:

	3 per cents.	4 per cents.	5 per cents.	Total
Amount refunded into 2 per cent. consols of 1930.........	$119,260,000	$351,578,000	$72,071,300	$542,909,960
Interest saved on old bonds to maturity	27,283,662	89,852,710	13,050,355	130,186,727
Interest to be paid on new bonds to maturity of old bonds	18,189,108	44,926,355	5,220,142	68,335,605
Premium paid for old bonds	6,239,833	36,432,250	6,872,572	49,544,655
Premium received for new bonds	407,606	1,513,778	....	1,939,384
Net profit	3,262,327	10,025,883	957,641	14,245,851

In this way the time-honored policy of the Government was reversed, and nearly $550,000,000 of the public debt was put beyond the chance of extinction for nearly a quarter of a century, except by purchase in the open market. For the privilege of making this swap the Government paid a bonus of nearly $50,000,000 on the old bonds, of which is recovered less than $2,000,000 as premium on the new ones.

The foregoing tabular statement purports to show a net profit on the refunding operation by ignoring the interest (amounting to $257,837,642) on the new bonds after the maturity of the old ones. After deducting the apparent profit shown above ($14,245,851) the loss on the whole transaction is something tremendous, but we can not reduce it to exact figures, because we do not known how much of the extended debt we might have paid off if it had not been thus extended. We do know that a surplus of $240,000,000 was on hand at the beginning of this panic, and that the interest on that amount might have been extinguished some time earlier. We know also that the premium on the maturing bonds would have extinguished itself. In 1881, when Secretary Windom was confronted with maturing debts that had been running at 5 and 6 per cent., and for which Congress had made no provision, he issued a circular to the bond-holders offering to pay them or to continue their bonds at 3½ per cent. during the pleasure of the Government by simply putting a stamp on them to that effect; and the latter alternative was generally accepted by the bond-holders. In this way he and his successors in office were enabled to pay and cancel the debt whenever they had surplus funds and to get rid of their surplus in a rational manner.

The 4 per cent. bonds of 1907 were not all included in the list embraced in the Treasury report quoted above. A portion were left to run to maturity (July 1, 1907) so that they might be paid if the Government should then have the money in hand. The Government did have the money, but instead of applying it to that purpose $50,-000,000 of bonds were extended for twenty-three years at 2 per cent. interest, and the money which might have been employed in debt paying was deposited in banks. The interest which the Government is thus obligated to pay, and which it might have wholly saved in this instance, was $23,000,000 literally cast away by a stroke of the pen.

The excuse for this odd kind of financiering was that if the Government's interest-bearing debt were paid there would be a shortage of bonds to be held as security for national bank notes. If that is a good reason for keeping $240,000,000 of bonds alive when the Government has the money in hand to pay them off, then the same reasoning would justify the selling of new bonds when there is no use for the money which they bring in except to deposit it back in the banks. And that is exactly what the Secretary of the Treasury did last November, but not to so great an extent as he had at first intended. Bank notes originating in this way might properly be called foolscap currency. Leaving out of account the money paid for the bonds and redeposited in the banks (as equal quantities on the opposite sides of an equation cancel each other) it is a case where Uncle Sam gives Mr. B. his note, bearing semi-annual interest, and payable at the end of thirty years and not before, and takes in exchange for it B.'s note, payable without interest at no particular time. What happens at the end of the thirty years? Simply extend the transaction for another thirty years, unless Uncle Sam has recovered his senses meanwhile. But even this device of extending a debt and continuing needlessly to pay interest on it will not suffice much longer, since population and

trade are growing more rapidly than our ingenious financiers can add to the public debt. *Hence the proposal to
use other bonds than those of the Government as security
for national bank notes.*

STATEMENT OF MR. T. C. DANIEL, OF VIRGINIA, BEFORE THE
BANKING AND CURRENCY COMMITTEE

The Chairman. Where are you from, Mr. Daniel?
Mr. Daniel. I am from Virginia. I will first state
to the committee that I am not interested——
The Chairman. You had a good bank at one time, before the war?
Mr. Daniel. I have watched the currency question, or
the money question, I would say, for twenty years, with
a good deal of interest; and, after reading pretty much
everything that everybody else had said on the subject,
I felt it rather my duty to come here and make a few
contributions to the educational fund myself. Before doing so, I will say that I traveled a good deal summer before
last in England, Ireland, and Scotland. When I was in
London I interviewed the Bank of England, and I also
made investigations in France; and recently I have returned from a trip through Italy. Having had practical
experience for many years in mercantile life in this country, I was investigating conditions there, to see, by comparison, whether we could profitably imitate anything that
they have in the way of a banking system. But, since
traveling around those countries I realize that the best
civilization the world has ever known, the best government the world has ever known, are right here in the
United States. And the responsibility of the best civilization in the world rests upon the representatives of the
people in the Congress of the United States.

Now, when going through the Bank of England I
presented a letter which I had from Secretary Hay, and
the official of the bank was very polite. He took me
through the bank, and when we got back into the reception room I asked him if he would allow me to put a
few leading questions to him. He said he would, and I
asked him if he could give me a statement of the Bank of

England. "We do not issue any statements." "Does not the House of Parliament sometimes call on you for some statement as to the condition of the bank?" "No, sir; they do not call on us." "How do you regulate this whole business? Is it a close corporation?" "Well, the stockholders get their dividends periodically, and that is all they have to do with it." "How is it that some of these revolutionists, so called, do not get up in the House of Commons and raise the devil to know something about what is going on down here? That would be the condition in our country." "Oh, most of them are very large borrowers from the bank, and we do not have any difficulty with them." (Laughter.)

I tell you, with my experience and observation of twenty years, there is a whole volume in that. Through the ramification of credit, thousands and thousands of the best minds in this country are subservient. You can not find to-day five men out of a thousand who would come up here and express their disinterested opinion. Why? Because they are borrowers.

Now, we come down to comparing this country with other countries of the world, and I can not see any reason why a country that has $117,000,000,000 of national wealth, and is creating about $3,400,000,000 of national wealth a year, and which has $25,000,000,000 of internal commerce, should ever defer to any other country in regard to establishing a money system. What has impressed me in this whole question is this: the Bankers' Association for several years has been meeting around the United States, and I suppose there is not a section of the world where men have not been trying to formulate something definite; but the great difficulty seems to be that they do not locate on a firm foundation; they do not get correct premises, and consequently there is no logical conclusion reached.

The money panic of 1907 has brought the issue at last squarely before the American people. It is no longer to be hidden in sophistry. The old catch phrases of *fiat, ratio, parity,* and *bimetallism versus the gold standard* will no longer mystify the average intelligence of the American citizen. They are up against a *money famine* in the most prosperous conditions the country has ever known.

Giving additional privileges, in the shape of class legislation of the worst kind, to an obsolete national banking system, whose creation was only justified by the losses attendant upon a great civil war, will never be tolerated as being in the interest of the people.

These banking corporations ever since they made large fortunes out of the war debt have been before Congress asking valuable concessions in order to perpetuate their existence.

Unfortunately the United States Treasury Department has become a training-school for presidents and vice-presidents of national banks; and unless something is done to protect the people they will be so merged as to be practically in the same business. The maxim of the money lenders of the Old World will then be in operation: "Let us control the money of a country and we care not who makes its laws."

This being the case, it is about time the American people who have created and own $117,304,211,917 of the wealth of this country should be heard. This question is of such vital importance to them that it throws into insignificance any legislation that simply deals with how the banks are to loan out $2,876,368,096 in the currency system.

We find in the Report of the Comptroller of the Currency at page 48:

"Of the total stock of money in the country 11 per cent. is held in the Treasury as assets, 35.51 per cent. is in reporting banks, and 53.49 per cent. elsewhere, the per capita not in the Treasury or banks in 1907 being $19.36 or $1.03 less than in 1906."

The Chairman. Will you repeat that last statement?

Mr. Daniel. "The per capita not in the Treasury or banks in 1907 being $19.36 or $1.03 less than in 1906."

The Chairman. What do you mean by saying "not in the banks"?

Mr. Daniel. I mean in circulation. The rest is impounded in the reserves of the banks and in the Treasury Department.

The Chairman. You do not mean by that the deposits?

Mr. Daniel. Well, it is a very plain statement from the Comptroller of the Currency. I do not want to alter his language.

The Chairman. But I thought that as you used the expression you might define it.

Mr. Daniel. I can define it from being perfectly familiar with it. This is the actual amount of money that is doing the work, or the money in circulation in the country.

Mr. Crawford. You speak of the actual money and not of the deposits?

Mr. Daniel. Yes. In other words, only $1,679,853,760 is in circulation and doing the work of money.

The question is now asked by over 86,000,000 people in this country, with no uncertain sound, How is the Congress of the United States, to whom we have delegated the authority, going to supply this need of a permanent addition of real money to our currency system? No other power has a right to obligate the people, no other power can issue a perfect money unit, a legal-tender dollar, the ultimate of payment. The money issued by the authority of Congress under the Constitution of the United States, exercising its sovereign power, derived from the 86,666,000 people of this country, is not only redeemable in everything owned by them, but a legal-tender for all debts, public and private, estimated at many billions.

It is only necessary to realize the above facts to see how essentially the people are interested in the money question. It directly and individually affects every citizen, from the lowest to the highest, every dollar representing the plighted faith of the poorest and the richest, one to accept it for his property and debts due him, the other for his daily toil.

This being the case, and the inventory of the national wealth of the people of the United States being taken, I ask if any country or people can issue as good a dollar or money unit, with as much back of it, as the Congress of the United States can, having full power under the Constitution to obligate the entire national wealth of $117,304,211,917 for its redemption, as well as the life-

work and services of the population of 86,666,000 of the
most robust, enterprising, and productive people known to
civilization, their homes and property being in a country
described by Gladstone "as having the natural base of
the greatest continuing empire the world has ever known,"
and producing everything necessary to the human family.

Now, I have a summary here of the gold coin and
bullion imported and exported in the years ended June 30,
1900 to 1906.

GOLD COIN AND BULLION IMPORTED AND EXPORTED YEARS ENDED
JUNE 30, 1900 to 1906

	Imported	Exported
1900	$44,573,184	$48,266,759
1901	66,051,187	53,185,177
1902	52,021,254	48,568,950
1903	44,982,027	47,090,595
1904	99,955,368	81,459,986
1905	53,648,961	92,594,024
1906	96,221,730	38,593,591

GOLD PRODUCTION, UNITED STATES, FOR YEARS AS FOLLOWS:

1900	$79,171,000
1901	78,666,600
1902	80,000,000
1903	73,591,700
1904	80,464,700
1905	88,180,700
1906	94,373,800

This table will show that gold, so far as international
exchange or trade is concerned, takes care of itself, as
the difference between imports and exports is only $47,-
694,629 covering a period of seven years, and the United
States produced during this time $574,448,500, or annu-
ally $82,064,071.

Now, look at this contrast. During this time the national wealth of the United States has increased over
$28,000,000,000, as shown by the report of the Depart-
ment of Commerce and Labor for 1907:

"It is the total quantity of money in circulation in
any country which determines what portion of that quantity shall exchange for a certain portion of the goods or

commodities of that country. It is the proportion between the circulating money and the commodities in the market which determines the price.''

The Chairman. Mr. Daniel, I would like to say this: We have $34 per capita, and Canada has $19 per capita. Is there that much difference in the price of commodities in the two countries?

Mr. Daniel. But you have not that much here. It is tied up. Only $19.36 is in circulation.

The Chairman. But Canada has not got $19 among the people. Canada's total circulation, all they have out, is only $19 per capita, and that includes their reserves, and what is in the treasury of the Dominion, and all. I think they have $10 or $15 in circulation up in Canada, and we have $20. How do you account for the prices across the line up here being the same?

Mr. Daniel. If you will make a memorandum of that, I will come back to it.

The Chairman. I would like to ask another question, and you can answer them both at the same time. In Belgium they have about $9 per capita and in France $35.

Mr. Daniel. France has $40.

The Chairman. That is so much the better.

Mr. Daniel. I am familiar with all those facts.

The Chairman. I just wanted to call your attention to that.

Mr. McKinney. In Alaska they have a circulation equal to that in the rest of the country, and the prices there are tremendous.

Mr. Daniel. A simple statement of fact is enough to show that the gold in our money system is no longer the standard by which the tremendous wealth of the country is measured. The so-called gold standard is a mere fiction of the mind, a pretext for banking systems, to issue credit money on.

The following paragraph from the report of the Secretary of Agriculture suggests a comparison:

''The grand total for 1907 is $7,412,000,000. This is $657,000,000 above the value of 1906. During the last nine years wealth was created on farms in the United States to the fabulous amount of $53,000,000,000.''

This would buy the whole stock of gold in the monetary systems of the world, December 31, 1906, as estimated by the Director of the Mint, as follows:

In banks and public treasuries $3,764,900,000
In circulation 3,124,000,000

It will be seen that the value of one year's products of agriculture, $7,412,000,000, in the United States, is more than all the gold money of the world.

The gold outside of the currency system has no effect upon the value of other property, and therefore should not be considered.

The value of money in any country is determined by the amount existing. That commodities should rise or fall in price in proportion to the increase or diminution of money I assume as a fact that is incontrovertible.

This economic truth is now so plain that he who runs may read. What then becomes of this mere fiction of the mind, that gold is the standard of value of other things in this country? In other words, how can only $1,489,-742,845 of gold in our currency system, containing $2,876,368,696, constitute the standard of values? Any one with ordinary intelligence knows that if you were to retire the other kinds of currency in our present monetary system prices of all other kinds of property would experience a tremendous fall.

The relative importance of the value of gold and the value of other property is as follows: Total value of gold money in the United States November 1, 1907, $1,489,-742,845. Value of other property, $117,304,211,917. Annual average production of gold in the United States, $83,000,000. Annual average production of value of other property, $3,400,000,000.

Page 89, Report of the Director of the Mint: "The coinage of gold in the mints of the world, outside of the United States, from 1900 to 1906, when figured out, averaged only $211,312,448 a year."

The balance of trade due the United States by the outside world in 1907 amounts to $446,489,653, which would buy their total coinage of gold and leave them still in debt to us $235,177,205 a year.

To show the relative importance of our internal commerce and our foreign trade, I would call especial attention to a report from the Department of Commerce and Labor, dated December 14, 1907, as follows:

Internal commerce, United States, 1907 (estimated) $25,000,000,000
Domestic exports, fiscal year ending June 30, 1907 ..   1,854,000,000

The above comparison is made to clarify this subject, as our statesmen and business men have attached so much importance to this international trade or foreign commerce idea that they seem to think the whole American system must be made to conform to it. It is a case of looking so hard at the fly on the barn door that we can not see the barn door, or of the tail wagging the dog.

To emphasize this fact, compare the relative positions financially of these countries and the United States, and ask which should *dominate the future money system of the world.*

1904-5	Population	National debt	Per capita debt
Great Britain	43,217,687	$6,196,038,685	$139.52
France	38,961,950	6,963,953,193	172.48
Italy	33,476,120	2,490,955,026	79.93

Page 218, Special Report of the Census, 1907:

"Measured by national wealth, or the ability to raise revenue, the public debt of the United States is only 27.1 per cent. of that of Great Britain, 20 per cent. of that of France, and 16.4 per cent. of that of Italy."

Page 2, Statistical Record, Department of Commerce and Labor:

1904, national wealth of United States $107,104,211,917

Page 33, Special Report Census:

Estimated increase to 1907.......... $10,200,000,000

Total to 1907 .... $117,304,211,917
1907, internal commerce annually....   25,000,000,000

United States	Population	National debt	Per capita debt
1907	85,593,303	$878,596,755.03	$10.26

We find the following statement on page 33, Special Report of the Census, 1907:

"Without financial panics or other disturbing factors the figures reviewed would indicate that the census estimate for 1910, if taken on substantially the same basis as the estimate from 1890-1900, will show an annual average per capita accumulation of wealth from 1904 to 1910 of not far from $40."

This would amount to $3,400,000 annually.

The tax-payers and those producing this wealth would like their representatives in Congress, to whom they pay annually an aggregate of $3,585,000 for their services, to study this statement and give them an American money system made up of real dollars as authorized by the Constitution, regardless of any other country on earth, and not in the interest of short-sighted banking associations who desire to handle the money of the country and control it as far as possible in order to make the most money out of it for themselves. I hardly think their best friends would call them philanthropists, running banks in the interest of the people.

On the other hand, Congress is paid by the people to look after their interests and not the interests of banking associations. Thus the question becomes an individual responsibility upon every representative of the people in Congress, and not a matter to be settled by a few men on the Finance Committee of the Senate in consultation with banking associations.

What the people expect of Congress is a permanent increase of full legal tender dollars to sustain $117,304,-211,917 of national wealth produced by them, and to carry on $25,000,000,000 of internal commerce. They fully realize that a crazy-quilt currency made up of $1,489,-742,845 of gold, and only $574,459,086 of that in circulation as real money, and the balance of $1,386,625,851 in outstanding obligations redeemable in gold, can no longer support the tremendous development of this country. It is a condition and not a theory that now confronts the owners and producers of wealth in this country, and the dominant party that shirks the issue will be held responsible for the results.

To demonstrate the actual necessity of this, the following conditions are set forth: The total amount of money of all kinds in the currency system of the United States November 1, 1907, was $2,876,368,696, a little over 2 per cent. of the national wealth of $117,304,211,917, the value of which it is expected to measure and sustain as well as carry on $25,000,000,000 of internal commerce, and, in addition, measure and support the value of the immense issues of bonds and stocks of the corporations of the United States.

It would be easier for a sensible man to believe all the tales of the Arabian Nights than to think that $2,869,-074,255 of money (and by construction of the Secretary of the Treasury, about one-half of that only promises to pay another kind of money) can any longer carry on the business of this country and sustain values.

Based upon the $40 per capita of France, a country that has not half the need, demand, or wealth to redeem her money in as the United States, yet the only country in the world free of panics, we should have based upon our present population, December 1, 1907 (86,666,000), $3,466,640,000, or an increase of $590,271,304 in our currency system.

The tax-payers now ask their representatives in Congress to get together and give them a plain square deal on this money question stripped of all its sophistry, and to settle it right and allow the legitimate business of the country to go on uninterrupted by speculations in stocks and bonds by the non-producers in the stock exchanges, in conjunction with the banks in the large cities.

The power to create money rests entirely with Congress as placed there by the people, and if the people are responsible for these dollars they want them issued direct, as perfect money units, and not indirectly as promises to pay through banking associations with the right to retire them whenever they find it profitable to do so.

After the present painful experience they are opposed to having this power to issue currency turned over to any system controlled by money lenders and capable of being used as an India-rubber money, under the attractive title of an elastic currency. (Laughter.)

This country has not stopped growing nor has it exhausted its boundless resources. What the people want is more money permanently in the currency system, to be steadily increased as wealth accumulates and the population increases, and not an emergency, elastic, or champagne circulation to bring about a tipsy prosperity, so enjoyed by frenzied financiers, who make fortunes on paper and add nothing to the national wealth, yet coming to a sudden end at any time and absolutely stopping the progress and prosperity of the whole country (now adding to its wealth $3,400,000,000 a year).

In opposition we have men, calling themselves statesmen, hiding their assumed ignorance behind such expressions as "We must not issue 'fiat money'"—a term without meaning when applied to the material question of an American dollar issued by the sovereign power of the United States with $117,304,211,917 of national wealth owned by the people, who are adding to the same at the rate of $3,400,000,000 a year, and doing $25,000,000,000 worth of internal commerce annually, pledged to redeem them, every dollar being a universal order on all things on sale, all services for hire, and the ultimate payment for all the debts in the United States. Is there a sensible man in this the twentieth century who will stand up in the American Congress and say that he would rather have a promise to pay a dollar issued by a bank, secured upon a segregated asset of a corporation, called a bond, than a full legal tender dollar redeemable in all the property of the people of the United States? If a full legal tender American dollar is called "fiat money," by a parity of reasoning, the same statesman would call a United States Government bond a fiat creation, although both have squarely back of them all the assets of the United States and the plighted faith of the American people. Any man calling himself a statesman who can not rise above politics on such a vital question, but who resorts to sophistry and subterfuge, would properly belong to the class characterized by Adam Smith, ''That insidious and crafty animal, vulgarly called a statesman, or politician, whose councils are directed by the monetary fluctuations of affairs;'' or described by Buckle, ''Such men are at best only the creatures of the age, never its creators; their measures are the result of social progress, not the cause of it.''

Mr. Weeks. It was suggested that it was desirable to hear from men of all classes on this question—not bankers alone, but other business men—and I would like to ask Mr. Daniel what his business is?

Mr. Daniel. If you will allow me to be a little personal, I will say that I started out, after the war, from Fredericksburg, Va. I lived in New York for quite a time and also traveled as general salesman for one of the largest commercial houses there—Tefft, Weller & Co.—who did a business of $15,000,000 a year. In looking over the situation, always keeping this money question before me, I came to the conclusion that the best way to make money was to buy some cheap property near the capital of the United States and let its growth enhance its value. For about twenty years I have been in Washington, and I have now arrived at a point where the increase in the value of my property is sufficient to enable me to pay some attention to the interests of the people at large.

Mr. Weeks. You are a capitalist, then?

Mr. Daniel. I do not claim to be a capitalist because I do not want to arrogate to myself any of the qualities that go along with that position.

Mr. Weeks. You belong to the leisure class of the United States?

Mr. Daniel. No, sir; I am in the real estate business, and I have been, and am right now, in touch with pretty much everything that is going on.

That is all I have to say. I have no interest in this matter beyond the fact that there are 86,000,000 people in this country who have a great deal of property and who are working very hard for it, and they have built up a civilization. They have more wealth than all the rest of the world practically put together, and it is time that they should have something to say about the question. I am simply presenting a brief in their interest.

Mr. Crawford. Your suggestion is to increase the circulating medium by the issue of legal tender greenbacks?

Mr. Daniel. I have stated it plainly. We want real money. Do not disturb present conditions, but put more real money in circulation.

The Chairman. What do you mean by real money— United States notes?

Mr. Daniel. I mean the actual money.

The Chairman. United States notes?

Mr. Daniel. It cannot be anything else. Under the Constitution of the United States you can only issue one kind.

Mr. Crawford. Do you think, with a gold reserve in the Treasury amounting to a total of three hundred and forty-six millions, that it would stay at par?

Mr. Daniel. It would have no effect on it at all.

Mr. Gillespie. Do you mean to issue United States notes, making them irredeemable, or redeemable in gold, or how?

Mr. Daniel. When you put out a perfect circulation unit in the country, it is not supposed to be a thing that is retired. It circulates and stays out.

Mr. Gillespie. I wanted to know if that was your idea —the issuing of irredeemable paper money by the Government?

Mr. Daniel. Not irredeemable money, but redeemable in everything, backed by the national assets of the Government and people.

Mr. Gillespie. But if it is not redeemable, why have assets back of it?

Mr. Daniel. For instance, when the Congress of the United States, representing the American people, issues a dollar, it is by my consent that I take it in payment for any property I have or in payment for any service I render, and it is a thing that the American people accept and agree to redeem not only now, but for all time. That is a perfect money unit.

Mr. Waldo. You have got to have it redeemable in gold, though.

Mr. Daniel. Not redeemable in *any one thing, but everything.*

Mr. Waldo. I mean to do business with any other country on a gold basis.

Mr. Daniel. We do not need that. We have only had a difference of about forty-seven millions in seven years in exports and imports of gold.

Mr. Waldo. But you have got to fix that some way, have you not?

Mr. Daniel. I am glad you have asked that question. When I was in England I went down, for instance, to the Morgan bank, and I handed in a $100 American silver certificate or Treasury note, and I got a premium on it— something like $1.50 or $1.75. I went over to Belfast and bought $175.00 worth of linen there. I handed my money into the bank at Belfast and got a premium on it. Last summer I was over in Italy, and they are crazy after American money. They will tell you it is the best money in the world. They do not question it for an instant. Why, the influence of this country to-day is the most potential in the world, as demonstrated by the fact that they are paying us a premium on money right along without regard to whether it is gold or silver. Why do they need it? They need $446,000,000 of it to settle the balance of trade with us every year. They need it to pay for $1,854,000,000 necessaries of life, most of it. They can not get along without it.

I stopped off at the Strait of Gibraltar and got all my foreign money changed into American money, and of course to get American money I had to sacrifice quite a discount. The fellow gave me a whole lot of nickels. A party got on at Gibraltar with a lot of grapes. Two or three Spaniards were standing around, and I took out five of these nickels and handed them out for the grapes. This fellow looked at it for a while and turned around to his partner and said, "What about that?" The fellow said, "That is American money; the best money in the world."

That is the universal thought. Why? Because we have

$117,000,000,000 of national wealth, with the best things in God's world to reinvest the money in. Railroad bonds and everything are here to redeem it in this country—as good as can be found anywhere.

Mr. Weeks. Did you say you were paid a premium on American money?

Mr. Daniel. Yes.

Mr. Weeks. Where?

Mr. Daniel. In London and in Belfast.

Mr. Weeks. Who paid it?

Mr. Daniel. Bank of Belfast in Belfast, and the Morgan bank paid it in London.

Mr. Weeks. How much premium were you paid?

Mr. Daniel. I think I got 6 shillings on the $100. That was about $1 and 50c.

Mr. Weeks. Was that in gold or bank notes?

Mr. Daniel. Both. Most of it was gold.

Mr. Weeks. The payment was made indiscriminately?

Mr. Daniel. Yes.

Mr. Weeks. And a premium was paid on it?

Mr. Daniel. Yes.

The Chairman. In London?

Mr. Daniel. In London. I tell you it is a fact that there is some exaggeration about that idea of gold being the necessary thing. It took me a long time to reach this conclusion. I was timid for four or five years about taking this position, but I find that I can not, as a sensible man, take any other position.

The United States Government should kindly request the banking corporations to cease to occupy the middle of the economic or business stage of this country. The power to issue money is a sovereign function of the government and through money the value of trade, commerce, and property is regulated. It is therefore of the first importance that banking corporations should be confined to their legitimate business as lenders of money owned by their depositors and not be allowed *to control the measuring medium of property*.

The Constitution of the United States does not contemplate that banks should ever go into the governing business by issuing or controlling the supply of money and regulating the affairs of the country. It is plain from the action of the banks in the panic of October, 1907, that they need no guardian to look after their interest. They simply stopped paying their depositors, issued them clearing house certificates and script, held and hoarded all the money of any kind they could obtain. They ceased to make loans, but demanded money on the loans outstanding, and asked larger curtails on negotiable notes with renewals for only thirty days and increased the rate of interest on call and time loans, the effect being to instantaneously stop the progress of business, causing infinite distress and irreparable loss throughout the country. Thus the magnificent procession of business is stopped, its step reversed, depression takes the place of prosperity.

Not being able to use the old excuse of the country being overstocked, as the cause of this panic, the wiseacre economists, getting their wisdom from the superficial financiers, say we have overtraded. The fact is well known that the demand for everything, as well as money, is beyond the supply. Such a prosperous condition in the country generally is the underlying reason for the people standing the strain as well as they have.

In the meantime money goes up in value, causing a great depression in the value of other property, thus putting those in possession of money in position to take advantage of the misfortune of others. It is an open secret that the funds of most of the banks in the large cities are controlled by inside rings, composed of officers of the banks, who farm out the money to the best advantage to themselves, as well as that of the banks. While the hoarding process goes on the little interest lost in dividends to the stockholders does not amount to a drop in the bucket compared to the immense profits made by these men out of forced sales that they take advantage of.

The effect of this fall of prices upon the whole country is a hundred per cent. worse than the immediate loss. It is human nature to hold on to the thing that is going up in value—money—and let go of the things that are consequently going down; this intensifies the situation, making the inadequate supply of money that causes the panic scarcer still.

Superficial observers complain during this condition that the people are hoarding their money. As a matter of fact, in the *present panic* the Comptroller of the Currency in his *last* report states that the banks are doing most of the hoarding.

There never was a panic that hurt the owners or controllers of money; such conditions are a harvest for them and offer a premium on money (and meanness). The only cure for this condition is an adequate addition of money—so as to arrest the general fall of prices; as soon as this is done money will seek employment.

If the business of a country develops and commodities increase, and the amount of money remains the same, it is contraction in the worst form, because to take care of the increase of property and wealth a credit system of promises to pay, checks, etc., is built up so high that it is obliged to break down for the want of a broader foundation or more money to sustain it.

The United States should steadily increase in business and wealth, as its resources are practically unlimited and supply everything necessary to the human family. It can, therefore, be stated as an economic fact that a scarcity of money in such a country will always cause panics, while a sufficient amount of money to keep pace with its growth, increase of wealth and population will bring prosperity that will continue indefinitely.

If purchasing power were commensurate with the productive power of the people of this country we would have a continuous prosperity and an increase of national wealth that would be the admiration of the world. As it is, purchasing power can only be obtained through the command of money or its representatives. As long as this money consists only of a scarce commodity, in itself absolutely inadequate to perform the service expected of it, the break between productive power and purchasing power can not be filled up.

Jonathan Duncan recognized the real nature of such a crisis. "We have shown that in the natural state of things, production can never exceed consumption, and that what is called overtrading in goods really means the underproduction of money. It means that more commodities are brought to market than can be distributed, not because people do not want them, but because the instrument of distribution is incommensurate. If the wharves of a maritime port were choked up with goods which another country desired to possess, as, for instance, corn at New York needed in England, but that there were insufficiency of ships to freight the corn to London or Liverpool, it would be very illogical to say that the Americans had overtraded in the production of corn; the case would be one of underproduction of vessels, manifesting the absence of the instrument of distribution.

"A railway station further illustrates the argument. If there were more passengers than the train could carry, the directors, looking to their own interest, would not insist that the passengers were excessive, and complain of overtraveling, but decide that the means of conveyance was inadequate, and at once increase the number of cars and locomotives. The question, then, amounts to this: Would there be any glut of produce if money were permitted to increase as fast as produce increased? But we may certainly answer this question in the negative, and the answer subverts the whole of Mr. Lloyd's theory. Whence arise the convulsion, pressure, and stagnation which Mr. Lloyd pronounces inevitable, and as certain to recur periodically in established cycles? Surely not from the reluctance of hungry people to consume food, or from the refusal of people in rags to wear warm and decent clothing; yet we are told all the evil proceeds from the fact of those very people having been too industrious; they have overtraded, they have created too much, and the penalty is famine and nakedness. Under this theory, the condition of the productive classes is truly pitiable; if idle, they are treated as rogues and vagabonds; if industrious, they are deprived of bread."

We speak of overproduction of clothing in a world in which millions have not half as much clothing as they need.

"Too many shirts? Well, that is a novelty in this intemperate earth, with nine hundred millions of bare backs," says Carlyle.

This panic has given the financial rigors to all the

bankers; they realize that with only $2,876,368,696 in the currency system of this country and only $1,679,853,760 in actual circulation they had to take care of over $13,-099,635,348 owed to their depositors and at the same time provide the money necessary to carry on $25,000,000,000 worth of internal commerce. It is safe to say that if the country had not been in a prosperous condition and the American people in a pleasant frame of mind, half the banking institutions in the country would have been closed or in bankruptcy caused by an angry and outraged people demanding their money.

As we are living under a written constitution, and the will of the people is the supreme law of the land, in contradistinction to all other forms of government, it is useless to copy or imitate banking or currency systems of any other country. If it were not out of place, it could be shown that the money lenders and banking systems of the old world have caused more poverty and prolonged suffering among the people than war. I have visited these countries in recent years and studied their conditions from a financial and economic standpoint, and will say we want none of their banking systems imported into this country. Their money systems mean the increasing domination of capital over labor, and the enhancement of the value of money.

The great oversight made by the bankers of this country is the tremendous advantage the United States has over the rest of the world in its resources and productive capacity. In cultivating a foreign market for the sale of stocks and bonds they have lost sight of the fact that if we had an adequate amount of money in our currency system, the handling of same by them in developing the tremendous resources of this country would make legitimate banking more profitable than ever before, and create among the people a better market for bonds and stocks than can be found abroad, and the interest on these American securities would be kept at home and deposited in American banking associations.

The American Constitution is the nearest realization in the concrete of the principles of eternal justice ever applied to human government, and this money question should be made to square with the Constitution in the interest of the American people. Banking associations and money lenders should be a secondary consideration. From the days of Aristotle to the present hour all intelligent thinkers on the subject know that money is a creation of law. The vital question now is one of more money to keep pace with the immense growth and development of the country. Therefore it is useless to try to settle this question by discussing it from the premises of banks and promises to pay issued by and controlled by banking associations.

Banks are organized by individuals to handle and loan the money of depositors, not to create money; this is an act of sovereignty, a function of government.

With this fundamental principle of our form of government recognized, as it must be, a sufficient amount of full legal tender dollars, the best money in the world, can be supplied with mathematical precision to our monetary system. At a great expense our Government has established the Census Bureau, Department of Commerce and Labor, Bureau of Corporations, Interstate Commerce Commission, etc. These departments, in connection with the Secretary of the United States Treasury, Comptroller of the Currency, and Director of the Mint, can supply all necessary data upon which sufficient addition of money can be supplied and regulated on a percentage basis by the Congress of the United States, according to the increase of wealth, business, and population. Thus the most perfect monetary system could be established ever known to the human family, as it would be in the interest of the whole people, and at the same time a fair standard of value between buyer and seller, and preserve the equity of time contracts between debtor and creditor.

Mr. Chairman, before closing my argument in regard to the questions asked at a previous hearing as to the redemption of the full legal tender American dollar, a simple illustration may best explain it. A has a hundred-dollar legal tender note. B has a horse, which A values at $100, and he closes the purchase; the horse redeems the $100 note so far as A is concerned. B then desires to pay a debt of $100, and the hundred-dollar note is then redeemed by the debt so far as B is concerned, and the process goes on ad infinitum, these legal tender dollars being a universal order for all things on sale, all services for hire, and the ultimate of payment for all debts.

Answering the chairman's question as to prices in Canada being the same as in the United States, am constrained to say he has been misinformed. The general level of prices in Canada is fully 20 per cent. lower than in the United States.

To my mind it is a self-evident proposition that the purchasing power of a dollar or money unit is not any so-called intrinsic value in the dollar, but the competition of all men to get dollars, and if the number of dollars do not keep pace with the growing demands for dollars, their value will increase and greater sacrifices will have to be made by the people to get dollars, demand operating against supply.

To deny the quantitative principle in money is simply questioning the law of supply and demand, which is as universal as the law of gravitation.

Since the panic of October, 1907, there had been forced into the currency system a temporary increase of money, viz., the coinage of $10,364,720 of gold in October, $33,-840,060 in November, and $12,929,085 in December, 1907. And in addition to this an increase of bank circulation on Panama bonds issued and Government certificates of indebtedness.

The people must not be misled by statements putting the per capita of money at $35 as of this date, as it is only temporary and an unfair way of putting it. To make this plain I refer again to the report of the Comptroller of the Currency for 1907, page 48:

"Of the total stock of money in the country 11 per cent. is held in the Treasury as assets, 35.51 per cent. is in reporting banks, and 53.49 per cent. elsewhere, the per capita not in the Treasury or banks in 1907 being $19.36, or $1.03 less than in 1906."

Owing to the scarcity of money, $112,535,852 in gold was imported into this country, yet only $57,133,865 has been coined into money up to December 1, 1907.

This would make the coinage account stand as follows (letter received by me from Director of Mint, January 3,

1908): Coinage executed at the mint during the calendar year 1907, $131,907,490. Deduct amount of this coined up to the ending of the fiscal year, July, 1907, of $79,-622,337.50. We put to the credit of the next fiscal year, 1908, $52,285,152.50.

Although the Secretary of the Treasury and the Comptroller of the Currency both admit there was no lack of warning indications of financial troubles and possible business disaster for the last year or two, and these conditions must have been well known among the financiers of the large banks of New York, with whom these officials of the Treasury were in close business relations, it is therefore passing strange that nothing was done by them to protect the people against such a crisis and the loss of untold millions.

It is a question of more money.

The Comptroller of the Currency admits it on pages 66, 67, and 68:

"For at least ten or twelve years there has been an era of advancing prices and great industrial, commercial, and speculative activity in all the countries of the world. *Credits have increased and multiplied until the limit has been reached in the amount of reserve money* on which they must be based."

.   .   .   .

"The difficulty in selling bonds has become so great that for several years many of the railways have had to raise money for their necessary expenditures and improvements with so-called short-time notes, instead of regular bond issues, the rate of interest on such issues rising higher and higher and each issue being harder to place. Merchants and manufacturers of the highest standing and credit have found it more and more difficult to secure or renew loans and the rates have risen steadily for months past.

.   .   .   .

"On October 26 the New York clearing-house decided to issue clearing-house certificates for use in the payment of balances, and to limit, if not suspend, the shipment of currency to out-of-town banks. In this the New York banks were followed by those of the other central reserve and most of the reserve cities. The result was to at once precipitate a most serious bank crisis and a famine of currency for pay rolls and other necessary cash transactions. All domestic exchanges were at once thrown into disorder and the means of remittance and collection were almost entirely suspended. Money has been withdrawn and hoarded by individuals, corporations, and even more, perhaps, by the banks themselves, all of whom at once drew and held all the money of any kind they could obtain, often really in larger sums than needed.''

"Factories have suspended, workmen have been thrown out of employment, orders have been cancelled, the moving of crops has been greatly retarded and interfered with, and exports have fallen off at a time of the year when they should be at their highest. Another result has been a reduction of the volume of the foreign credits available just at the time they are more needed to offset the large imports of gold which have been made.''

The conditions which led to the panic of October and November, 1907, were not due to the failure of a few individual banks. They were not due to the lack of confidence of the people in the banks, but more to a lack of confidence of the banks in themselves and their reserves. Banks have been fearful that the reserve system would break down, and in consequence it has broken down, and the reserve deposits have been only partially available. They were also fearful that not sufficient money could be supplied to meet the demand, and as they all made the demand at once, there has not been sufficient money. The result has been a money famine.

The normal trend of gold is shown by the following coinage of the mints of the United States and the world (p. 15, Director of Mint, 1907) for the fiscal years—

1900	$107,937,110.00	1904	$208,618,642.00
1901	99,065,715.00	1905	79,983,692.00
1902	61,980.572.00	1906	53.002.097.50
1903	45,721,773.00	1907	79,622,337.50

By reference to Statistical Record of the Progress of the United States, Department of Commerce and Labor, page 3, it will be seen there, under head of "Money in circulation," there was no increase in circulation of gold from 1900 to 1907.

By reference to page 81, 1906, Report of the Director of the Mint, we find the "Estimated stock of gold in the United States" for the fiscal years—

1900	.... $1,034,439,264	1903	.... $1,249,552,756
1901	 1,124,652,818	1904	 1,327,672,672
1902	 1,192,395,607	1905	 1,357,881,186

Report of Director of Mint for 1907, page 93:

1906 .... $1,368,612,051   1907 .... $1,328,768,271

A net decrease in fiscal year of $39,843,780.
Report of Director of Mint for 1907, page 102:

1873 coinage of gold in the mints of the world........ $257,630,802
1905 coinage of gold in the mints of the world........ 245,954,257

After a lapse of thirty-two years a falling off of $11,-676,545 in the coinage of gold in the world.
Report of Director of Mint for 1907, page 2:

1897 coinage of gold in the mints of the world........ $437,722,992
1906 coinage of gold in the mints of the world........ 366,326,788

After a lapse of nine years a falling off of $71,396,204 in the coinage of gold in the world.
Report of the Director of the Mint, 1906:

"Stock of money in European banks, notes in circulation, December 31, 1905. England, France, Germany, Scotland, Ireland, Austria-Hungary, Belgium, Bulgaria, Denmark, Spain, Greece, Netherlands, Italy, Sicily, Norway, Portugal, Roumania, Russia, Finland, Servia, Sweden, Switzerland all now designated as gold-standard countries. Total of gold, $1,867,661,000 (decrease from 1904 of $12,-352,000) ; total of silver, $525,153,000 (net decrease from 1904 of $17,370,000). Notes in money system December 31, 1905, $3,660,245,000 (net increase over 1904, $321,152,000). Now, being so-called gold-standard countries, we must add the silver to the notes, and the total will be $4,185,398,000 of notes to $1,867,661,000 gold. Percentage of gold to other kinds of money in European countries, 44 per cent.

"Gold in the United States money system as per last revised report of the Director of the Mint, United States, page 93, for June 30, 1907, $1,328,768,271; other kinds of money $1,679,473,312. Percentage of gold to other kinds of money in United States, 79 per cent."

Upon the basis of European countries, 44 per cent., the United States, based upon the gold in its money system, $1,328,768,271, would be entitled to an increased issue of notes of $1,296,967,615, or a total stock of money in the United States of $4,305,209,198.

"Percentage of gold to other kinds of money in France, 51 per cent.: Gold, $555,454,000; other kinds of money, $1,088,713,000."

Upon the basis of France the United States would be entitled to an increased issue of notes, based upon its gold money, of $1,164,090,787; or a total stock of money in the United States of $4,172,332,370.

Based upon the banking principle of 25 per cent. of cash to credit the amount due depositors in banks, trust companies, savings banks, and building and loan associations, United States, a total of over $15,000,000,000. Twenty-five per cent. of this amount would be $3,750,000,000.

COMPARISON

After eight hundred years we have the following condition in the United Kingdom, 1904-5: Area, United Kingdom, 121,371 square miles; population 43,217,687. England's national debt, $6,196,038,685. Gold in banks, public treasuries, $196,400,000; in circulation, $290,300,-000; total, $486,700,000, or 7 cents on the dollar of national debt alone.

France, after eleven hundred years: Area, 207,054 square miles; national debt, $6,963,953,193. Population, 39,300,000. Gold, $555,450,000, or 8 cents on the dollar of national debt alone.

Now hear the case of the United States of America. Area, 3,624,122 square miles; population 86,666,000. After one hundred and thirty-one years: national wealth, $117,304,211,917; annual increase, $3,400,000,000. Internal commerce, $25,000,000,000. Foreign exports, $1,-853,000,000, and enough gold in the money system to pay off her national debt and have more left over than any other country has in its monetary system.

Upon this showing the American people have the right to demand an immediate increase of money. For thirty-five years they have patiently waited for the Congress to settle this money question upon a logical and sensible basis. They have suffered the results of makeshift legislation resulting in panic after panic. And now they find the magnificent prosperity of this country has been legislated into a financial blind alley, and more makeshift legislation is suggested.

As a practical man, familiar with the causes and temporary cures effected by the issue of credit currency, I do not hesitate to say that if the Congress of the United States would authorize the issue of five hundred millions full legal tender American dollars to the monetary system and to be gradually placed in circulation through the appropriation committees of Congress in the same way that the money received from the taxes of the people is again put into circulation, the passage of such a bill would act like magic upon the whole business conditions of the country, and prosperity would be upon us again.

Congress can then take up the question as to the proper amount of money the monetary system of the United States should have to meet its marvelous development.

J. P. MORGAN & CO., AUGUST BELMONT & CO. AND MESSRS. N. M. ROTHSCHILD & SONS, LONDON, ENGLAND, AND THE UNITED STATES TREASURY

Fawcet, in a work on Gold and Debt, says: "It is a trick of capital in all countries to persuade the people that their honor is at stake in the payment of war debts at the highest valuation the avarice of the holders may set on them."

OPERATION OF THE SO-CALLED GOLD STANDARD UPON THE UNITED STATES TREASURY—THE FIDUCIARY INSTITUTION OF THE PEOPLE—WHEN PUT IN OPERATION BY THE INTERNATIONAL BANKERS—MORGAN, *et al.*

These gold advocates declare that it is dangerous to allow the gold reserve in the Treasury—created ostensibly to maintain the parity or equal value of the American dollars—to fall below $100,000,000. In March, 1894, it dropped below this amount and in February, 1894, it went down to $65,000,000—at which time the American paper dollar was bringing a premium.

At this time, as of old, through the past history of bond issues by the United States, the international bankers and saviors of the credit of nations appear upon the scene and enter into a secret contract with the Secretary of the Treasury, and approved by the President of the United States, whereby, Morgan, Rothschild, and associates buy $62,000,000 of United States bonds at about 104½ in gold—at which time these bonds were worth $117.00 in the open market, and a little later went up to $120.00. The syndicate, therefore, bought these bonds at about $10,000,000 less than their value and the American people were saddled with an unnecessary debt, which they have to pay, principal and interest, through taxation.

The following is a characteristic copy of such contracts:

[Copy.]
"CONTRACT.

"This agreement entered into this 8th day of February, 1895, between the Secretary of the Treasury of the United States, of the first part, and Messrs. August Belmont & Co., of New York, on behalf of Messrs. N. M. Rothschild & Sons, of London, England, and themselves, and Messrs. J. P. Morgan & Co., of New York, on behalf of Messrs. J. P. Morgan & Co., of London, and themselves, parties of the second part.

"Witnesseth: Whereas it is provided by the Revised Statutes of the United States (section 3700) that the Secretary of the Treasury may purchase coin with any of the bonds or notes of the United States authorized by law, at such rates and upon such terms as he may deem advantageous to the public interests; and the Secretary of the Treasury now deems that an emergency exists in which the public interests require that, as hereinafter provided, coin shall be purchased with the bonds of the United States, of the description hereinafter mentioned, authorized to be issued under the act entitled 'An act to provide for the resumption of specie payments,' approved January 14, 1875, being bonds of the United States described in an act to Congress approved July 14, 1870, entitled 'An act to authorize the refunding of the national debt.'

"Now, therefore, the said parties of the second part hereby agree to sell and deliver to the United States 3,500,-000 ounces of standard gold coin of the United States, at the rate of $17.80441 per ounce, payable in United States 4 per cent. thirty-year coupon or registered bonds, said bonds to be dated February 1, 1895, and payable at the pleasure of the United States *after thirty years* from date, issued under the acts of Congress of July 14, 1870, January 20, 1871, and January 14, 1876, bearing interest at the rate of 4 per cent. per annum, payable quarterly.

"First. Such purchase and sale of gold coin being made on the following conditions:

"(1) At least one-half or all coin deliverable hereinunder shall be obtained in and shipped from Europe, but the shipments shall not be required to exceed 300,000 ounces per month, unless the parties to the second part shall consent thereto.

"(2) All deliveries shall be made at any of the sub-treasuries or at any other legal depository of the United States.[1]

"Second. Should the Secretary of the Treasury desire to offer or sell any bonds of the United States on or before the 1st day of October, 1895, he shall first offer the same to the parties of the second part; but thereafter he shall be free from every such obligation to the parties of the second part.

.   .   .   .

"Fifth. In consideration of the purchase of such coin the parties of the second part, and their associates hereunder, assume and will bear all the expense and inevitable loss of bringing gold from Europe hereunder; and as far as lies in their power, will exert all financial influence and will make all legitimate efforts to protect the Treasury of the United States against the withdrawals of gold pending the complete performance of this contract.

"In witness whereof the parties hereto set their hands in five parts this 8th day of February, 1895.

"J. G. CARLISLE,
"*Secretary of the Treasury.*
"AUGUST BELMONT & CO.

"*On behalf of Messrs. N. M. Rothschild & Sons, London, and themselves.*

"J. P. MORGAN & CO.

"*On behalf of Messrs. J. P. Morgan & Co., London, and themselves.*

"Attest:

"W. E. CURTIS,
"FRANCIS LYNDE STETSON."

In return for a profit of about $10,000,000 these gentlemen obligate themselves not to raid the gold reserve of the Government by the use of outstanding credit money until they complete their contract.

At this time the endless-chain operation of the so-called

---

[1] This would allow the gold to still remain in the banks as legal depositories of the United States.

gold standard forced a total bond issue of $262,000,000 upon the tax-payers—which, with the interest added, will be not less than $450,000,000 to be paid by them. These financial experts now realize that the American people will no longer submit to these issues of Government bonds—so they now advocate the acceptance by the United States Government of railroad and other bonds, and miscellaneous assets of banks, as the basis and security for money they may issue, while they still own and collect the interest on these securities.

I desire here to emphasize the fact that the people—consumers and tax-payers—have eventually to pay both principal and interest of these bonds or have it added to their living expenses in one form or another.

In the Panic of 1907

"Washington, D. C., November 22, 1907.—J. P. Morgan, head of the Financiers' Protective Committee in New York, and George T. Baker, President of the First National Bank, arrived here at 10 o'clock to-night, and went directly to the White House. Assistant Secretary of State, Robert Bacon, former partner of J. P. Morgan, accompanied Mr. Morgan and Mr. Baker to the White House and participated in the conference. They were in conference with the President one hour and a half. Mr. Morgan mentioned he had seen Mr. Cortelyou, Secretary of the Treasury, before entering the White House."

The Situation at this Time

President Roosevelt had just returned from the cane-brakes of Louisiana, and these creators of panics as object lessons, had the President on unfamiliar ground. Our Presidents have made so little study of "The Money Question," that these men have them at a great disadvantage.

When they fail to influence an administration at Washington in other ways the final stroke is to put it up against a panic, and they then win out, as no administration or political party has the moral courage to be thought responsible for a panic and subsequent business depression in the country. Roosevelt, being a fighter, would probably have done so, if he had had clear conviction on the money question. These controllers of the money of the country knew this was his weak spot, as it has been with most of our Presidents, and brought their pressure to bear accordingly. The President, nevertheless, being a man well posted in New York business methods, discovered enough to convince him that the bankers were not playing fair with the Administration, and the people, hence the discussion at this time in reference to the establishment of a *Central Government Bank.*

The visit of Morgan in company with Baker, and Assistant Secretary of State, Robert Bacon, former partner of J. P. Morgan, was described in the public press as follows:

"Morgan Visits White House in Opposition to Government Bank

"*Washington, D. C., November* 22, 1907.—The establishment of a Central Government Bank has been earnestly discussed within the Administration circle for the last week.

"Two things have contributed toward making the Administration favor the plan.

"First, as has been stated, the relief funds released by the Government have not been handled by the banks in a way to bring aid to the real business interests of the country, but rather to build up cash reserve and favor specialized interests, the real business demands being ignored.

"Second, in the issue of the $100,000,000 certificates of indebtedness, the banks practically have demanded that the Government turn the money over to them without recompense of any sort. The Secretary of the Treasury was compelled to compromise with the bankers in order to get anything at all.

"Mr. Cortelyou announced this evening that he purposed to return to national banks subscribing for the certificates, as a deposit of public money, 75 per cent. of the cash paid for them. The remaining 25 per cent. will go for the time being to strengthen the cash balance of the Treasury.

"The transaction in the certificates of indebtedness leaves the Secretary of the Treasury in a ludicrous light as a financier. Briefly, summed up, it is revealed that for the first time in the history of the world probably a Government pays interest on its own deposits in the banks.

"Taking a round million as a basis under the terms made with the banks, the following transaction takes place: The banks put up $250,000 and we promptly returned $1,000,000 in certificates of indebtedness exchangeable for currency."

"HARD BARGAIN DRIVEN BY THE BANKERS

"These certificates of indebtedness carry 3 per cent. interest. The other $750,000 supposed to be put up is promptly returned to the banks as deposits.

"The purpose of the Treasury as announced by the Secretary to-day is to leave the money in the banks and to increase the supply in the banks in every manner possible.

"In order to carry through the arrangement with the banks in the most expeditious manner, the Secretary and the banks have completed plans by which the sale of the certificates, the payments in the manner described and the issuance of bank note currency may all be accomplished simultaneously.

"The banks will include in their offers for certificates applications for increased circulation. They will make the payments for the certificates in cash and securities to the sub-treasuries, and receive in return, not the certificates themselves, but bank notes to the full amount of the certificates purchased."

This last deal with the United States Treasury occurred less than a month after the Secretary of the Treasury had given these men the use of $34,033,000 of the money of the tax-payers of this country, at a critical time during the panic. This was in addition to over $150,000,-000 that had already been deposited of the people's money in national banks without interest, and by December 31, 1907, amounted to $245,556,944. This enormous amount of the people's money was deposited in these banks, when by the testimony before the Banking and Currency Committee of Congress these national banks were unable to pay into the United States Treasury the 5 per cent. cash guarantee to the Government to protect their bank-note circulation.

This brings to mind the one-sided partnership that exists between the Treasury of the United States and the banks. Here is a specimen of how the business is carried on by the fiduciary department of the Government representing the people, and the present banking system.

"The United States Treasury does queer things. On August 22, 1907, I personally directed the attention of Secretary Cortelyou to some $4,000,000 of false entries made daily at the sub-treasury in New York. These entries are described in the report on fiscal system (page 76) as receipts of checks 'converted into cash before final credit is given in the accounts involved'—that is, checks are received from the clearing-house and paid with other checks sent there for collection, the checks being exchanged or 'swapped' without handling any money except the difference—but the amount balanced is falsely entered as gold certificates, for the most part, with additional entries of United States notes, silver certificates, fractional silver, nickels, and copper to make up the exact sum. My letters to Secretary Cortelyou detailing falsifications to the amount of $1,279,563,526 for the fiscal year 1906 were printed in the Congressional Record March 2, 1908, pages 2829-31.

"False entries engender false ideas. The false entries I complain of are made to conceal the fact that every year checks aggregating several hundred million dollars are received at the sub-treasury in New York and paid by balancing accounts.

"In 1907 the Treasury Department had over $250,000,-000 of available cash balance on hand or in banks, and $111,000,000 of United States bonds to pay off. By the use of bank deposits and checks drawn on them the operation would have been as simple as checking $111 out of $250 deposited. The Treasury seems to have considered the operation impracticable. Secretary Cortelyou paid $61,000,000 of the bonds and to pay off $50,000,000 more, instead of using the cash on hand or in banks, borrowed $50,000,000 to be repaid in 23 years (1930), with $1,000,-000 a year interest, that is, the Secretary bound the United States to pay $23,000,000 before paying the principal, which was as purely a waste of $23,000,000 as if it had been stolen.

"JAMES C. HALLOCK, Washington, D. C."

It can be clearly seen that Congress and the United States Treasury no longer represent the people. The greatest standing reflection upon the boasted intelligence of our people is their thoughtless submission to the present infamous currency system—*money based on debts, Banks of Issue, and gold redemption.*

CENTRAL BANK OF ISSUE

After the panic of 1907 Congress had to face and recognize the absolute failure of our "Monetary System."

After long and protracted debates on the subject Congress passed H. R. 21871, approved May 30, 1908, creating the present National Monetary Commission, for the following purpose:

"Sec. 17. That a Commission is hereby created, to be called the 'National Monetary Commission,' to be composed of nine members of the Senate, to be appointed by the Presiding Officer thereof, and nine members of the House of Representatives, to be appointed by the Speaker thereof; and any vacancy on the Commission shall be filled in the same manner as the original appointment.

"Sec. 18. That it shall be the duty of this Commission to inquire into and report to Congress at the earliest date practicable, what changes are necessary or desirable in the *monetary system* of the United States or in the laws relating to banking and currency."

On page 3 of his statement of "The Work of the National Monetary Commission" Senator Aldrich, the chairman of this Commission, construes his duties under this law as follows:

"Credit furnishes a vital element in all healthy economic life. Credit is based upon confidence; and confidence in a monetary system rests upon belief in the strength, stability, and efficiency of financial institutions. To secure an organization of capital and credit by which confidence can be firmly established, and credit maintained under all circumstances and conditions, is the task committed to the National Monetary Commission."

The English language seems to have lost its meaning to those gentlemen with banking predilection. Monetary means money, not national banks and promises to pay issued by banking corporations, organizations of capital or credit or of confidence games. I would refer the Chairman of

148

this Commission to the Century Dictionary, in order that *he* may know the meaning of the distinctive term designating the main duty of the "National *Monetary* Commission."

Century Dictionary.—"Monetary. Pertaining to money. Consisting of money.

"Monetary unit. The unit of currency. In the United States this is the gold dollar.

"The unit is the pound in the British Empire, the franc in France, the mark in Germany."

If Congress had intended that this Commission was to investigate banking systems and credit institutions only, it would have so directed, and designated it a "Banking and Credit Commission," for this purpose and not a "National *Monetary* Commission."

Upon an examination of all the publications issued by the "National Monetary Commission" it will be found that not one of them treats of the subject of money, but all of them are devoted to worn out banking systems—incorporated kaleidoscopic schemes—constructed so as to make the most money out of the people.

It is now the object of the dominating force back of the Chairman of this Commission to take the control of money entirely out of the hands of the people—mark carefully the statement made by Aldrich, November 10, 1910, the chief speaker at the annual meeting of the Academy of Political Science, in New York City:

"Any plan which for one instant permitted of political control hereafter of any of the great functions of the organization which we might suggest would be fatal. I realize this, and I think my associates on the commission will bear me out when I say that this is not a new thought on my part."

No one will accuse Senator Aldrich of this being a new thought on his part. It's as old as the banking business. There never was a time when they wanted any interference by the people with their handling and controlling of the money of a country.

November 20, 1909. Frank A. Munsey in his Washington paper of above date writes editorially as follows:

"Whatever may be thought of its purpose and tendency,

there can be no doubt that the currency commission, headed by Senator Aldrich, is getting together a vast store of financial information.

"If any criticism were to be made of the commission's work thus far it would be that the central bank argument seems to have the floor pretty much to itself. The authorities engaged in writing books and brochures, essays, and pamphlets are almost all representatives of the central bank view, and of experience with central bank administration.

"It may be that there are no other authorities worth quoting, but certainly in the United States there are some men of distinction who do not indorse this plan of currency reform for application to this country. It is, therefore, not beside the matter in hand to suggest that some of the respectable authorities on the other side ought to be heard from in the work of the commission.

"Senator Aldrich will make a mistake if he prepares a great library for the express purpose of elucidating the central bank plan. That seems the tendency of his work thus far. The greatest financial and banking authorities in the world have been set at writing books for the commission. The list of them is most imposing and justifies the belief that there will be tremendous value in the great collection of contemporaneous authority on the whole question involved. But just so certainly as the literary product of the commission gives evidence of a desire to lead public opinion, instead of illumine the subject fairly from all sides, just so surely will there be a prejudice aroused which will work to the injury of the plan and the disadvantage of all efforts at currency reform.

"It will be better for whatever plan Senator Aldrich has in mind if he keeps the country in the belief that he is fairly and open-mindedly presenting all the authorities on all sides and inviting the people to help in making a decision."

After Mr. Aldrich, Chairman of the Monetary Commission, swung around the European financial centers and then on a so-called educational trip through the West, giving them the result of his great researches, we read in the *New York Journal of Commerce,* November, 1909, the following concise and true criticism.

"Senator Aldrich has spent a week in the West dispensing palaver to business men and bankers in the chief cities in behalf of the Monetary Commission, and we know just as much now as we did before about his purposes in reforming the currency and banking system."

We have the following which shows from what sources Mr. Aldrich is getting his information in Europe:

"GATHERING DATA FOR REPORT

"Paris.—Senator Nelson W. Aldrich of Rhode Island and Prof. A. P. Andrew, who are at present in Paris gathering information for the report of the American Monetary Commission, are the recipients of much attention during their stay here. They have been dined by M. Pallain, governor of the Bank of France; M. Cochery, minister of finance, and the heads of several important French credit institutions and they have had a number of interviews with financial experts.

"Signor Canovai, Secretary of the Bank of Italy, has come to Paris from Rome to submit his views on finance to the Americans.

"Senator Aldrich has repeatedly informed his friends here that the sole remaining ambition of his public life is to assist in endowing the United States with a financial system as solid as that of Great Britain or France."

"Special from Staff Correspondent. *Washington Evening Star.*

"New York, September 2.—Representative Vreeland of New York, Vice-Chairman of the Congressional Currency Commission, of which Senator Aldrich is chairman, made the following statement upon his return from Europe.

" 'The object of the visit was to obtain a more intimate knowledge of the workings of the banking and currency systems of the great commercial countries abroad than it is possible to obtain from a book or printed report.

" 'Under the laws of England, Germany, and France, there is no government supervision or inspection of banks, nor are they obliged by law to make regular and detailed reports, as in the United States, hence the inside knowledge of their workings could only be obtained from their managers.

" 'GOOD TREATMENT IN LONDON

" 'The commission was treated with the greatest kindness and cordiality by the great bankers of London. The Governor of the Bank of England and two of his managing directors came before the commission and submitted to interrogatories in detail in relation to the workings of their system. The managers of four or five of the great joint stock banks in London also came before the commission and gave freely and in great detail all the information desired. The Commission employed Professor Foxwell, a noted English economist upon banking and financial subjects, to prepare a treatise showing the conditions which led to the adoption of the act of 1884, upon which the present English system is based.' "

[In this connection it is interesting to read Professor H. S. Foxwell's comment on banks.] He states:

"I remember, too, once lecturing in the city of London on markets, and showing that their true function was to level fluctuations of price and give steady continuous values. An organ of the banking class held this up to scorn. 'We live by fluctuations,' they exclaimed. It was much as if a doctor had said it was not his business to remove disease, because he lived by disease, and it shows the narrow, greedy temper which is apt to be induced by the habit of dealing in money."

"The commission went thoroughly into the question of branch banking, of reserves, of the workings of their currency system and other important details relating to the subject. The bankers of Great Britain are greatly interested in the American situation because the money panic in the United States of October, 1907, put a very severe strain upon the Bank of England and the great banks of London. Similar interest in our monetary conditions exists also in Berlin and Paris.

" 'The commission received many invitations to dinner and other social functions in London, but decided to decline all of them except the dinner given by Ambassador

Reid at Dorchester House, which was attended by the Governor of the Bank of England, Baron Rothschild, and other great London bankers.' "

Do these gentlemen hear from or come in contact at all with the producing or debtor class of these countries? The toiling millions whose welfare constitutes the very existence of these nations and who carry the burden of debt and interest?

The first test of a government or a money system is the condition of the people where it is applied. Do you hear the chairman of this commission saying anything about the economic condition of the people in these countries from whom he is trying to borrow a central bank scheme?

First let him apply to these "Banks of Issue" countries the real test of their value, for "By their fruits ye shall know them."

Effects of the Loss of Gold Upon European Banks of Issue

I quote from Henry B. Russel's book on International Monetary Conferences, page 251. "Hardly had the conference of 1878 closed, when European governments began to be seriously alarmed over a difficulty to acquire and to keep gold in the *banks of issue*.

"They were painfully aware that under prevailing commercial conditions a succession of bad harvests at home and good ones in America would necessitate large payments to us in gold, unless they could increase their exports of merchandise.

"The *Bullionist* made the following statement at this time, 'Of late we have had a very sharp reminder, in our inability to attract gold to our shores, that an ounce of fact is more potent than a pound of theory. At a time *money* here has grown rapidly dearer, and is double in value what it is in some other European centers, we find ourselves unable to bring here the supply of capital of which we so greatly stand in need. The truth is, our indebtedness to other countries has assumed such large proportion that we are no longer in a position to command supplies of *gold* as we once could.'

"Fortunately for them, American railroad stocks, a good many of which were held in England, advanced rapidly in value, and foreign investors made large sales to realize the profits. This helped England to balance accounts and enable the bank to maintain its reserve at this time."

Thus America's securities paid for America's breadstuffs and carried England's "Great Central Bank of Issue" through this crisis.

"The bank was obliged to maintain a high rate of discount, although money was so plenty that it could be borrowed on good securities in the market as low as one-half per cent. per annum." (Letter of Conant to Secretary Sherman, September 20, 1879.) This shows great industrial depression in a great "Central Bank of Issue" country, when money goes begging at one-half per cent. a year and a high rate of discount is maintained in order simply to protect the gold held by the bank of issue, the effect being that while money is cheap on the market it is artificially made dear by the bank, in order to keep its gold. This is enough to everlastingly condemn gold as a basis upon which to issue currency.

Senator Aldrich, the agent of international bankers, while Chairman of the Finance Committee of the Senate and Chairman of the Monetary Commission, after gathering information in Europe, vouchsafed to the American people the following profound conclusion, and you will notice that although this was a Monetary Commission money is entirely left out of consideration, and he presents a faith cure pure and simple, yet this apparently harmless piece of sophistry is most significant, when considered in connection with the Aldrich-Wilson Federal Reserve Act.

To quote Mr. Aldrich: "Credit furnishes a vital element in all healthy economic life. Credit is based on confidence; and confidence in a monetary system rests upon belief in the strength, stability, and efficiency of financial institutions.

"To secure an organization of capital and credit by which confidence can be firmly established and credit maintained under all circumstances and conditions, is the task committed to the National Monetary Commission.

"The slightest tinge of partisanship would destroy any plan they might suggest.

"Any plan which for an instant permitted of political control hereafter of any of the great functions of the organization which we might suggest would be fatal."

In other words the American people can exercise freedom of thought on all other subjects necessary to self-government. Yea, more than that, they can doubt the evidences of Christianity and the salvation of their immortal souls, but, I, Aldrich, inspired by the financial powers that be, will create and endow you with a banking system so sacred in its character and functions that no American should profane it by an independent thought.

Yet the people through their sovereign power the Congress of the United States are asked to endorse this heterogeneous mass of promises to pay issued by banking corporations and obligate themselves to redeem it all in gold. It also being an endless chain by which gold can be taken from the Treasury, and millions of bonds forced upon the people to redeem these notes.

A few Government officials with high sounding titles may be added to the management of the "Reserve Association of America" in an attempt to make the people think they are represented, and thus differentiate the scheme a little from the Bank of England, of which it is an imitation.

Those back of Aldrich formulating this gigantic credit money system know from past experience they have no trouble with Government officials—even the President of the United States cannot under present conditions afford to be unfriendly to those controlling the banking interests of the country.

As a climax it is now declared by Aldrich, the stalking horse and spokesman of the moneyed and corporate interests, that such a money system should be put forever beyond the control of the people of this Republic.

I mistake the temper and independent intelligence of the American people if they continue to submit to this imposition. This money question can no longer be shrouded in mystery, it is now out in the open and before the people. Each Representative in Congress will have to assume his individual responsibility to the people and *stand* or *fall* by his record.

Under an evil money system, and in *violation* of the *law*, banking and industrial corporations, really in partnership, one with the other, have caused the issue of stocks and bonds upon the railroads and industrial resources until it is now seriously suggested that the fundamental principles of the American Constitution must be violated, and our form of government changed in order to protect the fabulous amount of watered securities dishonestly issued by and through these corporations.

The time of the voters is taken up during each campaign with furious debates over all kinds of issues except the most important one, a Sound Money System. In the meanwhile, Presidential candidates are syndicated by the moneyed interests. There is no patriotism in these men now controlling the politics and policies of the country. It is a cold-blooded, far-seeing, avaricious, and systematic greed for wealth and the power that goes with it. What do these men care for political creeds? Their maxim is, *Let us issue and control the money supply, and manage the United States Treasury, and we care not what political party is in power.*

WHAT WILL BE THE VALUE OF GOLD WHEN DEMONETIZED?

The history of the fall in the price of silver is the conclusive answer. Page 119, Report of the Director of the Mint, 1909.

No. 19.—Bullion Value of the Silver Dollar [371¼ Grains of Pure Silver] at the Annual Average Price of Silver each Year from 1837.

Calendar year	Value	Calendar year	Value	Calendar year	Value
1837........	$1.009	1861........	$1.031	1885........	$0.82379
1838........	1.008	1862........	1.041	1886........	.76931
1839........	1.023	1863........	1.040	1887........	.75755
1840........	1.023	1864........	1.040	1888........	.72683
1841........	1.018	1865........	1.035	1889........	.72325
1842........	1.007	1866........	1.036	1890........	.80927
1843........	1.003	1867........	1.027	1891........	.76416
1844........	1.008	1868........	1.025	1892........	.67401
1845........	1.004	1869........	1.024	1893........	.60351
1846........	1.005	1870........	1.027	1894........	.49097
1847........	1.011	1871........	1.025	1895........	.50587
1848........	1.008	1872........	1.022	1896........	.52257
1849........	1.013	1873........	1.00368	1897........	.46745
1850........	1.018	1874........	.98909	1898........	.45640
1851........	1.034	1875........	.96086	1899........	.46525
1852........	1.025	1876........	.90039	1900........	.47958
1853........	1.042	1877........	.92958	1901........	.46093
1854........	1.042	1878........	.89222	1902........	.40835
1855........	1.039	1879........	.86928	1903........	.41960
1856........	1.039	1880........	.88564	1904........	.44763
1857........	1.046	1881........	.87575	1905........	.47200
1858........	1.039	1882........	.87833	1906........	.52353
1859........	1.052	1883........	.85754	1907........	.51164
1860........	1.045	1884........	.85904	1908........	.41871

Demonetization of Silver started in 1873, at which time it was worth $1.00368. 1908 price, $.41371.

In all the international conferences (from 1867 to 1892) the great objection to coining more silver was the fear that it might be demonetized and the country having most of it in its monetary system would be the heaviest loser. In 1873 this demonetization commenced, and the above table from the report of the Director of the Mint of the United

States will show the effect upon the price of silver. The same would have occurred, and will occur, whenever gold is demonetized, or the money value given it by law withdrawn.

How long! Oh, how long! will an intelligent people be blinded by this delusion that a gold reserve of $150,000,000 maintains the equal value of each dollar in the money system of the United States or the parity of our dollars, as the parrots in finance are prone to call it?

The dollar is the American unit of value and contains one hundred cents, and a man's purchasing power depends upon the number of dollars he has and the value of each dollar is exactly the same.

When a man has one dollar or a hundred dollars he can get the worth of it in the things offered for sale. That held as a reserve in European banks and the United States Treasury does not add one cent to their value. He can buy a dollar's worth or a hundred dollars' worth, whichever the case may be. Apply the test and it will be demonstrated that it is the dollar in the gold that gives it its value and not the gold in the dollar. There is nothing mysterious in the value of money. It is only worth what it will bring in other things. The mystery and jugglery begins when every real dollar is made the basis of issuing innumerable promises to pay, or debts, in the place of dollars, by banking institutions.

As the American people have to accept the dollar for their property and debts, they are vitally concerned in the number of dollars issued and can be depended upon to limit the supply carefully to meet the legitimate demand of trade. To say that the people themselves should not regulate the amount of money through Congress is equivalent to saying they are not fit or capable of self-government. The Constitution of the United States has already decided this question in favor of the people.

In buying things offered for sale or paying debts, would an American citizen ever be asked to accept a discount on this legal tender dollar or surrender one of them for less than one hundred cents when he can convert them at their face value into everything for sale in the United States and get a premium on them in foreign countries?

A full legal tender American paper dollar will bring a premium over gold in Europe. Whereas if the United States would withdraw the legal tender dollar stamp from gold, and stop its coinage into dollars at the mint, the gold would not be worth more than 50 cents on the dollar in the markets of the world.

To authorize the issue of lawful money is the highest act of sovereignty, for it carries with it the plighted faith of the entire population of the country to redeem it.

Every dollar of lawful money in such a monetary system would have back of it the entire wealth of the richest empire the world has ever known, for its everlasting redemption. Thus endowed it would go forth needing no justification or explanation, and the civilized world would accept it as the American dollar issued by the sovereign power of the United States, a valid and universal order for all things for sale, all services for hire and the ultimate of payment for all debts in the richest country in the world.

Compare the integrity and real value of this dollar with a promise to pay issued by a banking system, ultimately redeemable in gold, when it is a well-known fact that the debts of the American people now payable specifically in gold amount to over forty billion dollars and we have $1,393,978,664 in our whole monetary system, June 30, 1909. (Page 59, Report of the Director of the Mint.) In view of this fact, that there is not in this country gold enough to pay 3½ per cent. on the dollar, it would bankrupt the world on a gold basis to get 1 per cent. on the dollar of debts specifically payable in gold.

I would ask any sane man, much less one occupying a fiduciary position with the slightest appreciation of his responsibility to those he represents, how he could be induced to entertain for one moment such an impossible contract. It is an absurdity on its face. Thus to continue to pile up these obligations specifically payable in gold approaches reckless insanity. Besides being impossible of performance they are unfair and indefensible from both sides of the agreement. If gold were demonetized, as it eventually will be, and relegated to its legitimate use as a metal, it would not be worth more than 50 per cent. on the dollar, or if a 5 per cent. demand payment on the debts payable specifically in gold were made by the holders of said debts, it would result in wholesale repudiation of contracts and put the United States in a discredited position all over the world.

If every dollar in the American money system were issued by the Government as a perfect money unit, full legal tender dollar, they would be universally accepted and draw a premium in every great commercial city outside the United States. Not because their value or parity is maintained by a little gold in the Treasury of the United States, but because they will settle our balance of trade against Europe, and will buy American products, property, bonds, investments, and securities of all kinds, and have back of them more real wealth to redeem them than any other money ever issued.

Lord Goschen states, "Trade balance and exports are not paid for in gold, but in money of the country adjusted to the currency of the debtor country—or settled by interest-bearing public securities of the same."

This being the case why should the business of this great country go into spasms, and a scramble for gold set in with all its depressing and destroying effects upon business in the United States, and at the same time weaken the purchasing power of our foreign customers by taking from them gold, which is the only basis of their money supply, and creating a world-wide depression, lessening our exports and thus greatly reducing our balance of trade against them.

Why should the international or export trade of the United States be any longer hampered and restricted by this commodity money—gold—being expressed back and forth across the ocean?

After fairly considering all that Goschen and others have said on the subject of foreign exchange, the practical conclusion is inevitably reached that the cost of settlement of all balances is either done by the exchanging of bills owed by the people of one country to another, with the final balance settled by a premium or extra cost equal to the express and insurance that would be charged upon the shipment of gold or the gold itself, or interest-bearing public securities in the shape of bonds, etc., by the debtor and acceptable to the creditor.

Eliminate gold from the transaction and you destroy the demoralizing element.

No one with a clear understanding of the subject will any longer contend that gold regulates the price or value of the things transferred in international commerce or bought and sold in the domestic market; or operates as a standard of value for same.

Gold is now an unnecessary dead weight so far as commerce is concerned, and the ridiculous spectacle of transporting it periodically back and forth across the ocean, and thereby giving financial rigors to the business conditions of the world generally, is a performance unworthy of the twentieth century.

Under modern conditions international balances can be almost instantly settled, without the intervention of gold, by corresponding banking houses.

Is it not better for the United States to take back its interest-bearing securities in settlement of the final balance of trade, and thus have the people of other countries working for us to pay interest upon their securities that we will soon hold under this process, than to pursue the American bankers' plan and break our necks trying to float American securities, such as railroad bonds, etc., in foreign countries, whereby we reverse the operation and have our people working for them to pay interest on American securities held abroad? And whenever they get hard up they unload these same bonds and stocks upon the American money market, thus taking gold money from us, which is now the narrow foundation upon which rests the vast superstructure of credit money, and promises to pay, issued by national banks, etc., the effect being to break down the present weak financial system of our country, a credit contrivance, liable to give way at any time.

The United States under normal conditions fixes the value of its own products and the outside world pays the price only because they want the goods.[1]

---

[1] On exported surplus of American products the price is fixed at the point of greatest demand in competition with similar products from other countries and in a free market.

There is no uniform price for anything in the different parts of the world; value is a relative thing affected by local conditions which make the cost price.

Credit money, tariffs, and combinations are the artificial influences affecting prices of commodities in the United States and elsewhere to a considerable extent at present. "The value of money is in the inverse ratio of its quantity: the supply of commodities remaining the same," which are subject to the law of demand and supply affecting each commodity. This law of demand and supply will ever affect prices and value, and is as universal in its application as the law of gravitation.

This brings us to another fallacy acquiesced in by a great many who claim to be students and authorities upon the subject of money. They lay down the dictum that only gold, or its full legal tender representative in paper, has any effect on prices of commodities, and constitutes the standard of value of other things.

It is only necessary to have actual and practical experience in the business world and watch the effect of the contraction of the currency on prices of things offered for sale and this theory vanished in thin air.

The panic of 1907 was a conspicuous object lesson or demonstration of this and destroys this theory for all time. Paper money of all kinds was bringing a premium in the financial centers and all kinds of money substitutes, clearing-house certificates, promises to pay issued on bonds, certificates of indebtedness, scrip issued by banks, were put out to arrest the fall in prices. Is there a monometallist who still contends that if silver, silver certificates, and national bank-notes, promises to pay, amounting to $1,730,-700,353, were taken out of the currency system there would be no fall in prices of other things? If there be such a man standing in the light of the twentieth century no other term describes him than a gold monomaniac.

The establishment of a perfect money system should be taken up as an original proposition to be adapted to our form of government, and in keeping with the twentieth century development of the greatest republic known to the human race.

We should first forget the semibarbarous money systems

of the past and be no longer hampered by their mistakes
—they are to be contrasted as the primitive man in the
dugout and the modern passenger in the swiftest ocean
liner.

The so-called gold standard is the Chinese shoe of the
ignorant past and can no longer be allowed to confine the
business development of the world. To slightly paraphrase
Dryden—

> "By education most have been misled.
> Habit continues what the nurse began,
> And thus the child imposes on the man."

THE RAT IN THE STATUE

Hung Fung was a Chinese philosopher, nearly a hundred years old. One day his Emperor said to him:

"Hung, ninety years of study and observation must have
made you wise. Tell me what is the evil in a government?"

"Well," said Hung, "it is the rat in the statue."

"The rat in the statue!" repeated the Emperor. "What
do you mean?"

"Why, this," replied Hung—"We build statues to our
ancestors. They are made of wood and are painted. Now
if a rat gets into one of them we cannot smoke him out
because it would be disrespectful to an ancestor. We cannot drown him with water because that would wash off
the paint. So the rat is safe because the image is sacred."

The Chinese philosopher embalms a crying evil of our
times. We tolerate a chain of errors because they are set
in sacred images. We follow strange lights because they
gleam from past histories.

The gold fetish is the rat in the temple of Christian civilization.

A PROPER MONEY SYSTEM

There is no such thing as real money without the impress upon it of the great law of legal tender. This exclusive power to issue money is so imbedded in our democratic form of government, and so essential to its perpetuity and the well-being of its people, that there would be little left if this highest act of sovereignty were destroyed or transferred to banks of issue.

The Supreme Court of the United States has long since decided this matter as applied to coin and paper money.

U. S. Rep. Vol. 110, p. 447.

This position is fortified by the fact that Congress is vested with the exclusive exercise of the analogous power of coining money and regulating the value of domestic and foreign coin, and also with the paramount power of regulating foreign and interstate commerce. Under the power to borrow money on the credit of the United States, and to issue circulating notes for the money borrowed, its power to define the quality and force of those notes as currency is as broad as the like power over a metallic currency under the power to coin money and to regulate the value thereof. Under the two powers, taken together, Congress is authorized to establish a national currency, either in coin or in paper, and to make the currency lawful money for all purposes, as regards the National Government or private individual.

The United States Supreme Court speaking of this same power—

Legal tender cases, 12th Wallace—declares:

It was for this reason the power to coin money and regulate its value was conferred upon the Federal Government, while the same power, as well as the power to emit bills of credit, was withdrawn from the States. The States can no longer declare what shall be money, or regulate its value. Whatever power there is over the currency is vested in Congress.

By the self-confession of bankers and financiers, who have grown rich while the people have grown poor, that after forty-five years, during which they have dominated and shaped all legislation on money, they all agree that the present system, which means a gold basis with "National Banks of Issue," is a dismal failure.

Under the operation of "Banks of Issue" and a gold basis for the redemption of credit money, promises to pay, we find all Europe staggering under a mountain of debt, created through, and manufactured by, the use of credit money put out by "Banks of Issue." These debts are then made permanent, and ever increased by the funding schemes put in operation until there is little left in the way of an equity above the assessed taxable value of their national wealth. If a country, state, or nation be bonded for all the assessed value of its property, the bondholders and not the people are the owners of it.

The people of these countries are crushed down by the weight of these debts to hopeless poverty; and ultimate failure is the economic fate of these nations.

Upon the historic side universal failure has been written upon the governments of the past.

America still hopes to demonstrate to the world a successful form of government. This cannot be done with a false money system, or by following false precedents. The same can be said of a country that is said of an individual: "He is wise who learns by the experience of others, and a fool who does not learn by his own." We see inevitable failure written in unmistakable figures of debts upon these European countries, and to-day the premonitory symptoms are being felt in the United States from the same monetary causes. Business depressions and panics, strikes and rioting in this great country of almost boundless resources and natural wealth, are the signals of distress, red flags of danger ahead.

We should not temporize with this great economic question; we should leave it no longer in the hands of bankers —so-called financiers. Yea, more than that, we should no longer leave it a question to be settled by politicians and so-called statesmen, all amenable to the powers that be. Wealth, fashion, caste, and office, are against the interest of the people on this great question. Now that the issue has been made by the confessed failure of the present monetary system of the United States, the people will find those who are against our democratic form of government are in favor of the European system of money, and will throw their influence to the bankers' side in favor of a "great centralized world banking system, based on gold," but if the American people are once aroused upon the subject, the fact cannot be concealed from them, that *Indirect Taxation, Debt Funding Schemes, Gold Basis Banks of Issue,* are the corner-stones upon which rest the plutocracies of the world.

Those who advocate this system virtually say to the people, "All industrial and commercial interests that we cannot control so as to own the surplus product of labor, be damned."

So outrageously un-American, un-Democratic, un-Republican, is the idea of a "Central Bank of Issue Money System," credit money issued and controlled by money-lending corporations, that its secret promoters are abashed to such an extent that they are afraid to come out in the open and declare that they even advocate such a system. Yet the evidence is so plain "that he who runs may read" that plans are now being formulated, to quote in the words of Senator Aldrich at Paris, "to endow the United States with such a banking system as they have in Europe."

The issue now before the voters of this country is no less than the control of our government in its financial affairs by bankers and promoters in New York and Europe, or its control by the people. It is, therefore, a matter of deepest and widespread importance to the whole country and to the latest posterity.

We can no more pattern our monetary system after that of Europe than rewrite the Constitution of the United States to conform to the monarchies of Europe. Our monetary system should stand for America, and for financial independence, and not chain this country to European thrones.

Money is so much value represented in a circulating medium, which constitutes so many universal orders, which the people agree to accept for anything they own, including debts and services. As such they have authorized its issue by their sovereign power, the Congress of the United States.

Originally money was a due bill issued by one person to another, now legal tender money is a universal order, issued by all the people against themselves, and is redeemable in the entire wealth of the country and the services of all its people. Originally the value of these dollars was expressed by the physical thing being stipulated in the due bill itself. Since, by an act of sovereignty taking on the character of universal orders, money is a creation of law and thereby being declared units of value, ''American dollars,'' their value depends upon their number or quantity, other things being equal, and the standard of their value depends upon the quantity of dollars out. A proper monetary system is, therefore, to be regulated by the number of dollars issued under the authority of the sovereign power.

Money has become the most important factor in the business of the world and the law governing it must now be definitely understood. First of all it must be known that money, like everything else desired by man, is subject, as to its value, to the law of supply and demand. Next, as the medium of the exchange of everything else desired by man, it becomes the most important thing to be regulated in quantity, as it affects the value, through its quantity, of everything else.

It therefore goes without saying that the value-purchasing and debt-paying power of money is far more important to regulate as to quantity than all things else. The law of demand and supply should be more carefully recognized in its effect upon money than upon any other economic question. For by the quantity of money—other things being equal—all things for sale are measured.

Should the *regulation* of this, the greatest *factor* in the business of the United States, be any longer left to accident, or the selfish manipulation of a certain class of men calling themselves bankers and financiers, but in reality professional promoters and exploiters of the people—all in the business for what they can get out of it—not once applying the principle of the greatest good to the greatest number to the usefulness of money? On the contrary their paramount thought is: *How can we, the money handlers, make the most money out of the people?*

While all the judicial machinery of the Government is being used to break up monopolies that now fix the price to the consumer of the things they control, it is proposed in this central bank of issue scheme to have the Government transfer to banks the monopoly of the one thing, ''money,'' which measures the value of the earthly possessions of every man, woman, and child in this republic. And the only reason they give for this is that Congress may abuse its sovereign right by an over issue of money. Therefore, the welfare of the American people should be turned over to the tender mercies of banking corporations!

It has been ably stated, ''If Congress can be trusted with the power of taxation, which reaches into every home and can take from the mouth of labor the bread which it has earned; if Congress can be trusted to levy taxes which collects from every man his share in the Government's support; if Congress can be trusted to enact our coinage laws and to regulate the value of our metallic money; if Congress can be trusted to adopt a criminal code affecting the lives and liberties of our people, surely, sir, there can be no good reason for fearing that it will not act wisely in regulating the currency of this country.''

THE NOMINATION OF WOODROW WILSON

Previous to the panic of 1907 the American Bankers' Association, representing the money power, made systematic efforts to induce Congress to pass an asset currency Bill.

In 1906 they introduced this asset currency Bill in Congress and it was referred to the Finance Committee of the Senate.

The Finance Committee of the Senate realized at once that this was an attempt on the part of the bankers to use the *assets* of the *banks*—upon which they could continue to draw interest from the people—as security for the issuing of the National Bank Notes.

This would enable the banks to draw interest on the assets of the bank and immediately enable them to multiply and pyramid more interest earning debts on the borrowers.

The members of the Finance Committee of the Senate— controlled by the Republican party—at once saw the great danger to their party of endorsing such a self-evident scheme on the part of the bankers to multiply interest earning debts upon the people, and declined to endorse the Bill.

But the panic of 1907 gave the Bankers the opportunity, and they had rushed through Congress, in the last days of the session, the Aldrich-Vreeland Emergency Currency Bill which incorporated in it the asset currency scheme.

In this connection it should be of serious interest to the public to read in *Leslie's Weekly* of October 19, 1916, an article by B. C. Forbes, Vice-Chairman of the Railways Investors League, from which I quote the following:

"Picture a party of the nation's greatest bankers stealing out of New York on a private railroad car, under cover of darkness, stealthily hieing hundreds of miles south, embarking in a mysterious launch, sneaking on to an island deserted by all but a few servants, living there a full week under such rigid secrecy that the name of not one of them was once mentioned lest the servants learn their identity and disclose to the world this strangest, most secret episode in the history of American finance.

"I am not mincing. I give the world the real story of how the famous Aldrich-Vreeland Currency Report (of 1907)—the foundation of the new currency system—was written."

He then names the following parties as present at this secret conference: "Senator Nelson A. Aldrich, Chairman Finance Committee of the United States Senate; Paul M. Warburg, of Kuhn, Loeb & Co., later made Vice-Governor of the Federal Reserve Board; A. Piatt Andrews, Assistant Secretary of the United States Treasury; Henry P. Davison, of J. P. Morgan & Co., and Frank A. Vanderlip, President of the National City Bank of New York."

At the same time the Monetary Commission was appointed to investigate the banking systems of foreign countries in order to divert the attention of the people from what had been done and keep them from investigating the banks in this country that were using the money system of the United States to plunder the people, thus by indirection and deception this pernicious principle of Asset Currency was first injected into the money system of the United States.

The Democratic Party went on record as unalterably opposed to an asset currency and voted solidly against this Bill in Congress.

Before describing the proceedings of the Democratic Convention at Baltimore I would call attention to the discovery of Woodrow Wilson by Col. George Harvey, manager of *Harper's Weekly,* financed and controlled by J. P. Morgan & Co.

Col. Harvey made this discovery a year before the Baltimore Convention.

Subsequent to this discovery was the phenomenal fact that Woodrow Wilson was allowed to denounce the Money Trust, without provoking the resentment of the banking interests that made up the Money Trust. And even the public press overlooked in Woodrow Wilson this heretofore heinous offense.

Bryan by advocating some of the fundamental principles

of democratic government laid down by Thomas Jefferson had drawn around him the rank and file of the democratic voters numbering 6,500,000. It was therefore plain that no democratic nominee of a convention could be elected president without his following.

The interests backing Wilson fully realized this, and Wilson himself willingly forgot his previous desire to rid the democratic party of Bryan, having before stated that he wished—"Bryan could be knocked into a cocked hat."

Soon after being discovered by Col. Harvey as a presidential possibility Wilson invited Bryan to visit him and they came to an understanding and soon thereafter Mr. Bryan speaks favorably of Wilson as a presidential candidate of the democratic party.

Col. Harvey became such an enthusiastic backer of Wilson in *Harper's Weekly*, which the Democrats of the country knew was a Morgan paper, that Wilson in order to rid himself of the appearance of being backed by the bankers, in the most public manner told Col. Harvey that he did not want the support of *Harper's Weekly* in his campaign and in an equally public manner declined a reputed offer of a contribution to his campaign fund from Thomas F. Ryan. This was all done with such effective staging that every newspaper of any size featured it for weeks in the Harvey-Watterson, Wilson-Ryan masquerade, which should have been entitled, "The seeming repudiation of Ryan, the bankers' representative, and the adoption of the silent Col. House as the representative of the 'invisible government' of money." The desired result was accomplished, the people had no further doubt but that Wilson and Bryan were in perfect accord and would fight the money trust to a finish, yet subsequent events have shown that the money trust as usual had gotten control of Wilson by discovering him first.

THE DEMOCRATIC NATIONAL CONVENTION
Baltimore, Md.   July, 1912

These proceedings are most important to the voters of this country and should be borne in mind when considering the action of coming National Conventions.

The Morgan, Belmont and Ryan Combination dominated this convention and elected Alton B. Parker temporary chairman over the opposition of Bryan.

Seeing this line-up in this Convention first for Champ Clark and then for Oscar W. Underwood, I sent the following letter to the Baltimore *Sun*.

It is inserted here for the guidance of the voters in selecting Presidential Candidates; and to show we have paid too much attention to parties and politicians and too little attention to the vital economic question of money upon which the prosperity and happiness of the people depend.

"Editor Baltimore *Sun*.
    "Dear Sir:
"The writer made an argument before the Rules Committee of the House of Representatives on the Resolution to Investigate the Money Trust.

"It is now recognized by those who take a deep interest in the future of our Government that the Money Power dominates the entire business and politics of this country, the other questions involved are mere side-issues.

"I would therefore call the attention of the delegates of the Convention in Baltimore to the fact that Speaker Clark and Mr. Underwood, now chairman of the 'Ways and Means Committee,' the most important Committee in the House of Representatives, in a Caucus of the Representatives of the Democratic party in Congress, opposed the passage of this Resolution to Investigate the 'Money Trust' now exploiting the people of the United States, and building up and maintaining the Trust Combinations of this Country.

"It is a historical fact that Speaker Clark and Chairman Underwood were willing to align themselves with the money power to prevent their Monopoly of Money and Credit being exposed.

"They allowed their delegates to make Alton B. Parker, the representative of these interests, Temporary Chairman of the Democratic Convention at Baltimore.

"In return for this Clark and Underwood received the solid vote of the New York delegation.

"This being the case the people ask the question, 'How

would these two men stand on the money question, now of paramount importance, if either was elected President of the United States?'

"This matter should be treated immediately in your editorial column, while the Convention is in Session.

"Very truly yours,

"T. CUSHING DANIEL.

"Washington, D. C., July 2nd, 1912.''

Woodrow Wilson received the nomination the following day.

As the Democratic Party had always opposed the So-called Gold Standard, the National Bank System, and an *asset currency,* I would call especial attention to the new and novel method of those in control of this Convention in reversing the Democratic party on the money question without attracting the attention of the voters of the United States.

This occurred in the adoption of the platform. It is more than strange as reported that Mr. Bryan should have suggested this remarkable innovation that the Candidates should first be nominated and then the platform adopted by this Democratic Convention. This remarkable program was then carried out. Woodrow Wilson was nominated and Mr. Bryan made Chairman of the Committee to write the platform.

Senator O'Gorman and Lewis Nixon of N. Y., Tammany delegates, were made members of the Committee and presented a report from the New York delegation containing their recommendations for the platform to be adopted.

To accept the nomination of a man who was not willing to enter into an open agreement with the American people, and pledge himself to stand upon a platform discussed and adopted by a National Convention representing the people, is unprecedented in American politics, and has the ear-marks of a financial deal between the bankers and politicians who eventually controlled this Convention. A careful reading of the money plank in this platform—and its careful omissions—in connection with the genesis and final passage of the Aldrich-Wilson "Federal Reserve Act" show conclusively that the Democratic party was absolutely reversed by this Baltimore Convention on the money question—without notice to the people, and the Wilson Administration subsequently forced the Democratic party to endorse the so-called "Gold Standard" an "Asset Currency" and the loaning of false money "bank credits" to the people by Banking Corporations, in the Federal Reserve Act.

All this forcibly reminds the writer of a statement made in his presence by two United States Senators of long experience in attending National Political Conventions. They admitted to each other that no man had been nominated by either the Republican or Democratic National Conventions in the last 25 years who had not first received the O. K. of the representatives of the "International Bankers" and they then cared little as to which was elected as they were secure in either case.

The money plank inserted in this Democratic platform shows that although Belmont, Morgan, and Ryan were dramatically read out of the party, the money power got what they really wanted by having this money plank put in the platform.

The Democratic Party had always denounced gold monometallism and the so-called gold standard as a fraud upon the people.

In 1912 the last Republican Platform declared, "The Republican Party is responsible for the resumption of specie payment and for the establishment of the Gold Standard." By referring to the Aldrich-Wilson Federal Reserve Act it will be seen that the money power was given all it required, and that had been heretofore opposed as fundamentally objectionable to the Democratic party, viz., "*An asset currency*," the *so-called "Gold Standard"* and the *National Banking System*.

This money plank in the Democratic Platform not only endorsed but proposed to enlarge the powers of National Banks, and allow them to loan their false money, "*bank credits*" to create permanent interest earning mortgages upon the farms of the United States.

The Committee appointed by Congress to investigate the control of money and credit in the United States, in its report to Congress states: "We find from the testimony

that the most active agents in forwarding and bringing
about the concentration of control of money and credit
through one or another of the processes above described
have been and are:

"J. P. Morgan & Co., First National Bank of New York,
The National City Bank of New York, Kidder Peabody &
Co., of Boston, Lee Higginson & Co. and Kuhn, Loeb &
Co., of New York."

Mellin, president of the New York, Hartford & New
Haven Road, testified under oath before the Interstate Commerce Commission that the papers had been made out to
indict J. P. Morgan, Sr., for violating the criminal clause
of the Anti-Trust law, and that Morgan's son came to
him in great distress of mind and told him if the papers
were served upon his father it would kill him.

Mr. Mellin then told Morgan's son he would assume the
responsibility for his father, which he did, and he was
indicted in the place of Morgan.

J. P. Morgan was summoned to appear at Washington
before the "Money Trust Committee"; he was there confronted in the Committee Room with a map summing up
the financial transactions of his life, representing billions
of stock and bonds created and issued dishonestly by the
operation of a false and indefensible banking and currency
system which the House of Morgan in connection with
foreign bankers had built up in the United States.

The press stated that J. P. Morgan returned to New
York after testifying before the Money Trust Investigating
Committee a sick man and would immediately leave for
Europe.

Before leaving where did he look for protection of the
system through which he and his foreign bankers worked?
Col. George Harvey, the discoverer of Woodrow Wilson,
says, that before leaving for Europe Mr. Morgan held an
impressive conversation with him at Mr. Morgan's residence, and that Morgan told him, when you see President
Wilson say to him that if at any time he needs assistance
our resources are at his disposal.

Think of the situation, in connection with what had
gone before, the time and the men, and draw your own
conclusion.

In order that Woodrow Wilson, if elected President of the United States, could not plead ignorance of the money question in allowing himself to be controlled by the Banking Combinations, I sent him a complete exposure of this infamous "Asset Currency" and "Corporation Bank Credit" money scheme in the following books.

April, 1911, "Daniel on Real Money" was published. In this book it is conclusively shown that there is no such thing as a Gold Standard, and that it is an economic fallacy used by Banking Corporations to prevent the Government from exercising its exclusive Sovereign function of creating and issuing for value received its full legal tender money as a circulating medium of exchange in the interest of the people.

The Banks' plain and unmistakable object being to restrict the Government to the use of gold alone as legal tender money in order that Banking Corporations may be able to create interest bearing debts upon the borrowers by loaning them "bank credits" non-existent or false money created by Banking Corporations.

Woodrow Wilson had the above unanswerable facts placed clearly before him in this book, the receipt of which he acknowledged.

The second book, "High Cost of Living," by T. Cushing Daniel, published by the Monetary Educational Bureau, was sent to Woodrow Wilson in Bermuda after he was nominated by the Democratic Convention at Baltimore, Md.

Woodrow Wilson after receiving the nomination at Baltimore made a visit to Bermuda and during this time he was reticent on the money question.

Immediately upon his return from Bermuda the Public Press stated that Mr. Wilson held conferences at Princeton with Professor E. Parker Willis on proposed currency legislation.

A short time thereafter it was stated in the Public Press that Congressman Glass of the Banking and Currency Committee of the House of Representatives had been called to Princeton by Woodrow Wilson to confer on Currency legislation. After this conference the papers reported Mr. Glass as saying that he found that Mr. Wilson already had very definite ideas on the subject. The said Prof. E. Parker Willis was in the Halls of Congress opposing the passage of the Resolution to Investigate the Money Trust, and was subsequently appointed by President Wilson Secretary of the Federal Reserve Board in the United States Treasury. The next appearance of Congressman Glass was as Chairman of the Banking and Currency Committee of the House reversing himself on all his previous convictions on what he considered an honest money system in the interest of the people.

Such is the power of the "Invisible Government of Money" over place hunters and politicians.

The New Banking and Currency Committee of the Senate decided to commence its Hearings by first sending out a list of questions to be answered by the bankers. After reading a list of these questions, I addressed the following letter to the Chairman of the Committee.

"May 5th, 1913.

"SENATOR ROBERT OWEN,

Chairman Banking and Currency Committee, United States Senate, Washington, D. C.

"Dear Sir:

"I notice in the public press that your Committee will send out a list of questions to be asked of 'prominent bankers and financial experts through the country soliciting their views on the "currency question." '

"From the list of questions printed in the papers it would seem the subject is being restricted to *Banking* and *Currency*.

"It is not likely that the people will be satisfied in having this most important subject before the country—barring none—'a proper money system' side-tracked by any more hearings simply on banking and currency in the interest of credit money lending corporations.

"On behalf of the honest workers and real producers of this country I would ask that the following questions be added to any list sent out in order that a sound and correct foundation may be established for the future money system of the United States.

"QUESTIONS

"What is money?

"What constitutes the money unit of the United States?

"Give your definition of a money unit.

"Should a dollar be a debt or a redeemer of a debt?

"State whether you believe in a Gold Standard.

"Define a standard of value.

"Give your reasons for believing in a Gold Standard.

"Give your reasons why the Government should not issue the money.

"Give your reasons why banks should issue the money; or credit substitute for same.

"I would be pleased to make a statement before your committee at an early date.

"Very truly yours,
"T. CUSHING DANIEL."

The fundamental principles sought to be brought out by these questions were not considered.

The whole question of money was side-tracked to give the right of way to this Corporation Bank Credit Scheme of the Bankers.

On May 8th, 1913, I addressed the following letter to President Wilson and sent a copy of it to Mr. Bryan, Secretary of State.

ATLANTIC CITY, N. J., May 8th, 1913.

"WOODROW WILSON,

"President of the United States.

"Sir: The Republican Party has foisted upon this country the English scheme of 'banks of issue' with the present result.

"In the present critical stage of American development I would call your attention to the following maxim of the 'money lenders' of the Old World: 'Let us control the money of a country, and we care not who makes its laws.'

"Those who favor the continuance of banks of issue in this country are to be classified in history with John Sherman and Nelson W. Aldrich and the money power.

"It makes no difference whether it is done under the name of the so-called national reserve association of the United States or 'regional banks,' as now suggested to Congress.

"The issue is at last squarely drawn, and the Democratic Party will stultify and absolutely discredit itself if it indorses banks of issue in any form.

"The majority of the 6,500,000 men who voted for Bryan believed that the issuing of the money was a Government function. The 4,000,000 men who voted for Roosevelt in 1912 voted on the money plank of his platform, which declared 'the issuing of money to be a Government function.'

"An organization of the Socialist Party in Chicago has declared that the issue of money should be by the Government.

"The Democratic Party, from the days of Thomas Jefferson, has declared in favor of the Government issue of money and against banks of issue. The Constitution of the United States unequivocally provides for the Government alone issuing money.

"I presented the side of the people in the hearings before the Banking and Currency Committee after the panic of 1907, and expect at an early date to make a statement before the Banking and Currency Committee of the Senate. I regret very much not being able to confer with you on this subject in the interest of the people as requested in my letter of April 22nd, 1913.

"With great respect,
"T. CUSHING DANIEL."

A NEW COMMITTEE WAS CREATED BY THE WILSON ADMINISTRATION AS SOON AS IT CAME INTO POWER TO TAKE CHARGE OF THIS LEGISLATION CALLED THE BANKING AND CURRENCY COMMITTEE OF THE SENATE

A slightly amended scheme was then suggested of Regional Banks as a substitute for the "Reserve Association of the United States" as recommended by the Aldrich Monetary Commission, and that these banks should have the power to issue their notes as a substitute for money.

I was astounded upon hearing that a Democratic Caucus

was to be held to force this bankers' bill through Congress. I sent President Wilson the following telegram and mailed a copy to Speaker Champ Clark and Mr. Oscar Underwood, Chairman of the Committee on Ways and Means of the House.

MOUNTAIN LAKE PARK, MD.
"August 10th, 1913.

"WOODROW WILSON, President of the United States.

"Do you propose to force the American people into partnership with a convicted Money Trust through a democratic caucus?

"T. CUSHING DANIEL."

Upon my return to Washington I attended the hearings before the Banking and Currency Committee of the Senate, and realizing the kind of bill the administration had indorsed and was then putting through the Senate, wrote the following letter to President Wilson:

"WASHINGTON, D. C., November 25th, 1913.

"WOODROW WILSON, President of the United States.

"Sir: The people of the United States have never indorsed an asset currency.

"No political party in the United States has ever suggested in its platform the issuing of an asset currency. The whole record of the Democratic Party is in direct opposition to the pernicious theory underlying the issuing of asset currency.

"The issuing of bank credits as a substitute for money in the United States and Europe has caused such inflation as to expose and absolutely destroy the so-called gold standard of values.

"In S. Doc. 232-63 Cong. 1st Sess-S. 2639 hearings before the Committee on Banking and Currency, the writer conclusively demonstrates that there is no such thing as a gold standard.

"If the pending bill is passed by Congress, the Democratic Party will absolutely reverse and stultify itself by indorsing an economic absurdity, and something that does not exist, after having opposed it for over 40 years.

"Mr. President, if you or Mr. Bryan had taken the

people into your confidence and had stated that you were in favor of an *asset currency*, and of the Government *issuing debts instead of dollars as money*, as provided in this bill, neither would have received the support of the people of this country.

"The issuing of real money, for which a valuable consideration is given, and not debts redeemable in gold, is a Government function, as provided in the Constitution of the United States.

"No incorporated banking institutions with *stock issues* are *necessary* as a *condition precedent* to *the Government's exercising* this *highest act of sovereignty.*

"In the light of experience and present conditions, it is plain as the noon-day sun that if the people are now forced into partnership again with this convicted Money Trust and those responsible for it, as contemplated in this bill (S. 2639), it can and will produce nothing but disaster.

"Bank credit inflation has swamped the so-called goldstandard theory until every man of ordinary intelligence can now see the economic fraud that has and is now inflicting untold loss and suffering upon the people. Is it any longer rational to pledge the people to maintain gold payment—under the fraudulent pretext of maintaining the parity of our dollars and the so-called gold standard of values—a thing that does not exist?

"Upon this false and fraudulent gold-basis system, it is now estimated that the banking corporations of the world have created out of bank credits as a substitute for money about 60 billions of debt against the people. Do you not consider it time to stop this bank-credit inflation that requires money from the borrowers that is not in existence, and that the Government should exercise its sovereign power and issue full legal tender dollars into the money system of the United States?

"In legislation on money you deal with the highest attribute of sovereignty of this great people. The Constitution provides that 'Congress shall coin (create) money and regulate the value (quantity) thereof.' This means money and not asset currency or debts redeemable in gold, the quantity of which is measured only by the debts that the banks can manufacture against the people by rediscounting debts already held against them. This currency is farmed out to banking corporations already burdened with interest charges, which the borrower eventually pays. This is done in order that banking corporations may multiply more debts with higher interest charges upon an already overburdened people.

"At this time to multiply more debts upon the people by the Government issuing an asset currency in partnership and coöperation with these banking corporations, redeemable in gold, would be the monumental fraud and absurdity of the age.

"Mr. President, allow me to say that nothing but deep concern for the people and the future of this country prompts this frank statement of the facts here presented.

"Very respectfully,

"T. CUSHING DANIEL.

"P. S. Those who control the money of the banks will control the so-called Government banks. The officials become mere figureheads, mere employees."

STATEMENT OF T. CUSHING DANIEL OF VIR-
GINIA, SEPTEMBER 25, 1913, BEFORE THE
BANKING AND CURRENCY COMMITTEE,
UNITED STATES SENATE ON H. R. 7837 (S.
2639)

A BILL TO PROVIDE FOR THE ESTABLISHMENT OF FEDERAL
RESERVE BANKS FOR FURNISHING AN ELASTIC CURRENCY,
AFFORDING MEANS OF REDISCOUNTING COMMERCIAL PAPER,
AND TO ESTABLISH A MORE EFFECTIVE SUPERVISION OF
BANKING IN THE UNITED STATES, AND FOR OTHER PUR-
POSES

[Reprinted from S. Doc. 232, 63d Cong., 1st Sess.]

Mr. Daniel. Mr. Chairman, in order to establish a
sound and safe monetary system in the interest of all the
people in the United States, it is first necessary to explain
the present gold-basis fallacy, the very foundation of the
present money system and upon which all credit substitutes
for money are issued by the Government and dealers in
debts.

As J. Pierpont Morgan, Irving Fisher, Lawrence Laughlin, and many professors of political economy in the great
universities of the United States have indorsed this economic fallacy, it therefore becomes of paramount importance that it should be most carefully considered by your
committee at this time.

I now quote from the sworn testimony of J. Pierpont
Morgan, as a witness before the Money Trust investigating
committee of Congress, December 19, 1912, Washington,
D. C.

"*Mr. Untermyer.* Money is a commodity, is it not?
"*Mr. Morgan.* Yes.

. . . . . .

"*Mr. Morgan.* Money is gold and nothing else."
183

A few months later Prof. Irving Fisher, of the department of political economy, Yale University, 1913, stated before the American Economic Association in Boston:

"We so seldom see gold coin that we are apt to forget that the ultimate unit of money in the United States is a certain weight of gold. Many people are under the impression that a dollar is something created by Government fiat. It is, as a matter of fact, a unit of merchandise. Underlying every bank note, greenback, or other form of money which we handle daily is a gold dollar with which this other money is interconvertible with 25.8 grains of gold bullion; mere merchandise fixes the purchasing power of the dollar. Every dollar must be worth what 25.8 grains of gold bullion is worth, no more and no less."

In New York, January, 1913, after Mr. Morgan had declared gold was a commodity and that gold was money and nothing else, Prof. Laughlin, department of political economy, University of Chicago, made the following statement:

"J. Pierpont Morgan was correct when he said 'Money is gold and nothing else.' "

In order to close the case against the people in favor of a gold basis for the redemption of credit money, issued by banking corporations and the manufacturers of debts, could a stronger trio be found to indorse this economic fallacy? A gigantic scheme to exploit the people. I want the people to realize the tremendous and far-reaching importance to them of this false basis of money—the very foundation upon which banking corporations, money lenders, and manufacturers of debt issue and draw interest on their credit substitutes for money.

Our whole system of money and currency is built upon this absolutely false foundation, which has and is now costing the people untold millions.

We are indeed fortunate in having these reputedly great authorities state unequivocally the economic basis or foundation of their money system. Especially true is it at this time, as the present administration at Washington is adopting this false system as the foundation of the money bill now being forced through Congress.

I will repeat those reputed authorities, J. P. Morgan,

Prof. Irving Fisher, and Prof. Lawrence Laughlin, unreservedly hold ''that 25.8 grains of gold fixes the purchasing power of the dollar.''

I will now show that this is an absolute fallacy and will first prove that the unit of value in the United States is the dollar and not the 25.8 grains of gold in the dollar.

The United States mint was established by the act of Congress of April 2, 1792, and it provides in section 9:

''That there shall be from time to time struck and coined at the said mint coins of gold, silver, and copper of the following denomination, values, and descriptions:

''Eagle: Each to be of the value of 10 dollars or units and to contain 247$\frac{4}{8}$ grains of pure standard gold.

''Dollars or units: Each to be of the value of a Spanish mill dollar, as the same is now current, and to contain 371$\frac{4}{16}$ grains of pure silver.

''Half dollars: Each to be of half the value of the dollar or unit.

''SEC. 20. *And be it further enacted,* That the money of account of the United States shall be expressed in dollars or units, dimes or tenths, cents or hundredths, mills or thousandths: A dime being the tenth part of a dollar; a mill the thousandth part of a dollar, and that all accounts in the United States shall be kept and had in conformity to this regulation.''

This act establishes $1 as the legal unit of value in the United States and then says that when gold is coined into a dollar or money unit it shall contain 25.8 grains of gold, and this gold shall be weighed according to the standard of weight used at the mints before being coined into money units or dollars.

The dollar or money unit is the creation of the sovereign power of the people and binds them and their property to protect its value and redeem it at par. In other words, it is a creation of law, lawful money of the United States, a legal tender for all things on sale, all services for hire, and the ultimate of payment for all debts, public and private.

This means that 96,000,000 people in the United States stand ready to receive it and redeem it at 100 cents on the dollar. In fact, its money value, its purchasing and

debt-paying power, would be the same if it did not have
one grain of gold in it.

Every legal tender dollar or money unit is redeemable
(continuously) in $134,000,000,000 of national wealth,
including all the gold and silver that we now have or
ever will have, and the services of 96,000,000 of the most
energetic, enterprising, and productive people in the world.

That money is a creation of law has been recognized by
the leading and most reliable economists of the world from
the days of Aristotle. This great thinker, whose complete
neglect of artistic forms and his adherence to "essential,
naked truths," induced Dante to speak of him as "The
master of those that know," and placed him at the head
of the philosophic family, speaking of money, says, in
Ethics:

"Money, then, has been made by agreement, as it were,
a substitute for demand, and is so called because it exists,
not by nature, but by law, and it is in our power to
change it and make it useless for the purpose. It is called
"nomisma" (from "nomos," law), because money is not
a natural product, but exists only through law, and it lies
with us to change it and rob it of its utility as we will."

Paulus, the Roman juris-consult, incorporated in the
Pandects of Justinian this economic fact:

"And this material—gold—stamped by the State, circulates with a power which it derives not from the substance but from the quantity. Since that time of the
things exchanged one is called merchandise and the other
is called price."

It is plain that the 25.8 grains of gold is not the unit of
value of the United States, but that $1 is the unit of value
and so declared by law.

I will now prove that the dollar puts the value into gold
and not the gold the value into the dollar.

What would be the value of gold if demonetized?

The history of the fall in the price of silver when demonetized is the conclusive answer. The demonetization
of silver started in 1873, at which time silver was worth
$1.00368. Present price after being demonetized (i.e.,
denied the use as money), 54 cents.

Fix the basic fact in the mind, that value depends upon

demand. No fair-minded man will contend that gold, if demonetized—or denied the use as money—would be worth more than 50 cents on the dollar.

Two-thirds of the present value of gold is based on demand (and is an artificial one) created by the law allowing it to be coined into money, only one-third of the supply being used in the arts. Its value as a metal has been entirely lost in a fixed value given it as money, allowing it to be coined into money.

I will now show that the purchasing power of the money unit, or dollar of the United States, does not depend, as stated, viz.:

"On the 25.8 grains of gold that fixes the purchasing power of the dollar."

This conclusion is based on the exploded theory of intrinsic value in gold.

Let us analyze the value of this commodity, gold. Has it intrinsic value?

Our common sense at once tells us there is no such thing as intrinsic value, for the simple reason all value is relative. In order that there may be no remaining doubt on this, I refer to the following leading authorities:

Prof. Jevons, "Essay on Value of Gold":

"There is no such thing as intrinsic value."

John Stuart Mill, "Principles of Political Economy":

"There cannot, in short, be intrinsically a more insignificant thing in the economy of society than money."

Prof. Perry, "Principles of Political Economy":

"This author is led astray by the worse than useless adjective 'intrinsic,' having never yet learned that there is only one kind of value in economics, namely, purchasing power."

Mr. MacLeod, speaking of the expression, "intrinsic value," says:

"This unhappy phrase meets us at every turn in economics, and yet the slightest reflection will show that to define value to be something 'external,' and to be constantly speaking of 'intrinsic value,' are utterly self-contradictory and inconsistent ideas.

"Thus over and over again it is repeated in economical treatises that money has intrinsic value, but that a bill of exchange, or bank note, is only the representative of value.

"Money will exchange for anything—corn, houses, horses, carriages, books, etc.—and each of these is the value of the money with respect to that commodity. But which of these is its intrinsic value? The incongruity of these ideas is so glaring that it is only necessary to call attention to it for it to be perceived at once. 'Yet from the very beginning of the science this phrase has infested it.'

"To say that money, because it is material, and the product of labor, has intrinsic value, and that a bank note is only the representative of value, is just as absurd as to say that a wooden yard measure is 'intrinsic' distance, and that the space of 36 inches between two points is 'representative' distance. It is of the first importance to economic science to exterminate this unhappy phrase 'intrinsic value,' which is clearly shown to be a contradiction in terms." (MacLeod: "Theory and Practice of Banking.")

Thus having disposed of this transparent fallacy of "intrinsic value" used so successfully for many years by those advocating the gold basis for the redemption of credit substitutes for money issued by banking corporations and manufacturers of debts against the people, we are now prepared to annihilate the entire premises or foundation upon which the present false and infamous money system is established, advocated, and indorsed by J. P. Morgan et al.

Here is the crux of their economic conclusion on money:

"The fact that every dollar, whether coin or paper, is practically interconvertible with 25.8 grains of gold bullion —mere merchandise—fixes the purchasing power of the dollar."

In other words this 25.8 grains of gold bullion constitutes the so-called gold standard of value.

There is only one standard of value in a money system, and it has long since been fully recognized and indorsed by leading economists and recognized authorities on money. Concisely stated, the standard of value in a money system is constituted by the number of dollars in the system. The value of the dollar is made by the demand for dollars, demand operating against the supply. Therefore, if the dollars are few and the demand great the standard of their value is high and their purchasing power great. And if the dollars are many and the demand small the standard of their value is low, and their purchasing power small.

Thus the value of the dollar or money unit is made by the demand operating against supply. I quote from John Stuart Mill, "Political Economy":

"The value of money, other things being the same, varies inversely as its quantity; every increase of quantity lowering the value, and every diminution raising it in a ratio exactly equivalent."

John Locke says:

"The value of money in any one country is the present quantity of the current money in that country in proportion to present trade."

Sir James Graham says:

"The value of money is in the inverse ratio of its quantity. The supply of commodities remaining the same."

John Stuart Mill says:

"Alterations in the cost of the production of the precious metals do not act upon the value of money, except just in proportion as they increase or diminish its quantity."

Again: In the case of metallic currency the immediate agency in determining its value is its quantity, Prof. Stanley Jevons declares:

"There is plenty of evidence to prove that an inconvertible paper money, if carefully limited in quantity, can retain its full value. . . . Such is the case with the present notes of the Bank of France."

Prof. Fawcett says:

"By limiting its quantity (paper money) its value in exchange is as great as an equal denomination of coin or of bullion in that coin."

Alexander Baring, of Baring Bros., says:

"The reduction of paper would produce all these effects which arise from the reduction of money in any country."

Ricardo states:

"A well-regulated paper currency is so great an improvement in commerce that I should greatly regret if prejudice should induce us to return to a system of less utility. The introduction of the precious metals for the purposes of money may with truth be considered as one of the most important steps toward the improvement of commerce and the acts of civilized life, but it is no less true that with the advancement of knowledge and science we discover that it would be another improvement to banish them again from the employment to which during a less enlightened period they had been so advantageously applied.''

Having shown that $1 is the money unit of the United States and that money is the creation of law and that there is no such thing as real money, unless created by the sovereign act of the people, and that the standard of value or purchasing power of a dollar depends upon the present quantity of the current money in the United States in proportion to present trade, I will now show the exact position and how gold entered into our money system in order that there may be no more mystery surrounding it.

The Troy pound, to regulate the coinage of metal into money, was obtained from England in 1827. It is made of brass and now kept in the mint in Philadelphia and constitutes the standard weight by which our coinage is governed and the commodity gold, turned into money by the highest act of the sovereignty of a people, making it lawful money of the United States, a full legal tender for all debts, public and private, and a universal order for all things on sale and all services of the people.

I desire to make indelibly plain and rivet in the minds of the people that the Troy pound is simply a standard by which the metal, gold, is weighed when coined into a dollar, or measures how many grains of gold will be equivalent to a dollar, or money unit, according to law. It weighs this gold just as it would weigh any other material substance and just as the yardstick would measure 36 inches of cloth or anything else. The metal gold does not measure the value of the dollar. The purchasing power of the dollar is measured by the dollar and the price of the things it will buy.

The value of the dollar when compared to other things depends upon the quantity of dollars out. Therefore the quantity of dollars constitutes the standard, affecting general prices, and not the gold in or out of the dollar.

I repeat, if the dollars in a money system are few in number, the standard of their value will be high and the price or value of other things low. If the dollars be many, the standard of their value will be low and the prices of other things high. It is only necessary to state this to prove it.

This brings us to the inevitable conclusion: That the number of dollars, or money units, constitutes the standard of value of each money unit, or dollar, in a money system, and fixes the purchasing power of the dollar, or money unit. This absolutely annihilates the false conclusions dogmatically expressed by Morgan, Fisher, and Laughlin, viz.:

"The fact that every dollar, whether coined or paper, is practically interconvertible with 25.8 grains of gold, mere merchandise, fixes the purchasing power of the dollar. Every dollar must be worth what 25.8 grains of gold is worth, no more and no less."

It would be just as logical to hold that a yardstick made of gold would make the gold in the yardstick a standard of length, instead of the 36 inches in the yard being the standard of the yard, as applied to length; or that if you destroy the gold yardstick and only had yardsticks made of steel the "standard" of length, 36 inches, would be destroyed. It would be just as reasonable to contend that the clock made of gold would constitute gold the "standard" of time or that the bushel measure made of gold would constitute gold as the "standard" of its cubical contents.

The yardstick in the Bureau of Standards at Washington is declared by law to be the model for all other yardsticks and is made of bronze, but bronze is not a "standard" of length. Stripped of sophistry, when applied to money, it means when gold, the metal, is coined into a dollar of the United States the said dollar shall contain in weight so many grains of gold.

The troy pound kept in the mint is simply the "standard" weight for weighing the gold bullion.

A dollar, or money unit, does not change. Fifty cents cannot be $1, or 200 cents be $1, any more than 18 inches could ever measure a yard or 72 inches be less than two yards.

The professors of political economy in the great universities who advocate this false theory of money are confounding the idea of a dollar, or money unit, the legal creation of a sovereign power, with the "standard" weight, a material substance, used as a model by which gold is to be weighed. That they are intellectually dishonest is the most charitable construction that can be placed upon the position they now take upon this most important economic question vitally affecting all the people.

I would earnestly impress upon the minds of this committee the vital importance of the difference between the dollar, or money unit, and the metal, gold.

The dollar, or money unit, is the creation of the sovereign power of the people, and binds them and their property to protect its value and to continually redeem it at par, or 100 cents on the dollar. In other words, it is a legal tender for all things on sale, all services for hire, and all debts, public and private. This means that 96,000,-000 people in the United States stand ready to receive it at 100 cents on the dollar. In fact, its money value, which is its purchasing and debt-paying power, I repeat, would be the same if it did not have one grain of gold in it.

To say the equality, validity, value, or purchasing power of the full legal tender dollars or money units of the United States, redeemable all alike, depend for their redemption at par upon the 25.8 grains of gold in the dollar or money unit in an unthinkable absurdity. Every legal tender dollar or money unit in this country is redeemable in $134,-000,000,000 of the national wealth, including all the gold and silver that we now have in the United States or will ever have, and the services of over 96,000,000 of the most enterprising and productive people in the world.

If our mints were closed to the coining of gold into money, you could weigh out 25.8 grains of gold and in six months thereafter it would not be worth 50 cents, yet the purchasing power of the dollar or money unit would be unchanged. When the sovereign power of the United States embodying the will of the people says this is a lawful dollar or money unit, and thereby pledge $134,000,-000,000 in the national wealth and the resources of 96,000,-000 people for its redemption at par, or 100 cents on the dollar, you have the best and soundest money unit in the world without one grain of gold in it.

To make it more explicit and so plain that no man can refute it, the lawful money of the United States is created by the sovereign power of its people, each dollar or money unit is complete in itself; each has the same value, the same purchasing and debt-paying power; their equality or parity is necessarily the same, as each has its redemption alike in all the property and services of the people without discrimination.

The parity or equality is cemented together by an unlimited and universal demand for dollars of the United States, all doing the same work and having the same purchasing and debt-paying power.

The demand for dollars of the United States is the greatest ever known in the history of the world—bringing a premium over gold money in Europe.

Ninety-six million people in this country place an incessant and unending demand upon them for their services and support.

Over sixty billion of debts demand them for payment; the perpetual call for interest demands them without end.

Twenty-five billion of internal commerce demand their services.

Europe demands hundreds of millions of our dollars to settle her balance of trade with the United States.

I would ask these jugglers of words, "Is not this demand sufficient to preserve the parity or equality of our dollars?"

In conclusion, I would impress upon the mind that a dollar is not a debt, but a redeemer of debt; therefore one dollar should not be redeemed in another dollar.

This idea is an invention of the money lender and manufacturer of debts: A reversal of all sound ideas of finance that ever existed. It is based on the absurdity that a dollar is a debt. A dollar has never been a debt. It is not made for redemption, but is made to be a redeemer.

If the paper dollar is treated as a debt, then the gold dollar must be treated as a debt, else the one dollar is not at a parity of function with the other dollar; then one has the quality that the other does not possess, and the two dollars are not treated on equal terms.

There is no sound and stable money system unless every

money unit in that system is legally equivalent to every other money unit.

I would ask these gentlemen who say they believe that 25.8 grains of gold fixes the purchasing power of the dollar and constitutes the standard of value in the United States to answer the following questions:

First. If the $750,523,267 of nonlegal tender bank notes —credit money—were withdrawn from the money system of the United States what would be the effect upon values? There is only one answer: Any man of average intelligence knows there would be a great contraction of the circulating medium, a consequent fall in prices, a tremendous increase in the purchasing power of the dollar, ending in a money panic.

Second. If the $727,886,731 of silver currency, now debts redeemable in gold, and the $344,221,741 of nonlegal tender greenbacks were withdrawn, what would be the result? A money panic would follow sufficient to create financial ruin and repudiation throughout the country and the present standard of values would be absolutely destroyed.

Is there a man who still believes that if the silver currency, greenbacks, national-bank notes, all nonlegal tender currency, were taken out of the money system of the United States there would be no fall in prices of other things, and that 25.8 grains of gold would still fix the purchasing power of the dollar or money unit? If so, no other term would describe him than a "gold monomaniac."

To demonstrate how this false economic theory of money has worked in the interest of those who created and maintain it, money lenders and manufacturers of debts, and to the greatest injury of the people, I call attention to the following statement from the last Report of the Comptroller of the Currency, 1912, page 50, viz.:

"June 14, 1912: Cash holdings of the 25,195 all reporting banks, $1,572,953,479.43."

Of this amount, only $881,936,455 was gold, or legal money. It is shown on page 49, same report of the Comptroller of the Currency, that upon this narrow foundation of real money these banking corporations have invested $5,358,800,000 in bonds and other securities, and then have made loans and discounts to the people, aggregating the enormous sum of $13,953,600,000. In other words, these banking corporations, after investing in bonds and stocks more than five times as much money as they had in their business, used their bank-credit substitutes for money, and manufactured $13,953,600,000 of interest-bearing debts against the people, held alone by these banks.

I will now give a typical illustration of how it is done.

There is, we assume, $1,000,000 of actual cash money in circulation in a community. A bank is opened by a few men who say to the people:

"More business can be done in this community, and you need more money with which to do it. Put your million dollars in our bank and we can arrange to accommodate this demand for more money with which to do it."

The $1,000,000 is deposited in the bank. Several of these men then apply to the bank for a loan to establish a cloth factory. The banker approves the loan and requests them to leave their notes for the amount, and securities against the property, places the amount to their credit, and gives them a check book for them to check against the amount, to pay for their machinery, etc.

Now, since all classes in the community are depositing their money in the bank, little money will go out in payment for these checks. Thus a great many loans can be made in this way, and new enterprises started and men put to work.

Plans are then submitted to this banker for ironworks, lumber yards, etc. They look to be safe and sound loans, and are made by the banker to the amount of half a million dollars, and they leave their notes and securities, and are allowed to check on the bank to that amount in payment for their needs in establishing these enterprises.

Everybody is now leaving their money and checks on deposit with the bank. The half a million of checks drift back to the bank in the course of a few days, and are not cashed, the money being left with the bank for safety.

More borrowers come in and leave their notes and mortgages and borrow, and the amount is placed to their credit in figures, and they also take their check book with them to check up on same.

The banker has now loaned out the $1,000,000, and only enough money has been taken out of the bank to meet the small necessities of those bringing in the checks, and while these small amounts of cash are going out other small amounts of cash are coming in, and the two about balance each other.

The banker has now loaned this million once, and drawing interest on it and still has it all in his bank, for the people who have brought in the checks against this million that had been loaned have not cashed them; in other words, have left them on deposit. So the banker when he makes up his "bank statement" for the United States Treasury Department reports that the bank has on deposit, not $1,000,000 but $2,000,000. And those who read this statement refer to this as evidence of the prosperity of their community, since the bank began doing business with them.

Other industrious and enterprising men come along to establish new enterprises, and borrow on stocks, bonds, and other securities. The banker sees they are good and makes the loans.

Checks are written to the extent of another million. They come back to the bank and are put on deposit, the cash going out being balanced by the cash coming in.

Now, the banker has loaned the million twice and is drawing interest on it twice at the same time. Another million is loaned in the same way. The third million is loaned, and only $1,000,000 is being used as the basis of all these loans, and the banker is drawing interest on the million dollars three times over at one and the same time.

In the bank's statement sent in to the United States Treasury it would now report deposits of four million. It makes no distinction between the deposits of actual cash and the deposit of checks drawn against the bank's credits.

These loans increase under this process until the bank draws its 6 per cent. interest as much or more than 10 times over on every million dollars, or over 100 per cent. on the actual money in the business.

While the people refer to the prosperity of their community as evidenced by the large deposits in the bank, the actual situation is this: The enterprises in this community have all been mortgaged by this process, and the people are working to pay interest and principal on these debts manufactured on them by these bank credits. They are, in fact, financially enslaved and working for the credit money lenders.

The banker or manufacturer of debts now grows most important, and talks about his manufactured loans out of nothing as "accommodations," and now advises and dictates to those doing the borrowing from his institution. Gets let in on the ground floor on promotion schemes, assumes a patronizing and advisory position to everybody else, considers every one else's business his business and his own business no one's but his own.

In the larger cities the clearing-house association of banks is the modus operandi. The New York Clearing House is a typical illustration in its charging off of checks one against the other to avoid paying out money. Report of the Comptroller of the Currency, 1912, page 775: Clearing-house exchanges for year 1912, $96,672,300,864; balances settled in money, $5,051,262,292; the per cent. of balances settled to exchanges, 5.22 per cent. Thus $100,-000 of incoming checks on a bank is paid with only $5,200, and this is not paid out to the depositors, but transferred from one bank to another.

This is the process by which the banking institutions of the United States, with only $881,936,455, or less than $1,000,000,000 of real money in hand, have manufactured, by the use of their credit substitutes for money, nearly 14 billions of debts against the people. payable to these banks, principal and interest, in money.

Present monetary condition of the United States as developed by the dealers in debts: Total amount of legal tender money, gold, in the United States, Report of Director of Mint, 1912, page 243, $1,616,538,976; debts, non-legal tender currency, redeemable in gold, $1,822,631,739.

On the gold-basis theory that every other dollar in the currency system is interconvertible with the gold dollar, these demand obligations would exhaust more than the entire gold supply. As the banking corporations have in their possession $881,936,455 of this gold, and $940,695,284 of this credit currency convertible into gold, it is evident that they control the entire money system of the United

States. A mere statement of these facts proves this control. J. P. Morgan, the recognized authority among the bankers, practically admits this, as evidenced in his testimony under oath December 19, 1912:

"*Question.* If a man controls the credit of a country, he would have control of all its affairs?

"*Mr. Morgan.* He might have that, but he would not have the money. If he had the credit and I had the money, his customer would be badly off.

.   .   .   .

"*Mr. Morgan.* What I call money is the basis of banking.

"*Question.* But the basis of banking is credit, is it not?

"*Mr. Morgan.* Not always. That is an evidence of banking, but it is not the money itself. Money is gold and nothing else."

He admits that those who have control of the credit of a country would have control of all its affairs. He then states that those who have control of the gold would have control of its credit, which is a self-evident fact.

Having shown that the gold basis of our money system is false, the whole system is false.

Restricting money to gold has been used successfully so far by dealers in debts as a subterfuge to prevent the Government from issuing its real money—redeemers of debts—in order that they might issue a cheap credit substitute to manufacture debts upon the people, and have the debts paid back in money.

It should be remembered that in the operation a debt is created against the borrower by loaning him the bank's credit instead of money, and that there is no corresponding amount of money in existence represented by this substitute in which the debt can be paid. Therefore the scarcity of money in comparison to the debts demanding payment necessitates constant borrowing, refunding, and multiplication of debts and interest and other charges on the people.

A counterfeiter is prohibited by law from creating that which he passes as money, because, in passing it to others, he is getting from them something of value for that which cost him nothing. Why, then, should banking corporations be allowed to create a substitute for money, bank credits, etc., which have cost them nothing, yet when loaned to the people can only be paid back, principal and interest, in money which the borrower has to obtain under the most adverse conditions before he can ever pay the debt, if at all, in money?

Under this debt-creating system, money, the medium of exchange, the most important factor in civilization, has been transformed into a gigantic system of oppression. It absolutely perverts the correct economic system, that money to circulate and not money to loan is what the industrial well-being of the world needs. Out of this perversion comes the pernicious and infamous theory that money shall be based on debts.

The following is the result of this false economic money system on the people of this country: Manufactured debts —National, State, municipal, corporate, real, and personal —amounting to not less than $90,000,000,000.

Upon a 5 per cent. basis, this would be an annual charge of $4,500,000,000 a year upon the people in interest and dividend charges alone, to say nothing of payments on the principal. These interest and dividend charges of $4,500,-000,000 can be paid only in two ways, viz.: Adding it to the cost of the things that the people buy and use, or reducing the price of the labor which produces them. No other term can properly describe this system than as being a monumental fraud perpetrated upon an unsuspecting people that no power on earth can much longer conceal from them.

This false economic system of money has been maintained by the dealers in debts by assuming the intrinsic value of gold; then, the importance of maintaining the parity in value of gold and silver; next, the establishing of the so-called gold standard; and now the false contention that 25.8 grains of gold is the unit of value and fixes the purchasing power of the dollar. Having assumed these premises sound, they decline to discuss them further and proceed to reform the credit superstructure in which they are most interested, the banking and currency system, and object to saying anything about the false foundation upon which the whole system must rest.

In order to reform this banking and currency system,

they again assume false premises, as follows: That a dollar is a debt, and has to be redeemed in gold alone in order to be a redeemable dollar; and that a dollar redeemable in over $134,000,000,000 of national wealth, including gold, is an irredeemable dollar. Also, that full legal tender dollars, secured for their redemption upon the entire wealth and services of the people of the United States, and redeemable in everything they possess (including debts and gold), is fiat money, unless redeemable in gold alone. The logical deduction from this would be that, by lessening the security back of a dollar or money unit, its value would be increased.

This is all based upon the false theory that a dollar is a debt to be redeemed, instead of a redeemer. When you put a perfect circulating money unit of value in a money system, it is not a thing supposed to be redeemed in any one thing. It circulates and stays out, as a part of the circulating medium, redeemable in everything.

It should be remembered there can be no sound and stable money system unless every dollar or money unit in that system is legally equivalent to every other money unit. Therefore, all money issued by the Government should clearly be made a legal tender for private debts as well as for public debts. Otherwise, it places it in the power of the people to repudiate individually what they have done collectively, and they would not stand on the same footing with respect to their Government or to each other.

Money, to be real, must have upon it the impress of the law of legal tender, delegated to Congress by the sovereign States. This exclusive power to issue money as provided in the Constitution of the United States, is so imbedded in our democratic form of Government, and so essential to its perpetuity and the well-being of its people, that there would be little left if this highest act of sovereignty was destroyed or transferred to banks of issue.

The Supreme Court of the United States has long since decided this exclusive right of the Government, as applied to both coin and paper money, as follows (U. S. Rep., vol. 110, p. 447):

"This position is fortified by the fact that Congress is

vested with the exclusive exercise of the analogous power of coining and regulating the value of domestic and foreign coin; and also the paramount power of regulating foreign and interstate commerce. Under the power to borrow money on the credit of the States, and to issue circulating notes for the money borrowed, its power to define the quality and force of those notes as currency, is as broad as the like power over a metallic currency under the power to coin money, and to regulate the value thereof. Under the two powers, taken together, Congress is authorized to establish a national currency, either in coin or in paper, and to make the currency lawful money for all purposes as regards the National Government or private individuals.''

The United States Supreme Court, speaking of the same power, declares (Legal Tender cases, 12th Wall.):

''It was for this reason the power to coin money and regulate its value was conferred upon the Federal Government, while the same power, as well as the power to emit bills of credit, was withdrawn from the States. The States can no longer declare what shall be money, or regulate its value. Whatever power there is over the currency is vested in Congress.''

By the self-confession of bankers and financiers who have grown rich during which time they have shaped all legislation on money, they now agree that the present system (which means a gold basis, with national banks of issue) is a dismal failure.

Under the operation of banks of issue and a gold basis for the redemption of credit money, promises to pay, we find all Europe staggering under a mountain of debt created through, and manufactured by, the use of credit substitutes for money devised by banks.

These debts are then made permanent and ever increased by the funding schemes put in operation, until there is little left in the way of an equity above the assessed value of their national wealth.

If a country, State, or Nation, be bonded for all the assessed value of its property, the bondholders, and not the people, own it.

The reason now given by bankers to reform the banking

and currency system is the need of "more elasticity."
Elasticity is the curse of the present credit money system,
yet they want more of it, because it is most profitable to
them.

It is now shown that with only $1,616,538,976 of real
money (gold) in the money system they have, by the use
of credit substitutes for money, pyramided $13,953,600,000
of debts against their borrowers, and with $750,472,349 of
their credit currency (national-bank notes) injected into
the system it can readily be seen that the whole system is
made up of elastic inflation, invisible credit, and india-
rubber currency.

By extending or calling in bank credits, they can inflate
or contract the currency.

If they desire to create a fall in prices or influence politics, give an object lesson to an administration, it is only
necessary for them to call in their bank credits and retire
a part of their bank-note circulation and it is accomplished.

Having reached the limit of this credit inflation, and not
yet being satisfied, they now demand an asset currency in
order that they may have the use of more of this india-
rubber money under the attractive plea of an elastic currency.

In the meantime the people are being deceived by official
reports from the United States Treasury, circulated through
the press, that the people have on deposit in the banks,
June 14, 1912, $17,024,067,606.89 of money, when, as a
fact, it is almost entirely made up of debts owed the banks
by the people, being the proceeds of loans entered on their
books as if it were cash deposited in the banks by the people.

This immense sum of debts owed the banks by the people
is used as an evidence of the great prosperity of the country; again used as an evidence of prosperity in making up
the banking power of the United States to the grand total
of $22,548,706,835 for 1912. Report of the Comptroller of
the Currency, page 42, where he states:

"Since 1900 the banking power of the country has more
than doubled, the increase being 111 per cent."

As the debts against the people increase and they become
more and more financially enslaved, the banking power increases. Such a system is good for the banks and dealers

in debts, but means untold suffering, poverty, bankruptcy, and ruin for the people.

I respectfully submit the following as absolutely essential to a proper reform of our money system on sound economic principles.

First. Absolute control of the monetary system by the Government.

Second. Government supervision over all banks and financial institutions doing business with the public and dealing in the circulating medium of the country.

Third. The issuing of money being a Government function means the issuing of full legal tender money, not an asset currency or debts, redeemable in gold, as a circulating medium. The only effect of which would be the pyramiding of more debts upon the people by the use of credit substitutes for money.

It simply means the issuing of debts instead of dollars as a circulating medium.

Fourth. There shall be no further issue of circulating notes by any national bank beyond the amount now outstanding. The Government will offer to purchase at a price not less than par and accrued interest, the 2 per cent. bonds held by national banks and deposited to secure their circulating notes. The Government shall take over these bonds and assume responsibility for their cancellation (upon presentation) of the outstanding notes secured thereby. The Government shall issue, on the terms herein provided, its full legal tender notes, lawful money of the United States, as fast as the outstanding notes secured by such bonds, so held, shall be presented for redemption, and may issue other notes from time to time to meet business requirements, it now being the policy of the United States to retire as rapidly as possible, consistent with the public interest, bond-secured circulation, and to substitute therefor real lawful money of the United States in place of banks-of-issue promises to pay—credit money. All notes issued by the Government shall be full legal tender, and payable for all debts, public and private, and constitute a first lien upon all the assets and services of the people of the United States for their redemption.

Fifth. The following amendment:

"And be it further enacted, That all the money heretofore issued by the Secretary of the Treasury of the United States, authorized by act of Congress, shall be substituted by lawful, full legal tender money of the United States, thus destroying forever the operation of the endless-chain process upon the United States Treasury.''

Sixth. That no banking or other corporations or association of men shall be allowed to issue any kind of money, currency, or any credit substitute for same.

I will now call attention to the warnings of our great statesmen, so long neglected by the representatives of the people:

William Pitt, chancellor of the exchequer of England, predicted this result when the First (so-called) Bank of the United States was established by Alexander Hamilton. He stated:

"Let the American people go into their debt-funding schemes and banking systems, and from that hour their boasted independence will be a mere phantom."

Thomas Jefferson declared of the money power of his day:

"I hope we shall crush in its inception the aristocracy of our moneyed corporations which dare already to challenge our Government to a test of strength and bid defiance to the laws of our country."

The great founder of Democracy declared:

" 'Carthago delenda est'—bank paper must be suppressed and the circulating medium must be restored to the Nation, to whom it belongs. Let banks continue if they please, but let them discount for cash alone or for United States notes.''

Salmon P. Chase, ex-Secretary of the United States Treasury, knew the present conflict would come, and said:

"My agency in procuring the passage of the national-bank act was the mistake of my life. It has built up a monopoly that affects every interest in the country. It should be repealed. But before that can be accomplished the people will be arrayed on one side and the banks on the other in a conflict such as we have never seen in this country."

Horace Greeley saw the pernicious principle concealed in the system and said:

"We are careful to conceal the ugly fact that by our iniquitous monetary system we have nationalized a system of oppression more refined, but none the less cruel, than the old system of chattel slavery."

Abraham Lincoln clearly anticipated present conditions. He said:

"I see in the near future a crisis arising that unnerves me and causes me to tremble for the safety of my country. As a result of the war, corporations have been enthroned, and an era of corruption in high places will follow and the money power will continue its sway by appealing to the people until all wealth is aggregated in a few hands, and the Republic destroyed. I feel more anxious for the safety of my country than ever before, even in the midst of war."

6. Henry Cernusche, years ago, denounced this gold-basis system by saying:

"Pernicious in Europe, pernicious in America, pernicious in Asia, the monometallic gold scheme has produced, and can produce, nothing but disaster."

The time has at last come to establish a money system on sound and correct economic principles. Bankers, money lenders, dealers in debts, should not be taken as authorities on this subject. Their personal interest in the banking and currency system should disqualify them as witnesses. It is obvious that their interest and those of the people in establishing a money system are absolutely antagonistic.

If any of the members of the committee would ask those representative bankers whether they were in favor of reforming the money system to enable the people to pay off their debts, their logical answer would be no, for the reason that their business consists in dealing in debts, and the more debts the more money they obtain from the people.

Is there anything in the record of these high financiers, or the methods they have adopted in manufacturing debts upon the country, calculated to inspire the confidence of the people in any money system that would meet with their approval?

There is no mystery surrounding an honest money system established on sound economic principles. The mystery and dishonesty begins when one dollar is made the basis for creating from eight to ten imaginary credit dollars, drawing interest from the people and controlling the money system of the country in the interest of manufacturers and multipliers of debts.

The ruinous effects of this system can no longer be concealed from the people, who now feel daily the intolerable burden in the high cost of living. The great sovereign power of the 96,000,000 people must now be felt and reckoned with. No more makeshift legislation on money can save the people's representatives from their direct responsibility, and their votes will now determine whether they are with or against the people.

A majority of the 6,500,000 people who voted for Bryan believed the issuing of money to be a Government function.

The 4,000,000 people who voted for Roosevelt indorsed the plank in the Progressive Republican platform declaring that the issuing of money is a Government function.

The great army of real workers, the American Federation of Labor, believes the issuing of money to be a Government function.

The vital question is, Shall the Government any longer issue debts redeemable in gold as a circulating medium and allow banking corporations to issue their credit substitutes for money; or shall it exercise its sovereign power, as provided in the Constitution of the United States, and issue real money and regulate the value thereof in the interest of all the people?

Having exposed this gold basis scheme upon which banks issue their credit substitutes for money, in the name of the American people I call upon Congress to do away with this gold basis credit money system, establish property as the thing of value, money as the medium of exchange, make man the master above the dollar, free the people from financial bondage, and save this Republic.

NOMINATION OF PAUL M. WARBURG AS A MEMBER OF THE FEDERAL RESERVE BOARD

Saturday, August 1st, 1914

I quote the following from the opening of this remarkable performance.

The Committee on Banking and Currency of the Senate assembled in *Executive Session* at 2 p. m. (This means a secret session behind closed doors.)

Hon. Robert L. Owens (Chairman) presiding. Present: Messrs. Hitchcock, Reed, Pomerene, Shafroth, Hollis, Lee, Nelson, Bristow, Crawford, and Weeks.

An attempt was made not to have the testimony of Mr. Warburg recorded at all, then followed—

THE CHAIRMAN: I have advised the reporter that this meeting is *strictly executive,* and under no circumstances are the notes of the proceedings to be given out to any one, and that he is under obligation not to divulge the notes.

SENATOR SHAFROTH (interposing): Nor the substance of them.

THE CHAIRMAN: Nor the substance of them.

Seeing in the public press some time after this hearing that the testimony of Warburg had been made public, I called up a Senator, one of the members of the Banking and Currency Committee, and asked if I could get a copy of Paul M. Warburg's testimony. He replied he did not have a copy, but if I called up Senator Owens, Committee Room on Banking and Currency, I might get a copy, I did so immediately and received the reply that they did not have a copy, and did not know how I could get one. I then called up the same Senator and so informed him, whereupon he said he would get a copy if possible for me. I then asked him if the testimony of Warburg had been given to the public would the Senate have confirmed his appointment. He said, No.

Later I received from this Senator by mail a copy of this testimony of Paul M. Warburg.

There is no avoiding the conclusion that the nomination and confirmation of Paul M. Warburg was forced upon the people of the United States by the bankers in collusion with the Senate Banking and Currency Committee. The examination of Mr. Warburg was unavoidable, the committee having summoned him to appear, and the testimony plainly shows that it was held simply to whitewash him, and enable the committee to report his nomination to the Senate. The documentary evidence conclusively proves that the committee suppressed Paul M. Warburg's testimony until August the twelfth and upon the face of this document will be found in large type the word "Confidential," ordered printed in confidence for the use of the Senate—made public August 12th, 1914.

Paul M. Warburg's confirmation having been rushed through the Senate on August 7th, 1914. The statement "made public" stamped on this document is absolutely false as it has never been made public.

Paul M. Warburg testified that he came to the United States in 1893, then went back to Hamburg and became a member of the firm of Warburg and Warburg. In 1895 he married the daughter of Mr. Loeb of the firm of Kuhn, Loeb and Co., New York, and his brother, Felix Warburg, married the daughter of Mr. Schiff. Kuhn, Loeb and Co., firm consists now of Jacob H. Schiff, Otto H. Kahn, Paul M. Warburg, Felix Warburg, Jerome J. Hanauer and Mortimer L. Schiff. This combination made a close connection between the banking houses of Kuhn, Loeb and Co., of New York and Warburg and Warburg of Hamburg, Germany.

Paul M. Warburg states that since his marriage in 1895, to the daughter of Loeb, he had been in this country every year for a few months. Came to the United States permanently in 1902, but did not become a citizen of the United States until 1911.

Mr. Warburg was practically unknown to the American people until he was mentioned as one of the partners of Kuhn, Loeb and Co., one of the six banking houses found to constitute the "Money Trust" of the United States, by a committee of Congress. To give the public a further insight into the record, character and moral standard of Mr. Warburg, I will quote from his own testimony before the Banking and Currency Committee of the Senate August 1st and 3rd, 1914.

Mr. WARBURG: "I may add this: That a thing which had a great deal of influence on my making up my mind to remain in this country and work here, and become part and parcel of this country was the monetary reform work, because I felt I had a distinct duty to perform here and I thought I could do that; and in fact I have been working on it since 1906 or 1907.

"Then I felt it was the right thing for one to become an American citizen and work here and throw in my lot definitely with this country."

How did he throw in his lot with us as an American citizen? Was it on the side of the people or the banks and corporations?

The record shows in 1912 his firm of Kuhn, Loeb and Co. had acquired a stock interest in 32 banks and trust companies, and according to his own testimony this was during the time he was working to reform the money system of the United States. If he had told the whole truth he would have said that he had been working as the agent and tool of the Money Trust and under their directions and instructions, to reform the money system of the United States in the interests of the banks and to enlarge their power to exploit the people of the United States by manufacturing more debts upon them with their "bank credit" substitutes for money. To substantiate this I will quote from the record of this hearing to show that Warburg was the representative of the banking interest and as such approved this Aldrich-Wilson Federal Reserve Act, from its very origin to its enactment into law, amplifying and legalizing their control over the money and credit of the United States.

SENATOR BRISTOW: When did you first become active in promoting the monetary reform of the United States?

Mr. WARBURG: 1906.

Question: Were you consulted in regards to the report of the Monetary Commission in any way?

Mr. WARBURG: Yes, Senator Aldrich consulted with me about details and I gave my advice freely.

Question: And in regard to the bill which was prepared by Senator Aldrich in connection with the commission, were you consulted in regard to that?

Mr. WARBURG: Yes.

Question: What part did you have in the preparation of that bill, directly or indirectly?

Mr. WARBURG: Well, only that I gave the best advice that I could give.

Question: What did you think of the bill as a whole?

Mr. WARBURG: I think, on the whole, the bill proceeded on fundamentally sound principles. As for the idea of centralizing reserves and of creating discount markets was concerned; that is the same principle that *our present or rather, it is the same object that our present bill achieves.* I did not quite agree with the construction of it: but on the whole, so far as the fundamental ideas are concerned, I thought it was a good bill.

Question: Yes. Do you think it was a better bill than the present law?

Mr. WARBURG: No. I do not. In some respects I may prefer some features of that, and in other respects I think this is a better one.

Question: What are the fundamental differences between the two?

Mr. WARBURG: Well, the Aldrich bill brings the whole system into 1 unit while this deals with 12 units and unites them again into the Federal Reserve Board. It is a little bit complicated, which objection, however, *can be overcome in an administrative way.*

Question: You think by administration that you could so organize the present system as to make it conform to the desirable features of the Aldrich bill so far as centralization and control are concerned?

Mr. WARBURG: I think so.

This representative of the banks on the Federal Reserve Board states only a fact when he says the Federal Reserve Act and the Aldrich Bill are fundamentally the same, and that the *Federal Reserve Board by their administration can make* it *a central bank system* so far as *centralization* and *control is concerned.*

Thus it is admitted before a committee of the United States Senate that Woodrow Wilson as President of the United States adopted this despicable subterfuge of creating 12 Federal Reserve Banks in the place of one and then united them in the Federal Reserve Board, thus deceiving and betraying the American people into the hands of a legalized Money Trust. Woodrow Wilson as President of the United States violated this plain declaration in the money plank of the Democratic platform, upon which he was elected president of the United States, which declared, "We oppose the *so-called Aldrich Bill* for the *establishment* of a *Central Bank.*"

Woodrow Wilson not only betrayed his own party, but the 4,000,000 progressive Republicans who voted on the following plank in their platform, "We are opposed to the so-called Aldrich Currency Bill because its provisions would place our currency and credit system in private hands not subject to efficient public control."

Mr. Warburg appointed by Woodrow Wilson as a member of the Federal Reserve Board is an intimate friend of W. G. McAdoo, who was affiliated with Kuhn, Loeb and Co. in his large financial deals in New York, made treasurer of the Democratic campaign fund, then appointed by Wilson, Secretary of the United States Treasury, and under the Federal Reserve Act, Ex-officio Chairman of that board.

When we consider the moral turpitude of this witness when testifying in his own behalf we can readily understand why the bankers selected him to represent them when fabricating this gigantic financial swindle upon the American people, embodied in this Aldrich-Wilson Federal Reserve Act.

SENATOR BRISTOW: When a banking house like yours owns the stock of another bank, say the National City Bank of New York, and has directors in that bank, do you think it proper for your firm, when you are getting a commission for the sale, to sell that security to your own bank?

Mr. WARBURG: I do not think it makes a bit of difference.

When Mr. Warburg's attention was called to the report of Commissioner Lane of the Interstate Commerce Commission on the financing of the Union Pacific and Chicago and Alton by Kuhn, Loeb and Co., in which Mr. Lane says, "The testimony shows that Kuhn, Loeb and Co. received $5,000,000 on the $100,000,000 of Union Pacific convertible bonds. On the 750,000 shares of Southern Pacific which the Union Pacific purchased at $50.61 per share the same banking house received $2.50 a share."

They received a like commission of $2.50 per share on the Chicago and Alton stock sold the Union Pacific at $86.50 per share. It is significant that a member of this firm (Kuhn, Loeb and Co.) refused to disclose the extent of its interest in these securities.

The following questions were then put to Mr. Warburg:

SENATOR BRISTOW: Do you think it was legitimate business for your firm to charge these excessive rates to these *railroad companies* for *handling* this *business*, when *they were directors* in the *companies and were practically selling bonds as Kuhn, Loeb and Co., bankers,* to the *railroad companies which they controlled largely and collected commissions from both—practically selling to themselves and exacting a commission?*

Mr. WARBURG: I told you in the beginning I could not discuss the affairs of our firm.

SENATOR BRISTOW: Reading from the report of the Interstate Commerce Commission—"Incidently it may be observed that the bankers—Kuhn, Loeb and Co., who *managed these corporations appear to have been richly rewarded."*

Now I want to know if you think that is legitimate business, financing?

Mr. WARBURG: Well, of course, what I said before I have to say in reply to that, that I could not under any circumstances pass judgment on transactions of my firm.

Question: But your firm did handle the finances of Mr. Harriman in his acquisition of the Southern Pacific by the Union Pacific?

Mr. WARBURG: *Yes.* But now again, Senator, you are getting into my firm's business, and I am *driven all the time into the very thing that I do not want to discuss with you; you are coming again to things which I decline to discuss.*

Question: I am only coming to the transactions of your firm that you as a member of the firm participated in.

Mr. WARBURG: I participated in every transaction of the firm since I became a member. Consequently you could just as well ask about any transaction of my firm.

SENATOR BRISTOW: And it seems to me that that is a perfectly proper thing to inquire about.

Mr. WARBURG: Well, it does not seem so to me, and I do not think we should lose so much time as it is very important for me to get back to New York.

Question: I understood you to say that you approved of the things which your firm did when you participated in the profits of the concern. Now do you approve those methods?

Mr. WARBURG: I made it plain in my letter to this committee of two weeks ago that I cannot consistently be asked to pass any judgment on the *acts* of *other* people in connection with my appointment to office. I will not do that.

Question: Well, when Mr. Harriman bonded the Union Pacific for $100,000,000 to get control of the Southern Pacific, do you think that was legitimate?

Mr. WARBURG: That was perfectly legitimate.

(The Supreme Court of the United States took a different view of this action, not only considered it illegitimate, but a flagrant violation of law, as they were competing lines, and ordered that the Union Pacific should not hold the Southern Pacific, in its decree against those roads.)

SENATOR BRISTOW: Do you approve, as a citizen, of the methods employed by Mr. Harriman in the acquisition of these railroads through the Union Pacific, with which, of course, your firm was connected?

Mr. WARBURG: The same answer, Senator.

SENATOR BRISTOW: That is, you will not say whether or not you believe the actions of Mr. Harriman as carried out by the members of your firm, through the assistance and agency of your firm—were right or wrong?

Mr. WARBURG: No; I will not discuss it.

SENATOR BRISTOW: Now you think it is altogether proper for one of these roads then to acquire part of the stock as a basis for capitalizing and increasing its capital stock?

Mr. WARBURG: Yes: it is all right.

SENATOR BRISTOW: Do you think it was wisely done in the Harriman cases?

Mr. WARBURG: There again you are asking me a question which I decline to answer.

SENATOR BRISTOW: How do you think we can find out your opinion about these shady transactions in Wall Street if you decline to answer questions of this kind?

SENATOR BRISTOW: You decline to state whether you think Mr. Harriman's methods in the Southern and Union Pacific and the Chicago and Alton and other deals of a similar kind were good or bad?

Mr. WARBURG: Yes.

The entire testimony of this witness, and representative of the bankers, was a desperate effort to conceal the dishonest character and methods employed in the business by his firm, Kuhn, Loeb and Co., J. P. Morgan and Co., National City Bank, First National Bank of New York, et al.

All having been convicted by a Committee of Congress as composing the money trust of the United States. Mr. Warburg knew if such disclosures were made by him before this Senate Committee, and became known to the public, he could never be confirmed by the Senate, as it would absolutely disqualify him from serving on any committee or board representing the people, or of holding any fiduciary position under the Government of the United States. More than this it would have damned eternally the whole corporation credit money system that he represented.

The following is only one of many attempts of Mr. Warburg to conceal the dominating control these bankers exercised over the business of the corporations in which they owned stock or were directors.

SENATOR BRISTOW: Investigation showed that your firm owned stock in some thirty approximate different banks and trust companies and banking concerns?

Mr. WARBURG: I want to say that these thirty trust companies in which we are supposed to be owners are a surprise to me. I mean that there may be some stock in our name; if there is, it must be of very unimportant sizes because I have no idea, whatsoever, that we have *any holdings worth mentioning* in that number of companies. There are only three or four of them in which we have any holding of any important number of shares.

It should be remembered that Mr. Warburg was actively engaged in reforming the banking system of the United States in the interest of the banks since 1906 and during this time his firm had acquired interest in twenty-three banks and trust companies; yet he says such ownership was a surprise to him.

SENATOR BRISTOW: Has your firm any stock, as a firm, in any bank?

Mr. WARBURG: So far as I know, they have not.

Answering conclusively these statements of Mr. Warburg I refer to the sworn statement made by a member of his firm on page 1696 when testifying before the Money Trust Investigating Committee of Congress, which shows that the firm of Kuhn, Loeb and Co. owned stock in thirty-three banks and Trust companies Nov. 1st, 1912.

SENATOR BRISTOW: I want to ask you in regard to some other matters. A little further on, to illustrate, this Money Trust report shows that your company, in a period of years, within six years, from January, 1907, to December, 1912, marketed $100,000,000 worth of Southern Pacific securities?

Mr. WARBURG: I could not tell you offhand whether that amount was handled by our firm at all, because probably our firm acted in each case as syndicate managers for a syndicate which purchased those amounts and did not act alone.

But we are getting here again into transactions of my firm.

SENATOR BRISTOW: Ah! But when you participated in the profits of the transaction is it not a part of your business life?

Mr. WARBURG: But as a matter of principle I think we should not get into a discussion of the business of my firm.

SENATOR BRISTOW: I am discussing your business.

Mr. WARBURG: No, you are discussing the firm's business.

SENATOR BRISTOW: Did you get any part of the profits that came from the handling of this $100,000,000?

Mr. WARBURG: You may take it that whatever my firm did I got my profits—my share in the profits.

SENATOR BRISTOW: Your share of the profits, now, without being specific, I take it for granted that this was quite material, and that you are one of the important members of the firm.

Mr. WARBURG: I am one of the important members of the firm.

SENATOR BRISTOW: We may take it for granted, then, that whatever profits accrued to your firm in handling of this business here since you became a member of it, you participated in the profits as one of the partners?

Mr. WARBURG: Yes, sir.

SENATOR BRISTOW: What is the amount of your holding in the American Surety Co., Mr. Warburg?

Mr. WARBURG: I think 100 shares or a little more. I could not tell offhand.

SENATOR BRISTOW: Why did you become a director in that company if you only had a small holding?

Mr. WARBURG: I will be glad to answer that, but you can see in what a position it places me; I would like to have the Committee protect me somewhere from these questions.

The protection was given in the following suggestion by a Senator, a member of the Banking and Currency Committee of the Senate.

SENATOR SHAFROTH: In a committee hearing, no matter how irrelevant or objectionable the question may be it goes in the record, but whether you answer it or not is entirely within your own discretion.

Mr. WARBURG: All right, I understand.

SENATOR SHAFROTH: So you can refuse to answer any question without seeking protection from the Committee.

SENATOR BRISTOW: You are a director in the Baltimore and Ohio Co.

Mr. WARBURG: Yes, sir.

SENATOR BRISTOW: What interest did you represent on the directorate of the company?

Mr. WARBURG: The interest of the *bankers* that placed the securities of the Baltimore and Ohio and who want to protect as far as it is necessary, and as far as they consistently can, the securities they have sold.

SENATOR BRISTOW: How much of the securities did your firm market?

Mr. WARBURG: Oh, I could not tell you offhand certainly a very large amount; several hundred million dollars.

SENATOR BRISTOW: How much of the stock of the National Bank of Commerce did you own?

Mr. WARBURG: About 900 or 1000 shares.

SENATOR BRISTOW: And you represented yourself on the directorate of that company.

Mr. WARBURG: I represented myself and my partners because my partners are also holders in that company.

SENATOR BRISTOW: Your partners are holders also; you are a director of the National Railways of Mexico?

Whom do you represent on that board?

Mr. WARBURG: I represent my firm, because at that time we reorganized that railroad and marketed its securities.

He also admitted that he was a director and represented the same interests in the same way in the following corporations: The United States Mortgage and Trust Co., The Title Guarantee and Trust Co., Wells Fargo Express Co., The Western Union Telegraph Co., and that other members of the firm of Kuhn, Loeb and Co. were directors and held stock interests in like manner in many other banks, trust companies and industrial corporations.

Kuhn, Loeb and Co. are the Bankers for the Baltimore and Ohio Railroad and The Penn. Railway System, and it is an open secret at the Treasury Department that Paul M. Warburg represents the International Hebrew Bankers in the United States. The Committee appointed by the Congress of the United States to investigate the "Money Trust" made the following report in its findings after many months of careful investigation.

This Committee reports that a Money Trust exists in this country composed of J. P. Morgan and Co., The First National Bank of New York, The National City Bank of New York, Lee Higginson and Co., of Boston and New York, Kidder, Peabody and Co., of Boston and New York, and Kuhn, Loeb and Co., of New York.

And that this banking combination worked together in placing securities and divided the profits.

It has been conclusively shown that this combination conceived the Aldrich-Wilson Federal Reserve Act for their profit and protection.

The evidence shows that Kuhn, Loeb and Co., during the ten years, 1897 to 1906, purchased in association with other banking houses $821,289,000 of securities of corporations in the United States, and in the six succeeding years the firm of Kuhn, Loeb and Co. purchased, in association with their banking houses, stock in corporations in the United States, amounting to $704,000,000, and purchased as a firm, securities of railroads, etc., aggregating $530,000,000, making a total of $2,055,289,000 of American securities dealt in by this firm of so-called bankers during this time.

Yet they consider this private business; and when a Committee of the United States Senate, supposed to represent the people, attempts to inquire from this man, Warburg, a member of this firm, he refuses to give them any information about the method in which Kuhn, Loeb and Co. et al. fraudulently manipulated these debts upon the great public carriers of this country upon which the people have to pay the interest, dividends and principle, if ever paid.

Yet the astounding fact remains that this German Jew, Paul M. Warburg, the characterless and degenerate product of the false money system of Europe, a representative of the International Money Power, is elevated by President Wilson and the American Senate to a controlling position over the money system of the United States upon which absolutely depends the prosperity and happiness of a hundred million people in this Republic.

For obvious reasons this Combination of Bankers, with a verdict of being a Money Trust against them by a Committee of the Congress of the United States could not come out in the open and advocate and endorse such a bill, as they knew such action on their part would have killed the bill.

Therefore Woodrow Wilson, President of the United States, Paul M. Warburg et al., were selected as sponsors for the Bill.

From the indisputable facts there is no escaping the conclusion that the Aldrich-Wilson Federal Reserve Act is a heartless betrayal of the people, and Woodrow Wilson the scholastic Judas of Democracy.

INTERNATIONAL PLUTOCRACY FORCES THE FEDERAL RESERVE ACT THROUGH THE CONGRESS OF THE UNITED STATES—USING A DEMOCRATIC CAUCUS TO ACCOMPLISH IT

The Federal Reserve Act, enlarging and attempting to further legalize this false gold basis, debt manufacturing, banking and currency scheme, gives these Banking Corporations the power to loan ten dollars of false and fictitious money, having no existence and represented only by "Credit and Debit" figures upon the books of the banks, called "Money of Account" or "Bank Credits," for every dollar of lawful money of the United States they have to loan, thus giving a lawful dollar of the United States ten times the earning power in the possession of these Banking Corporations that it has in the possession of the man who earns it. It also gives the banks the preposterous and ruinous privilege of rediscounting debts held against their borrowers, and have the amount credited *as reserve* to their account with the Federal Reserve Bank, and upon this reserve so created loan ten times the amount in "Bank Credits" to other borrowers.

Gives these banks that make and hold the debts against the people the control of the means of their payment.

Gives these banks the control of the medium of exchange upon which the business of over a hundred million people depends.

Gives these banks the means to increase and pyramid interest-earning debts upon the people without increasing the money in which these debts can be paid.

Gives these banks the control of the "Money and Credit" of the United States, thus enabling them to restrict the opportunities of our people to develop the great and varied resources of this country in their own interest.

Gives banks the astounding and ruinous power to say to over a hundred million people in this Republic how much or how little money or credit they shall have.

Under the operation of these Federal Reserve and Farm Loan Acts, if $2,000,000,000 of debts created against borrowers of "Bank Credits" at the member banks were rediscounted at the twelve Federal Reserve Banks, it could be considered by the member banks as reserve held in the Federal Reserve Banks. On the basis of this reserve it would be possible for the member banks to, in turn, extend credit or *create additional interest-earning debts upon borrowers* of approximately $20,000,000,000 without having put another dollar in the money system in which debts can be paid. Thus it will be seen that a *discounted* debt of the borrower is made the basis of the banks creating *ten additional interest-earning debts upon borrowers.*

And if the interest and principal of the *debts so created* are not paid, the property of the borrower is taken from him.[1]

The Federal Reserve Act embodies and enlarges the Bank of England scheme of creating debts without lending money. The Federal Reserve Act was hailed as establishing an institution that would furnish the people with adequate money to meet all the demands of business, and that the Government would issue the money. The fact being that the Government cannot issue a dollar under this act, or even a Federal Reserve note, unless a bank borrows it on a debt already created against a borrower; and this note is itself *a debt, not money,* being redeemable at the United States Treasury, by the people in gold.

The banks get the interest on the Federal Reserve notes they borrow, in the shape of dividends on the stock of the Federal Reserve Banks which they own. Banks will not put enough of these Federal Reserve notes in actual existence to furnish an adequate medium of exchange, for this would stop the loaning of "bank credits" as a substitute for money.

Thus the Federal Reserve notes are issued for and entirely controlled by Banking Corporations organized for

---

[1] Assets of the banks in the United States, in 1914, $18,517,732,879. R. C. C., 1914, page 41.

Assets of the banks in the United States, June 28, 1918, $39,082,800,000. R. C. C., 1918, page 11.

private gain, and are in no sense Government notes issued in the interest of the people.

Although banks can take out Federal Reserve notes when they rediscount debts of borrowers at the Federal Reserve Banks, and can put these notes in actual circulation, they have no intention of doing so permanently, as this would put into circulation a debt paying currency. The action of the banks demonstrates this to be a fact. The Federal Reserve Scheme was inaugurated November 16, 1914, and up to October 31, 1916, the total amount of Federal Reserve notes issued was $238,496,920, of which $223,523,-070 were exchanged for a like amount of gold and lawful money, leaving the net amount of notes issued only $14,-973,850. During this time billions of dollars of debts, payable in money, have been put upon the people by loaning them "bank credits."

For banks to create debts upon borrowers, by loaning them a fictitious substitute for lawful money, is an infamous transaction, but in addition to this, under the Federal Reserve Scheme, debts so created can be rediscounted at the Federal Reserve Banks, and the proceeds of these debts placed to the credit of the "banks' reserve;" and upon this reserve the banks can create from six to eight times this amount of additional debts against borrowers by loaning them additional "bank credits" or "money of account," represented only by credit and debit figures on the books of the banks.

I ask the question, could the ingenuity of the most cunning and unscrupulous minds conceive a more ingenious and dishonest scheme, to rob the people by putting them in debt by loaning them money that has no existence?

A CONCRETE CASE

It should be borne in mind that the Federal Reserve Banks are owned by the Bankers, who subscribe to their capital stock, and in this way get their earnings, and are under the management of the board of directors, two-thirds of whom are elected by the bankers.

I ask the most careful reading of the following correspondence:

"W. G. McAdoo,
    "Secretary U. S. Treasury.
"Dear Sir:
    "Kindly let me know to what amount the banks can expand their loans to relieve the cotton owners of the South upon the $15,000,000 of gold deposited in the Reserve Banks at Richmond, Atlanta and Dallas, Texas, and greatly oblige,
                            "Very respectfully,
                            "(Sgd.) T. Cushing Daniel."
    This letter was referred by Mr. McAdoo to the Federal Reserve Board for reply. In the reply of the Federal Reserve Board dated September 13th, 1915, they state:
    "If the member banks took this accommodation in the form of a deposit the deposit would count as reserve, and if the borrowing bank were a country bank $12 of reserves would sustain $100 of loans."
"W. G. McAdoo,
    "Secretary U. S. Treasury.
"Dear Sir:
    "Kindly let us know the rate of interest charged on the $15,000,000 deposited in the Southern Banks to help the owners of cotton, and oblige,
                            "Very respectfully,
                            "(Sgd.) T. Cushing Daniel."
    In reply under date of October 13th, 1915, I quote:
    "Replying to your letter of 8th inst., you are advised that the Federal Reserve Banks at Richmond, Va., Atlanta, Ga., and Dallas, Texas, are loaning the fifteen million dollars deposited with them by the Secretary of the Treasury, for use in connection with the moving marketing or storing of the cotton crop, to member banks at three per cent."
                            (Sgd.) Wm. P. Malburn,
                            Ass't. Secretary U. S. Treasury.
    The following analysis of this transaction is a concrete example of how this infamous copartnership of the Government and banking corporations operates under the Federal Reserve Act, and illustrates the profits made by the loaning of "bank credits" as a substitute for money by the banks. This is the real reason why banking corporations and bankers so violently oppose the Government's

exercising its sovereign function of issuing and loaning real money for a valuable consideration direct to the people.

The Government deposits $15,000,000 of gold, the people's money—received into the United States Treasury as taxes from the people—in the three Federal Reserve Banks of the South. The stock of these Federal Reserve Banks belongs to the member banks.

STATEMENT

The $15,000,000 of the people's money earns the stockholders of the Federal Reserve Banks by being deposited with the member banks 3 per cent. a year . . . . $ 450,000

On this $15,000,000 the member banks loan borrowers on cotton—the farmers—$125,000,000 of "bank credits" at 6 per cent. Earned by the banks out of the farmers $7,050,000 a year $7,050,000

The people whose money furnishes the basis of the whole transaction receive nothing.

This vicious principle, ruinous to the people, underlies the whole Federal Reserve System.

Stripped of its technicalities and misleading verbiage the Federal Reserve Act resolves itself into a deliberate and well thought out financial conspiracy whereby the banks through the agency and coöperation of the Government steal by indirection the earnings of the people.

To illustrate: A farmer or a laborer by years of hard work has saved $1,000. If he loans it out at 6 per cent. it will only earn him $60.00 a year. On the other hand, $1,000 in the possession of the bank can be converted into reserve money and the bank can loan $8,000 of "bank credits" that at 6 per cent. will earn the bank—the nonproducer—$480.00 a year.

Suppose this $1,000 of lawful money in a bank's reserve is used as the basis of loaning $8,000 of "bank credits" on stock collateral at 3 per cent., this $1,000 is loaned eight times and is earning 24 per cent.

The loaning of "bank credits" at 3 per cent. on stocks

as collateral creates speculation and gambling in stocks. As the stocks are supposed to pay not less than 6 per cent. dividends and are bought on a margin of 10 per cent. or 20 per cent. it seems to be a profitable investment and wild speculation follows in the stock market. When the banker's limit has been reached in making these loans the interest rates are run up on the borrowers. This immediately causes a fall in the prices of the stocks, and to protect them the borrowers are called on to pay from 10 to 50 per cent. on their "bank credit" loans.

This debt manufacturing and money-making scheme enables the banks in the reserve cities to offer sufficient inducements to those controlling the money in the banks of the interior or agricultural sections of the United States, to send their money, having actual existence, to the banks in the reserve cities in order that it may be converted into reserve money and furnish the basis of loaning from six to eight dollars of "bank credits" for every dollar so received.

Here we have the basic cause of the prosperity of bankers, dealers in debts and non-producers on one side, and the poverty and distress of the real producers and laborers on the other. This is the real cause of the under-development of the country and the over-development of the cities, and it is the fundamental cause of the conflict between capital and labor which is rapidly intensifying into anarchy which means the destruction of life and property.

The International Bankers, fully realizing the possibilities of this money-making scheme when applied to the development of the great resources of the United States, established Clearing House Associations at which incoming checks could be matched and cancelled in order that the banks could avoid paying out actual money and loan "bank credits" as a substitute for money.

Stock Exchanges were organized upon which to list bonds and stocks and thus make ready market for them in the United States and Europe.

In applying this debt-manufacturing scheme on a large scale the possibilities and earning power of the railways of the United States offered great inducements and were selected as a basis for bond and stock issues, now amounting to $20,000,000,000.

Great Industrial Trusts were then formed to consolidate the great industrial enterprises of this country in order that they might be subjected to this bonding, and stock issuing, debt manufacturing scheme.

The *Bank Panic Preventive of this act* is the privilege given the bank to rediscount the debts of borrowers and get the cash in case of a run on the bank. But it leaves the borrower in a helpless condition, absolutely at the mercy of the banks, for by calling in loans held against the borrower the banks can ruin millions of people by taking from them their property.

In other words, the Federal Reserve Act protects the banks while the people may be financially ruined. In short, the prosperity of the banks under the operation of this banking and currency scheme is built upon the ruin of the people.

I unreservedly state without fear of successful contradiction that in all the annals of time, no such ingeniously dishonest and ruinous piece of legislation has ever been inflicted upon an unsuspecting people.

1. The genesis and passage of this Federal Reserve Act will show that International Bankers, the Associated Banks and beneficiaries of this banking and currency scheme exerted their all-powerful influences over the mental hireling of the public press, and through a systematic educational propaganda throughout the United States deceived 95 per cent. of the people into believing that this indefensible and damnable piece of legislation was a beneficent law enacted by their Representatives in Congress in the interest of the people.

2. No greater demonstration could be had of the power of the subsidized public press to deceive and ruin a people.

It is absolutely useless to talk about ideals of Government, the "self-determination of peoples" and establishing a Democracy in any country of the world where this scheme of debt slavery of the people is allowed to exist.

THE BANKING PROCESS OF MANUFACTURING DEBTS

J. P. Morgan and Co., Kuhn, Loeb and Co., and associate banks controlling the railroads, make a contract with themselves, as bankers, to underwrite $50,000,000 of railroad securities. These securities are listed on the stock exchanges and delivered to the banks who agree to accept them as collateral security for loans and then offer them for sale. Thus these securities are given immediately an artificial market value that otherwise they would not possess; these banks can then increase or decrease their market value by increasing or decreasing the amounts they will loan on them, or they can practically destroy their market value by declining to accept them as collateral security for loans. Under the present banking system the banks control the money and credits of this country and thereby control the market value of these securities.

Having by this process, the loaning of "bank credits," manufactured the larger portion of about $90,000,000,000 of interest and dividend earning debts upon the resources and people of the United States, the stupendous credit superstructure erected by the banks was about to collapse.

The banks had so overloaded the borrowers with debts and fraudulently created securities by their underwriting schemes that they had overtaxed their ability to loan even "bank credits."

In fact, they had so disregarded the rudimentary principles of common honesty and so flagrantly violated the laws of the land, that they could but realize that if a real investigation was made into the affairs of the banks and the true character of their transactions once known by the public, the whole system would be destroyed.

With this condition confronting them, a large percentage of bankers were apprehensive of runs on their banks, exposure and quick transition from private palaces to public jails. They fully realized that something had to be done to protect them and the system. You will find their carefully worked out solution in the Aldrich-Wilson Federal Reserve Act, allowing the banks to reduce the amount of money they must keep as reserves, and allowing them to increase the amount of "bank credits" they can loan the people and rediscount debts.

These bankers and plunderers of the people, represented by Warburg et al., call it mobilizing reserves and liquefying their assets.

Mobilizing their reserves, simply means increasing the amount of "bank credits," or false money they can loan the people. Liquefying their assets means obtaining from the Government currency on the debts they have already created, and can create, on the people by the loaning of this false and non-existent money.

The Federal Reserve Act, as admitted by the Comptroller of the Currency, allows the banks to increase their "bank credits" loans, as a substitute for money, from two to three billion dollars; it thus enlarges the powers of the old system to multiply debts upon the people by loaning them "bank credits."

To show that the bankers fully appreciate this fact I will quote from the statement made by Frank A. Vanderlip, President of the National City Bank of New York, before the Pan-American Conference, May 25th, 1915:

"This country and other countries should understand the position we are in concerning our reserve. The new law reduces the reserve requirements, and we have, I should say off hand, $736,000,000 more reserve than the law requires for national banks. There is a similar plethora in the State banks. This gives us an enormous capacity for the expansion of loans. We can probably expand loans $2,000,000,000 or $3,000,000,000. We may not be in a state of preparedness for war, but we are in a state of preparedness to expand loans abroad, and credits at home."

The banks, in order to disarm suspicion and disassociate themselves from this bankers' scheme—to keep control of the money and credit of the United States, and pyramid more interest-bearing debts upon the people—adopted their usual methods of deception.

They allowed Wilson to attack them as a "Money Trust" without resentment. They did not object to his making high sounding promises to the people—"to free the credit system of the United States and if necessary 'hang the bankers as high as Haman' in order to bring about a 'new birth of freedom.' " Neither did the bankers object to Wilson being nominated at the Democratic Convention at Baltimore, although he had thus anathematized them in public. After Wilson was elected President, the record shows he fully coöperated with these bankers and forced this Federal Reserve Act through Congress which the Chairman of the Banking and Currency Committee admitted, during its final passage through the Senate, to be a bankers' bill pure and simple; and it has been so demonstrated in operation. Instead of freeing the credit of the United States as promised the people, Wilson saw it organized and then turned it over bodily to the bankers in the Aldrich-Wilson Federal Reserve Act.

To divert the attention of the people from this financial conspiracy, commissions were appointed to study the European banking and currency systems instead of investigating the system at home that needed the reforming. The International Bankers, not wishing to be recognized as principals, allowed Paul M. Warburg et al., to arrogate to themselves the framing of this monetary monstrosity to rob the people of the United States.

The Federal Reserve Act embodies in it the legislation required by the bankers in order that they may still control "money and credits" of the United States and *continue to create debts upon* the *people* by *loaning them* "*bank credits.*"

ILLUSTRATION OF HOW BANKING CORPORATIONS CREATE INTEREST AND DIVIDEND EARNING DEBTS UPON THE PEOPLE—WITH NON-EXISTENT MONEY, "BANK CREDITS"

The bankers loan $100,000 of "bank credits" to discount the notes of borrowers for 90 days. At the end of 90 days a curtail of 20 per cent. is made by the borrowers in actual currency—which under the Federal Reserve Act can immediately be *converted* into legal tender money and upon same being placed in their reserve fund the banks can loan as high as $10.00 for $100 so placed, or $200,000 of "bank credits" on the $20,000 paid in by the borrowers on the debts.

Here we have an illustration showing why the banks believe in this "Federal Reserve System"; it gives the bankers the privilege of loaning as high as ten dollars of "bank credits" for every dollar they can put in their reserve. It also accounts for the insistence on the part of the banker that all other forms of money shall be converted into "reserve money," the result being that the legal tender money, issued by the government, by being placed in a *bank's reserve* has *ten times* the *earning power* that it has in the hands of the man who earns it. Here we discover the great moral and economic evil underlying this whole system, as it gives to the bankers—non-producers—not only the control and use of the *money issued by the government,* but endows this money with ten times the earning power that it has in the hands of honest workers and real producers. It puts in the control of bankers and non-producers, the only *substitute for money*—"bank credits." The bankers therefore have every reason, as bankers, to restrict the legal tender money of the Government to gold which enables them to create and loan as high as ten dollars of "bank credits" for every dollar of real money in their possession.

The wide world over the object of the bankers and dealers in debts in confining real money to gold alone is that they may multiply debts upon the people by the use of *their cheap substitutes for money—bank credits.* This system has now *loaded down the people of the world with unpayable debts—earning interest—paid directly and indirectly by the people.*

Thus the sovereign power of the Government, representing the people, furnishes the *money and means to the bankers whereby the people* are *financially enslaved.*

To state it more plainly, this Government no longer represents the people, but diverts and prostitutes its highest attribute of sovereignty by the endorsement of this robbery of the people.

As the 27,062 Banking Associations in the United States now hold about 23 billion dollars of debts against the people, it will be seen that if they call for 10 per cent. curtail on these debts it will take all the *money in actual circulation* and leave the borrowers no means of payment other than by borrowing more "bank credits," which the banks can deny at any time and place the debtors absolutely at their mercy, which means holding them up for higher interest, commission for renewals of loans or selling them out, taking their property and anything else they have to pay these debts contracted by borrowing "bank credits" false and fictitious money, created by Banking Corporations.

THE BANKERS ESCAPED, THROUGH THE PROTECTION OF
    THE PRESIDENT OF THE UNITED STATES, AN INVESTIGA-
    TION THAT WOULD HAVE DISCREDITED THE WHOLE
    SYSTEM AND PREVENTED THE PASSAGE OF THE FEDERAL
    RESERVE ACT

The Money Trust Investigation House resolutions 429-504 passed by Congress authorizing the investigation of *Banking and Currency conditions in the United States as a basis for remedial legislation,* provides as follows:

"The Comptroller of the Currency, the Secretary of the Treasury, and the Commissioner of the Bureau of Corporations, and their respective assistants and subordinates, are hereby respectively directed to comply with all directions of the committee for assistance in its labors to place at the service of the Committee all the data and records of their respective departments, to procure for the Committee from time to time such information as is subject to their control or inspection and to allow the use of their assistants for the making of such investigation with respect to corporations under their respective jurisdictions as the Committee or any sub-committee may from time to time request."

The principal National Banks in the reserve cities of New York, Philadelphia, Boston and St. Louis refused or omitted to make any returns whatever and denied the power or jurisdiction of the Committee to inquire into their affairs. Whereupon

On December 26th, 1912, Counsel for this Committee wrote the Comptroller of the Currency as follows:

"The sub-committee of the Committee on Banking and Currency of the House of Representatives which is engaged in investigating the question of the concentration and control of money and credit under House Resolution 504 has been satisfied from the beginning—and experience has confirmed its then stated views—that no exhaustive investigation can be conducted such *as is provided by the resolution, without access to the books* of *account and affairs* of the principal National Banks in the great reserve cities.

"The data we require at the moment relate to the loans made by the principal National Banks in the reserve cities and involves a disclosure to the Committee of the *names* of *the borrowers and the security for such loans,* from 1905 to the present time."

As early as September, 1912, this Committee asked the Comptroller of the Currency to supply certain data concerning the business and practices of the larger National Banks. He referred the request to the President for instructions, in obedience, as he claimed, to the general Executive order, issued by President Roosevelt and reissued by President Taft, which prohibited any head of department or other official thereof from furnishing information without the permission of the President.

It was not until December 17th, 1912, however, that President Taft rendered his decision declining to allow the Comptroller of the Currency to furnish the information requested.

Thus the President of the United States aligned himself with the banks and protected them from an exposure that would have absolutely discredited the system and prevented the passage of the Federal Reserve Act.

Plainly stated, the position taken by the banks and upheld by the President was that the banks, the creatures of the Congress, were superior to their creator and that the Comptroller of the Currency was the only official of the Government whose acts or omissions were beyond its scrutiny.

Here we have the mandate of nearly a hundred million people, through their Representatives in the Congress, repudiated and set aside by the President of the United States in order to prevent the exposure of the dishonest methods and business transactions of those controlling the "money and credits" of the United States.

This caused the failure of the completion of the Money Trust Investigation, which would have discredited the whole system. This Committee so reported to Congress and urged further investigation into the monopoly of money and credits which they found to exist.

What is the result of the last financial frame-up on the people, tested by the facts? In 1908 the so-called National Monetary Commission, Nelson W. Aldrich, chairman, authorized by the Congress, spent $287,259.35 of the taxpayers' money ostensibly to investigate foreign banking and currency systems in order that they might improve the banking and currency system of the United States.

In 1913 the Money Trust Investigating Committee spent $57,471.97 in trying to investigate the banking and currency system of the United States, that needed the reforming.

During the five years that these investigations were carried on $334,731.32 of the people's money was spent and the President of the United States then stopped the investigation in order to protect this false banking and currency system from exposure. The Wilson administration came into power and utterly ignored the testimony of this Committee, utterly ignored its recommendation to complete their investigation which would have exposed the plundering of the people by this Money Trust, and would have destroyed the system.

President Wilson before his election declared he knew that a money trust existed, and this Committee stated in its report that a money trust did exist in the United States; yet this Wilson administration legalized and amplified the power of this money trust in the Federal Reserve Act and gave it the additional privilege of loaning about three billion more of "bank credits," or false money.

INTEREST AND DIVIDEND EARNING DEBTS MANUFACTURED UPON THE RESOURCES OF THE UNITED STATES BY THESE PLUNDERERS OF THE PEOPLE

It is a self-evident fact, now mountain high, and can be observed of all men, that the great railroad systems and industrial enterprises of this country have not been developed honestly or legitimately, but have been used by banking corporations, promoters and plunderers of the people as a basis for fraudulent over issues of bonds and stocks.

Thomas F. Ryan, a representative of the bankers, admitted under oath that 90 per cent. of all the stock issued on the railroads of this country was water.

Daniel Willard Prest, of the Baltimore & Ohio railroad system, testified before the Interstate Commerce Commission that it was the policy of his company to put back from its earnings one dollar in the road for every two dollars they paid on their stock. In other words about two dollars out of every three paid into the treasury of these public carriers by the public is used to pay dividends on watered stock.

The International Bankers and Banking Corporations are responsible for the present bankrupt condition of the railroads.

The condition of the railroads as admitted before the Interstate Commerce Commission, March 6th, 1915, *Railway Credit Poor.* Able to obtain loans only at high rates, says Festus J. Wade, St. Louis banker. "Asserting he had much experience with the credit' of Southwestern roads, Mr. Wade said that the roads' ability to obtain money on bonds in recent years was steadily decreasing."

On March 13th, 1915, James J. Hill, railroad builder, said—"Railroads at Last Ditch."

"The railroads of this country are staggering under too great a burden now and are right at the last ditch. They are no longer able to compete with each other, or any one else. They are too busy trying to solve their financial problems that will enable them to live a while longer."

Chicago, Jan. 1st, 1916—"Fewer miles of railroad were built in the United States during 1915 than in any other year since 1864, and more miles of railroad were in receivers' hands during the year than ever before, according to railway statistics compiled from official sources by the *Railway Age Gazette.*"

The Stock Exchange was established through which to market the securities thus created. With this false system for loaning "bank credits" in full operation, and controlled by them, the so-called great international banking houses and those controlling the banking system of this country entered into their gigantic underwriting schemes to float these interest and dividend earning debts upon the resources of the United States and by this process absorb the earnings of the people.

All based upon the damnable theory, fabricated by the lenders of false money, ''bank credits,'' that borrowing is a condition precedent to the use of a circulating medium of exchange, and that debt is a necessity.

Under the rulings of the Interstate Commerce Commission as reorganized everything must conduce to the payment of interest and dividends on excessive bond issues and watered stock in which the Money Trust trades.

So well pleased are these interests in the rulings of this Commission that on March 21st, 1916, most of the presidents of the large railroad systems appeared before the Senate Committee on Post Roads and requested that the Interstate Commerce Commission be given the power to fix the rate the Government shall pay the roads for carrying the mail for the people.

Senator Vardaman put the following question to Mr. L. M. Felton, president of the Chicago Great Western Railroad:

Senator Vardaman. Some years ago the roads were opposed to regulation by the Commission; now they are asking it. How do you account for that?

Mr. Felton. We have grown older and wiser.

It does not require much wisdom to reach this conclusion in the face of the following figures just issued by the Interstate Commerce Commission comparing the net revenues of the railroads as shown for January last, with the same month of 1915, after the rate increases were made by the Commission. These figures show the *net* revenue of the Eastern roads increased from $307 to $609 a mile and *net earnings* increased from $227 to $423 a mile, more than 130 per cent. Southern roads show $316 per mile against $187.

When the Bankers and Railroads won their fight before this reorganized Interstate Commerce Commission for increased freight rates, the public press declared that Wall Street and President Wilson were happy.

This dishonest system of loaning "bank credits" under the false and misleading designation of "capital" has given Banking Corporations, promoters, non-producers, speculators and parasites an unfair advantage over real producers and honest workers in the distribution of all wealth. Under this absolutely false economic system, so-called "capital" will ever control and absorb the earnings of labor. *For the interest and dividend upon these perpetually increasing debts can be paid only in one of two ways: Either by adding it to the cost of the things the people buy or use, or by reducing the rate of the wages that produce them.*

This system creates perpetual debts, breeds usury, speculation, gambling and corruption in its insidious and all powerful influences wherever felt.

Mr. F. A. Delano, the substitute for Thomas D. Jones on the Federal Reserve Board, calls this Federal Reserve System the "National Shock Absorber." In fact and in practice it is the "Bankers' Bulwark" for the protection of the Plunderers of the people.

It effectually ties the hands of the Government so that it can not issue another dollar into the money system to protect the people from financial ruin, unless permitted to do so by the banks. Then grants the banks the exclusive right to lend "bank credits" instead of money to the people. Thus the absolute control of "money and credits" is given to the banks with the astounding power to say how much or how little money or credit the people of the United States shall have.

The people should study the false foundation upon which rests this money-making scheme—called a Banking and Currency system—and upon which the business of this country now has to depend.

The cold figures from the Report of the Comptroller of the Currency for 1915, pages 122-5, tells the story. "Total cash held by 27,062 Banks and Trust Companies, $1,457,-702,138."

Amount borrowed by the Banks from each other, $2,783,-312,258.

Showing a shortage in cash to pay the debts they owe each other of $1,325,610,120.

Total Capital Stock Paid In $2,162,841,369
Surplus earnings $1,732,918,047

A large percentage of this capital stock was paid for out of surplus earnings from borrowers; leaving the large surplus here shown. All evidencing usurious exactions from the people.

Invested by Banks in bonds and other securities $5,881,-900,000. This shows these banks and trust companies have invested $1,986,140,584 more than their entire paid in capital and surplus.

This statement shows these bankers have already invested $1,986,140,584, more than they had to invest, and the statement they make of loaning ''bank capital'' or anything they own or have paid for, under this term, is a snare and a delusion.

The machinery of the present Banking and Currency scheme is too overloaded with expenses to be of any use to the people. The running expenses of the 27,062 banks now amounts to about $1,100,692,626

Interest on the $2,783,312,258 at 2 per
  cent. borrowed from each other   55,666,245
Interest on the $2,485,396,398 at 3 per
  cent. borrowed from time depositors   74,561,891
                                         _____

                            Total $1,230,920,762

To this should be added the extravagant management of the New Federal Reserve System.

All of which is eventually paid by the borrowers.

THE PEOPLE BEING MISLED BY FALSE STATEMENTS FROM UNITED STATES TREASURY

The United States Treasury, the fiduciary department of the people's government, should send out truthful and plain statements of the condition of the money system, upon which the business of over a hundred million people must depend. I therefore call your attention to criminally misleading statements sent out from the United States Treasury, and published in the public press throughout the country.

On August 1, 1917, the United States Treasury sent out the statement, repeated in the public press:

"Money in circulation in the United States reached on August 1st the total of $4,852,084,469, an increase of nearly 23 per cent. within a year. The *per capita circulation* August 1st was $46.53.

"The amount of gold in the Treasury and in circulation was $3,086,218,498, an increase of $586,000,000 within the year and approximately $1,300,000,000 since the European war started."

This statement conveys an absolutely false impression to the minds of the people. It would make them believe that the amount of money the people could use was rapidly increasing, and that there was $4,852,084,469 of money in actual circulation in the United States. This statement, when analyzed, brings out the following facts:

Proceeds of loans are treated as deposits of cash by the people. Report of the Comptroller of the Currency, June 30th, 1916.

Individual deposits in banks, $22,773,714,074.98. The average reader believes from this statement that *the people* have in banks this amount of money, and, therefore, are in a most prosperous condition, and that there is an immense amount of money in the country that can be used by the people. The fact being that the people have gone in debt to the banks $21,301,514,084.98 and are heading for bankruptcy; the total amount of cash in all the banks June 30, 1916, being only $1,472,200,000.

A truthful statement from the United States Treasury showing how the people are plunging into debt would warn them of rocks ahead, and that it was time for them to protect themselves instead of living in a fool's paradise, with no chance of ever paying their debts, and heading for bankruptcy. A truthful statement from the United States Treasury would show that after deducting the gold and other money, impounded as reserves of banks, which has to be subtracted from the total amount of money in order to ascertain the amount left in circulation, it would show that there is less than $1,900,000,000 of money in actual circulation to do all the business of over a hundred

238   REAL MONEY VERSUS FALSE MONEY

million people. The per capita *circulation* being about
$19.00 instead of $46.53.

The statement that there is "$4,852,084,469 of money in
circulation in the United States" is absolutely false and
misleading to the people. The $1,300,000,000 of gold
brought from Europe by the war has already been used
by the banks as the basis of creating about $13,000,000,000
of debts. In other words, $13,000,000,000 of additional
interest earning debts, demanding money in payment,
have been created with only $1,300,000,000 with which to
pay them.

CREDULOUS BORROWERS OF "BANK CREDITS"

The borrowers, with a superficial knowledge of money,
will ask the question: "If I borrow from the bank and
the bank puts the amount to my credit, and I can draw
a check on the bank and pay my bills, why is not that as
good as money?"

In the immediate relief the borrower feels in paying
his pressing obligations he fails to realize that he has
created another debt that calls for money in payment,
and that a new demand for money has been created while
no corresponding additional money has been put in existence to meet this new demand. The borrower has not paid
his debt, he has only transferred it to the bank in exchange
for "bank credits."

Every borrower is in competition with every other borrower to get money to pay his debt, and every new debt
increases the competition for money that does not exist.
Example: A borrows $500 of "bank credits," the bank
puts $500 to A's credit—which is a false entry for A has
not deposited one dollar in money. A then pays his bill
with a check for $500 to B. A's check is deposited and
credited to B's bank account and charged to A's account.

The check is then cancelled, so the circulating medium
that closed the transaction no longer exists, but A is
pledged to the bank to return $500 in money.

As the Clearing House enables the banks to act as a
unit, it matters not in which banks checks are deposited.

As the official reports of the Comptroller of the Currency show that in these settlements only five per cent. of money is used.

To illustrate the process: Ten banks have discounted with "bank credits" ten notes of ten thousand dollars each and placed to the credit of the borrowers one hundred thousand dollars as if they had deposited one hundred thousand dollars in money—the fact being, they have not deposited one dollar. When the borrowers draw their checks upon these "bank credits" for one hundred thousand dollars, these are paid at the "Clearing House Association" with five thousand dollars in money simply divided among the banks as their balances appear against each other. Result—One hundred thousand dollars more of interest bearing debts have been created and not one more dollar has been added to the money in existence wherewith they can be paid.

Will the time ever come when money will be at a reasonable rate of interest, or the conditions more favorable for the debtors to pay their debts? Under the present false Banking and Currency system this is absolutely impossible.

Every borrower of "bank credits" joins that ever increasing army of debtors, struggling to get hold of money to pay the banks for the use of the fictitious money loaned them, which has ceased to exist, as money, and is now only represented by the debt against the borrowers. Every debt created by bankers in loaning "bank credits" is a new demand for money. Hence this universal and perpetual demand for money on the part of the people to pay these debts.

Money loaned by the Government direct to the people and surplus money in the possession of its owner, would be loaned for a long term of years in order to have it earn interest.

Just the reverse is the case under the present false banking and currency system.

In addition to this ruinous exploitation of the people by this system, I desire to call attention to the enormous economic waste of time from useful pursuits, the exhaustion of mental and physical energy, the anxiety, suffering and humiliation felt by the larger portion of our people, who are debtors, in getting extensions and paying curtails on thirty, sixty and ninety day loans.

Under this indefensible system we have the great majority of our people supplicants and absolutely dependent upon these banks for a medium of exchange by which to carry on the legitimate business of this country.

RURAL CREDITS

The Federal Reserve Act as passed by Congress did not originate with the people. The influence of the money power framed the bill and it is acknowledged to be a banker's bill.

As an evidence of this I quote from the hearings before the Senate Committee on Banking and Currency, referring to the testimony of H. Parker Willis, this advocate of the so-called exploded gold standard theory, an expert on money, who gives a fair indication of his qualifications as a go-between and expert adviser to the President of the United States and the Banking and Currency Committee of Congress, in the following statement of his economic conclusions on money:

"*Senator Reed.* Well, is it not true, as a matter of financial law, that, taking prices in the aggregate and not picking out a particular year, but taking a period of time great enough so that you can strike a fair general average, the rise of prices has always followed the increase of per capita circulation?

"*Mr. Willis.* I honestly do not think so. You ask me for an opinion, and it is my duty to tell you what I think.

"*Senator Reed.* Certainly.

"*Mr. Willis.* I do not think so. But I also add to that there is scientific opinion in favor of the view you have expressed, but that, in my judgment, the weight of scientific opinion against it—closing, then, with the statement that, while there is a great deal of evidence on behalf of both sides, my own studies of the subject have led me personally to the conclusion that the quantitative theory of money is not a sound, is not a tenable one.

"*Senator Reed.* Then, if that is true, it will not make any difference how much per capita circulation we have out, as long as it is good money it will not affect prices.

"*Mr. Willis.* Provided it is good money, and instantly

redeemable, I do not think the mere quantity in circulation makes any difference.''

In order that there may be no further doubt on this question, I will state that there has been only one standard in the money system, and it has long since been fully recognized and indorsed by the leading economists and recognized authorities on money. Concisely stated the standard of value in a money system is constituted by the number of dollars in the system. The value of the dollar is made by the demand for dollars, the demand operating against the supply.

Therefore, if the dollars are few, and the demand is great, the standard of their value is high, and their purchasing power is great, and if the dollars are many and the demand is small, the standard of the value is low and their purchasing power is small. Thus, the value of the money unit is made by the demand operating against the supply.

Mr. Willis declines, at this late day, to recognize the universal law of demand and supply affecting the value or purchasing power of money.

After reading the statements of political economists and so-called experts in their endorsement of these bankers' bills, one has a painful realization that there is a great deal of truth in the statement of Lord Macauley, the English historian, when he said that for a valuable consideration he could get men of high standing and ability to question even the law of gravitation; and the recent statement of Vice-President Marshall that he could, for $500, get expert testimony on any subject in this country.

Thursday, March 12, 1914, by previous appointment with both the Chairmen of the joint sub-committees of the Senate and House on ''Rural Credits,'' I was making the foregoing statement before this Committee at one of the public hearings on the above date, in the interest of the people, and began to expose the Banker's Rural Credit scheme to exchange ''bank credits'' or false money created by banking corporations for interest-earning mortgages upon the farms of the United States.

At this point the Chairman of the Committee became very restive and impatient and asked me if I could not confine my remarks to *the bill* the committee was considering, fully realizing the bill they were considering was another frame-up on the people prearranged by the bankers. I stated to the Committee that if the rest of my written statement would be printed in the hearings for the benefit of the people, I would conclude my oral presentation of the case.

At a meeting of the sub-committees of the two Houses they refused to let this exposure of the Bankers' Rural Credit scheme be known to the people, and declined to let it be printed in the record of the so-called ''Public Hearings on Rural Credits'' of the Committees on Banking and Currency of the Senate and House of Representatives.

With great difficulty I had this manuscript returned and it is here inserted in order that the people may know the facts and understand how their interests are being treated in legislation on money.

RURAL CREDITS—THURSDAY, MARCH 12, 1914—UNITED STATES SENATE, WASHINGTON, D. C.

As none of the bankers and so-called experts on Banking and Currency—and their name is Legion—who have appeared before the Banking and Currency Committees of Congress care, for obvious reasons, to explain to the people the loaning of ''bank credits'' as a substitute for money, I will now do so.

The curse of the money system of the world is the manufacturing of debts by the banks on the borrowers by a dishonest substitute for money, created by the banks by debit and credit figures on their books. These debts, when created by the banks in this way, become demands for money, and it should be clearly borne in mind, there is no corresponding money in existence wherein they can be paid.

Bank Credit is purely fictitious, dishonest, dangerous and panic-breeding substitute for *money that does not exist*. Its use is absolutely indefensible, applying to it the rules of common honesty. No man or corporation should be allowed to make a substitute for money that costs comparatively nothing, and loan it to his fellowman as money. It is a fraud and flagrant injustice upon the borrowers for a corporation to enter into an agreement to lend money, then substitute a fictitious credit of their own making after causing a scarcity of money themselves in order to lend this substitute, and then compel the borrower to pay the debt in money. It is an economic swindle of the most pernicious and ruinous character. These debts are manufactured by a trick of bookkeeping and little cash is used. The matching of incoming checks at a Clearing House Association cancels them by the use of about 5 per cent. in money. This Clearing House device, not incorporated, having no legal existence, was organized in New York in 1854. Clearing House Associations of like character have been organized by the banks in every city of importance in the United States. All the borrowers usually receive is a credit on the bank's books. In most transactions, where "bank credit" is used, the only money that ever passes is when the borrower curtails or pays the note. Professor Sidgwick, an English authority, in his work, "Principles of Political Economy," states:

"In such a country as England, where deposit banking is fully developed and payments by check customary, the greatest part of such money must consist of what has been called 'money of account,' that is, of bankers' liabilities or obligations to pay in coin on demand, *not embodied* or *represented otherwise than in rows of figures on their books.*"

Here a favored class, licensed by law as banking corporations, are allowed to issue a substitute for money simply by a process of bookkeeping to create debts against the rest of the people.

Is this a system to be tolerated by a people where government was created to establish justice and "equal rights to all, special privileges to none"?

A very simple illustration that the experience of any man familiar with banking methods will verify, explains the process.

A applies for a loan. The banker asks A if he needs the money, or only an account to check against, and is told substantially that the bank does not have the money to spare, but if A merely wishes an account to check against, it is "all right." A gives the note for the amount needed and the banker makes an entry in A's deposit book to the effect that A has deposited the sum, which was in fact a false statement.

The banker does this as he has "confidence" that most of A's checks will be presented, not for payment, but as deposits, to be credited to other accounts and charged to A.

The bank's debt to A is thus settled by bookkeeping, that is by mere *transfer of bank credits*. There was no loan of real money; it was simply a loan of "bank credit," based on a banker's "confidence" that *A could be paid in that way*.

The borrower should realize that there is no similar way in which he can pay the loan. He must eventually pay it back in money. How can you apply to this infamous system the fundamental principle of our Government of "equal rights to all, special privileges to none," when these banking corporations are allowed to create debts against the people with their cheap substitutes for money by a system of bookkeeping?

The bankers call these transactions "loans of money" and the courts enforce them as such, although it is a plain financial and economic fraud upon the people.

1st. In the fact that the bankers are getting something practically for nothing.

2nd. They are creating fictitious money and using it as money.

The Constitution prohibits the creation of money or the emission of bills of credit as a substitute for money even by a sovereign State. Why should banking corporations be allowed to do so? The law prohibits the counterfeiting of money as a circulating medium, for the reason that he who makes it is getting something for nothing, thereby committing fraud upon the people.

The issuing of "bank credits" as a substitute for non-existent money not only manufactures unpayable debts upon the people, drawing perpetual interest, it inflates the currency system and advances the prices of the things the people buy or use. Thus the borrower and the people are caught at both ends of the transaction.

After my statement before the Banking and Currency Committee of the Senate in which I had annihilated the bankers' fallacy that gold was the standard of value, Prof. Irwin Fisher, Professor of Political Economy at Yale University, was again before the Committee and made the following admission:

"In fact I am very strongly of the opinion, based on considerable study, that the present high cost of living is largely ascribed to this check inflation, which is going on all over the world. They are increasing daily all over the world. I believe the rise in price is about half due to that alone. I am very glad you mentioned that, Senator, because, while I think the expansibility and contractibility of the currency, of the money, is important, the expansibility and contractibility of the 'credit' is the much more important."

Inflation could be prevented by prohibiting banks from loaning "bank credit" as a substitute for money. The Government gets its real money—that is made by the sovereign act of the people—into actual circulation by paying it out for something of real value in the interest of the whole people, as directed by their Representatives in Congress assembled. It is not returned to its creator; not being loaned, it has not to be returned, but continues to circulate. Therefore, there need be no harmful contraction or inflation.

This money, when in the monetary system, responds to the natural law of demand and goes where it is needed, in the healthful development of the country.

The man who borrows money from the Government keeps it no longer than he needs it and pays it back to the Government in order to stop the payment of interest as soon as possible.

Mr. Horace White, author of "Money and Banking," ex-editor of the New York *Evening Post* and the Chicago *Tribune,* in his testimony before the Banking and Currency Committee of the House of the Sixtieth Congress, hearings on the Aldrich-Vreeland Bill, clearly understood this and testified as follows:

Mr. Theodore E. Burton. Is it not one of the defects of our system, that it is so difficult to contract the currency? Has not that been one of the greatest difficulties for years past with it, to retire redundant currency?

Mr. White. No; I do not think that is so.

Mr. Burton. Under our present system?

Mr. White. Under any system. A banker can not put his notes out. That is all nonsense. He can not do it. He can just grant a credit to the depositor and then the depositor can draw out the notes, if the banker has them and the depositor wants them; but when the notes are no longer wanted, they will come back.

Mr. Burton. You do believe in that idea of a redundant currency?

Mr. White. No, I do not. That is all in the imagination, I think.

Mr. Burton. It is true, though, is it not, that stock speculation increases whenever——

Mr. White. Yes, but that does not increase on account of the currency. The currency circulates from hand to hand.

Mr. Burton. You do not trace that to the currency?

Mr. White. That is an inflation of deposit of liabilities. This means the loaning of ''bank credits'' as a substitute for money.

The owner of real money, if he finds no borrower for his idle money, goes out into the business world and uses it in developing some useful enterprise. In this natural and legitimate development of wealth, the dollar hunts for labor and new opportunities, thus creating unincumbered individual, and national wealth, and man is the master above the dollar.

Under this proper system of money, man is of first importance, property of all kinds next in importance, and money, issued by the sovereign power of the Government, a medium of exchange for all the people. This is the economic order of any proper system of government.

THE REASON GIVEN BY BANKERS

In order that the people may have the reasons furnished by the bankers in opposition to the Government issuing legal tender money—

I quote from the two leading authorities representing the bankers in opposition to the Government issuing money.

Mr. J. Barton Hepburn, Chase National Bank, New York, was one time Comptroller of the Currency and recognized leader among the great bankers in New York. I mention this to show that he is thoroughly qualified to state all the objections that can be made to the Government's issuing money, legal tender notes.

Mr. Glass. Would you have the Government issue the notes?

Mr. Hepburn. No; I would not and for the reason: you can not have anything better than the Government under which you live. You can not have any credit better than the credit of the Government under which you live, and crises will occur, and when they do occur, then let the banks come in for criticism and let the Government stand one side.

The Government should not issue the notes, because the Government cannot ever redeem a note except from the proceeds of taxation or sale of bonds, which is simply taxation deferred, and the reason why the banks can issue it is that they have better means of meeting their obligations in a stress and other times than the Government has. They have established assets on which they can realize.

The Government has no means of obtaining funds except by taxation or by sale of bonds which is taxation deferred.

Mr. Buckley. Have you now stated all the objections to Government issues so far as you know?

Mr. Hepburn. The impracticability of Government issue by our Government at the present time would be the most serious.

Mr. Buckley. Impracticability, meaning that they would have no way to get the notes into circulation?

Mr. Hepburn. Yes; no legitimate, proper way for putting notes into circulation.

He was then asked if these were all the reasons he could give against the Government issuing money.

He stated they were at that time, but if the Committee desired it he would file a brief setting forth the reasons.

A member of the Committee requested him to file such a brief.

I wrote to Mr. Glass, Chairman of the Banking and Currency Committee, to insist upon Mr. Hepburn filing this brief, and allowing me to answer same. The Chairman of the Banking and Currency Committee never complied with this request and Mr. Hepburn never filed his brief.

Answering paragraph 1. Mr. Hepburn admits the credit of the Government is the best that can be had, which can only mean that money issued by the sovereign power of the Government and redeemable in all the assets of the United States is infinitely better than a note or obligation issued by a banking corporation, secured upon its questionable assets. Answering the last part of this paragraph where he says: "In case of crisis, let the bank come in for criticism and let the government stand aside." This is rather a strange suggestion in view of the fact that this bankers' bill that is now the law and now universally approved by all these bankers, provides for gold payments of about $30,000,000,000 of obligations specifically payable in gold, now outstanding, with only $163,000,000 in the Treasury to meet such demands, yet they leave the doors of the United States Treasury wide open for this gold to be withdrawn at any time and he then suggests that the Government stand aside and let the banks come in for criticism. He does not seem to see that this is sacrificing the people to the banks and fails to realize that the people are the Government in the time of crisis. It is a well-known fact to which the people can testify from their veritable and painful experience that instead of being protected by the banks in these crises, they are immediately put between the upper and nether millstone by the banks denying them loans and usual discounts and calling upon them for the *payment* in *money*—which they have made scarce—by calling loans that they created by loaning Bank Credits—fictitious money—of the banks.

In time of panics those having actual money on deposit have been unable to get it from the banks; and while the people are suffering untold losses, the banks have protected themselves by violating the law in issuing clearing house certificates and other credit substitutes for money to settle their obligations.

Answering paragraph 2, where Mr. Hepburn states that the Government should not issue the notes, because the "Government cannot ever redeem a note except from the proceeds of taxation or sale of bonds."

This false economic theory of money is based upon the self-interested assumption of the bankers, that a dollar is a debt, instead of a redeemer of a debt. They fail to recognize that only the Sovereign Power of a people can create money.

The Constitution of the United States provides that Congress alone shall create money and regulate the value thereof. This means that Congress shall create and issue money, not debts, as a circulating medium, and that every dollar issued by the Government shall have all the power of money that the Sovereignty of Government can give it. It should be a perfect money unit—a legal tender dollar, good for all debts, public and private, and redeemable in all things for sale, all services for hire and the ultimate of payment for all debts.

That only is money, the acceptance of which consummates a business transaction and leaves nothing more to be done.

When the government, exercising the sovereign power of the people, issues a dollar, and gets full value for it in the interest of the people; the Government is in no way obligated to redeem it, but being a legal tender dollar, a medium of exchange, it stays out continuously, doing the work of money, not to be redeemed at the U. S. Treasury or Government institution, but as a legal tender and universal order, or acceptance, redeemable by the people on whose authority it was issued for value received.

Answering the last part of this paragraph, where it is stated—"That the reason why the banks can better issue the notes is that they have better means of meeting their obligations in a stress and other times, than the Government has. They have established assets on which they can realize. The Government has no means of obtaining funds except by taxation or by sale of bonds." This is a rather violent assumption, as it is a well-known fact that at no time are these banks in a position to pay in cash the money due their depositors and if the clearing house associations were to refuse to cancel their incoming checks by the matching process, there is not a bank in one of the large cities that could meet its obligations. We had a striking illustration of this inability in the case of the "United States Trust Company of Washington, D. C.," which, in order to meet the demands of its depositors, for money, had to call on the United States Government to furnish them a million dollars of the people's money to protect the banking situation in Washington. On the other hand, the Government, when exercising its sovereign power, under the Constitution of the United States is the creator of money and can issue same upon all the assets of the country and services of its people. This money, so issued by the Government, is a demand order for everything that money can buy, or man can want, in the country, and owing to the balance of trade against Europe, it would bring a premium over gold as it can be used in settling this balance in favor of the United States, thus saving the debtor the cost of express charges and insurance on sending the gold to the United States.

Gold is a handicap in international trade. A trade balance should be settled by interest-bearing securities of the debtor country.

Answering paragraph 5, where it is stated that "the Government has no way of putting its notes in circulation." This is based on the bankers' and money lenders' false theory that the only way the Government can get its money into circulation; it is first necessary for somebody to borrow it. The Government's function is to issue money and the proper way to put it into circulation is *to get a valuable consideration for it*. The method of getting it out is through the Congress of the United States representing the best interests of all the people. For example, $25,000,000 of legal tender money could be advantageously used annually for the improvement of the roads of the country. Large sums could be used to develop water-power sites and the improvement of rivers and harbors of the United States. Thus real money could be put into the monetary system for constant circulation—answering to the laws of demand would go where it was most needed. It would take the place of "bank credit" inflation, which should be prohibited in future by law, as its use inflates the currency, breeds panics and multiplies unpayable debts and is a wholesale fraud upon the people.

In order that the arguments of the bankers may be fully stated, in opposition to the Government issuing money, I now quote from Mr. Wexler, representing the American Bankers' Association before the Banking and Currency Committee of the Senate, stating the reason why the Government should not issue its legal tender money.

"*Senator Nelson.* If the Government wants to issue its money and get its money out into circulation beyond what is necessary to pay its current expenses, it can only be done by allowing borrowers to deposit their commercial paper with the Government.

"*Senator Nelson.* And you cannot get the Government's money into circulation in any other way?

"*Mr. Wexler.* No, sir; none in the world."

Such a statement coming from the chosen representative of the American Bankers' Association should disqualify them from testifying any further on this subject.

For the Government to get its legal tender money into circulation, it would be only necessary for Congress to authorize the United States Treasury to issue the money necessary for carrying out an appropriation by Congress for good roads, improvement of rivers and harbors, for water-power sites, and the money could be expended for other purposes, carefully and conservatively in the interest of all the people.

In answering the suggestion that the Government issue its notes to retire the national bank notes and pay off the United States bonds securing same, I quote Mr. Wexler:

"What kind of note have you given? How are you going to meet it? When are you going to meet it? Are you going to pay it in gold? Will we get it when we want it? If you will say what you are to pay for it, can you pay it? You have to provide all that kind of machinery."

This gentleman evidently does not comprehend *what a legal tender dollar issued by the sovereign power of the people really is.* A sufficient answer to all these questions can be given to satisfy the doubts of these gentlemen on this subject for all time.

A legal tender dollar issued by the Government is good for one hundred cents on the dollar, as long as this Republic lasts; it is redeemable continuously in $140,000,000,000 of national wealth, and all that may be added to it hereafter, including its gold and silver. It is a legal tender to pay all debts outstanding—it is a universal order for all things on sale, and all services for hire and the ultimate of payment.

There is a false idea among the people generally that money has to be taken back to the treasuries of the United States to be redeemed. This is not so. When the Government puts out a perfect circulating unit—or dollar— for value received, it is not a thing to be retired; it circulates and stays out and it is continuously redeemable by all the people.

The bankers' opposition to the Government's issuing money is, of course, due to the fact that it would deprive them of the privilege of loaning their credit substitutes for money; thus preventing the multiplying of debts upon the borrowers. The more real money in circulation the fewer debts, fewer banks, fewer non-producers.

After these bankers advocate their system as being a bulwark of strength and better fitted to issue these notes than the Government, we find this astounding admission in the testimony of Mr. Hepburn before the Banking and Currency Committee January 7th, 1913:

"Mr. Taylor. And what is the basis of all bank checks and other ways of dealing with business, the settlements really made? It is confidence, is it not?"

"Mr. Hepburn. You know your man."

I will quote from a letter printed in pamphlet form signed by J. P. Morgan & Co., and sent broadcast all over the United States, just after Mr. Morgan was examined by the Money Trust Investigating Committee: "To banking the confidence of the community is the breath from which it draws its life. The past is full of examples where the slightest suspicion as to the conservatism, or the methods of a bank's management, has destroyed confidence and drawn away its deposits over night."

How long will the prosperity of the country and the business of 100,000,000 people be allowed to rest upon this gigantic "confidence game"?

GENESIS OF THESE BANKING AND CURRENCY BILLS

As the Bill that passed the extra session of Congress is the basis upon which the "Rural Credits Bill" now before the Committee will depend, it should first be taken into consideration, and the people of the country should know the origin of this Federal Reserve Act, perpetuating this infamous "bank credit" money system in the United States.

This Federal Reserve Act did not originate with the people. The influences of the money power framed the Bill, and it is acknowledged to be a Bankers' Bill.

In confirmation of this, I first desire to call attention to the following testimony before the Banking and Currency Committee of the Senate, by Mr. G. H. Shibley, Director American Bureau of Political Research, as to the origin of this Bill.

Senator Reed. I want to interrupt you just a moment. Do I understand you to say now that the Money Trust got up the Citizens' League?

Mr. Shibley. The bankers—

Senator Reed. You think the bankers got up what I call a conspiracy to control and get a bill that suited them?

Mr. Shibley. Certainly.

Senator Reed. And they got up the Citizens' League as a means of propagating their ideas without apparently doing it themselves in the open?

Mr. Shibley. Exactly.

Senator Reed. And they got Prof. Laughlin to be the mouthpiece of that League?

Mr. Shibley. Their bulletin states that such is the fact.

TESTIMONY OF PROF. E. PARKER WILLIS

Senator Hitchcock. Mr. Willis, you are employed upon a financial Journal, are you not?

Mr. Willis. Yes, sir; the Journal of Commerce of New York.

Mr. Willis then states: "I was appointed *expert adviser* April 1st, 1912, to the sub-committee on Banking and Currency of which Mr. Carter Glass was Chairman; was then reappointed at this session of Congress in the same relation to the full committee on Banking and Currency.

Senator Nelson. You said you were the only official expert. Who were the non-official experts that appeared before you when you were framing the bill?

Mr. Willis. Their names are given in the hearings. I could hardly give them all, Senator, but some of the principal ones were Mr. A. Barton Hepburn of New York, who I think was Chairman of the American Bankers' Association Commission; Mr. Paul M. Warburg, of Kuhn, Loeb and Company; Prof. Laughlin, of the Department of Political Economy of the University of Chicago; Sir Edmund Walker, a Canadian banker from Toronto; and *a considerable number of other well-known bankers.*

Senator Hitchcock. Mr. Willis, have you any practical experience as a banker?

Mr. Willis. None whatever.

Senator Hitchcock. Have you ever been in business at all?

Mr. Willis. No, sir.

I would ask what chance would a man of such limited practical or business experience have in framing a banking and currency bill in the interest of the people, when surrounded by such men as he mentions, who knew exactly what they wanted. The record will show that Prof. Willis was an agent of the banking interests.

Senator Reed. Did you say you were Secretary of the Indianapolis Monetary Commission?

Mr. Willis. I did. Yes, sir, in 1897.

Senator Hitchcock. You had something to do with the drafting of that bill?

Mr. Willis. Yes, sir. I had expert charge of the work. This bill was introduced in the House in the Autumn of 1898.

THE BASIC FRAUD THAT UNDERLIES THE WHOLE MONEY SYSTEM

Until the seventeenth century the human family was too busily engaged in trying to establish some stable form of government to formulate any correct money system. In fact, they were oblivious to the importance of the subject when the Bank of England was established in 1694. This was the origin of the present bankers' money-making scheme. This, the so-called Bank of England, was organized for private gain, being allowed to call itself the Bank of England, just as if it was a government institution established in the interest of the people. As a matter of fact, the government had no interest in it or any control over it. The bank established the scheme of discounting the interest-bearing notes of borrowers by lending them the non-interest-bearing notes of the bank. Then by discounting the notes of the borrowers and crediting the borrowers with the proceeds of the notes on the books of the bank allowed them to draw checks against the amount. This was called in England "money of account," it is now called "Bank Credits." In reality it is a false substitute for money created, loaned and controlled by banks.

This brings us to the basic fraud that underlies the whole Bank Reserve System, the convertibility of all forms of credit currency into reserve money, and on each dollar of the credit currency, so converted into real money, the banks can loan from eight to ten dollars of "bank credits."

This vicious and ruinous principle which the people have never understood is reincorporated in Sec. 26 of the Federal Reserve Act.

The whole gold standard banking and currency system is based on the dishonest principle of creating debts without loaning actual lawful money.

Federal Reserve notes when issued to rediscount notes held by the member banks can also be converted into reserve money under Sec. 16 of this act which provides: "The said notes shall be redeemed in gold or lawful money at any Treasury Department of the United States or in gold or lawful money at any Federal Reserve bank."

It should therefore be readily seen from this exposure that unless this bankers' privilege is entirely eradicated from our money system it cannot be reformed in the interest of the people.

BANKING CORPORATIONS ORGANIZED FOR PRIVATE GAIN, CALLED NATIONAL BANKS—AND TRADING UNDER THE NAME AND INDORSEMENT OF THE UNITED STATES GOVERNMENT, COMMIT ROBBERY AND USURY ON THE PEOPLE AS SHOWN BY THE AUTHORITATIVE STATEMENT OF THE COMPTROLLER OF THE CURRENCY, JOHN SKELTON WILLIAMS, OCT. 6th, 1915

FACTS WOULD STARTLE PUBLIC

Should a Senatorial investigation of the activities of his office be inaugurated, the Comptroller declared that he was prepared with facts which would not only startle and horrify the public, but rouse a storm even among bankers themselves.

"We read much of the infernos of the slums of the great cities, of degradation and misery and squalor, of the grinding callousness of tenement landlords and sweat-shop operators," said Mr. Williams. "Here in the country we find bankers, men in business that should be the most respectable, as it is the most responsible of all secular avocations, literally crushing the faces of their neighbors, deliberately fastening their fangs in the very heart of poverty. Yet we are told by a United States Senator that 'the banker' —the 1,000 per cent. banker lending to a straitened and sorely pressed farmer— 'is a man to determine that'—the rate of interest. We are told that when the Government tries to use its power to prevent these thefts and rapes on the prosperity of communities it is guilty of impertinent intrusion and unwise interference with business and private judgment.

"I have in my hand, not to be shown, but I have it here

for reference, the report of a national bank in a certain State, from which I will give you some instances. *Here is a loan of* $109 *to a woman for* 30 *days, charges for interest,* $10—120 *per cent. Others are:* $380 *for* 90 *days, interest* $30, *or* 34 *per cent.;* $133 *for forty days, interest charged,* $10, *or* 75 *per cent.;* $145 *for* 80 *days, interest* $20, *or* 70 *per cent.;* $30 *for one month, interest charges* 360 *per cent.* I thought we had reached the limit when we found a national bank reporting a loan at 360 per cent., but on this paper is a record of a loan by a national bank, mind you, of $3.50 to a woman, for six days, with an interest charge of $1, which figures out about 6 per cent. a day, or 2,400 per cent. per annum. 'The banker is a man to determine that,' Senator Weeks tells us.

"LEADS TO ANARCHISM

"Surely, the Massachusetts Senator to the contrary, the Government can have no duty more solemn or urgent than to do all possible to end such heartless oppression of its citizens and such shameless degradation of its institutions and its name. When we allow one class or element of our citizenship anywhere to be destroyed, to be deprived of hope and self-respect, and to be doomed to despair and misery, we injure the entire country. We sow the seed of future general ruin, because when we leave people to feel that they have been despoiled, robbed, drained to death and can find in the law no rescue or remedy, they turn to lawlessness. The farmer floundering in the cruel tentacles of a 300 per cent. Government bank learns quickly to be disloyal to the Government, and to hate bitterly all banks and bankers and representatives of wealth and money. He is hurt and ruined, and he bestows his wrath not on the individual, but on the entire system. *Three hundred per cent. will make anarchists silently faster than all the I. W. W. apostles who can bawl. Interest rates which mean failure and the steady absorption of the results of sweat and labor foment revolution faster than all the demagogues and reckless ranters who may go howling about the land.* When national banks chartered by the Government disappoint and deprive toil of its just reward and stimulate resentment, we have prepared and fertilized the soil for a fearful crop of disaster.''

On Nov. 23rd, 1915, the Comptroller made the following statement:

''The sworn reports of the banks also show that, on Sept. 2nd, 1915, two thousand seven hundred and forty-three (2,743) national banks out of a total of seven thousand six hundred and thirteen (7,613), being more than thirty-six (36) per cent. of all the national banks of the country, were charging on some of their loans ten (10) per cent. per annum or more, in hundreds of banks very much more.''

If 2,743 out of 7,613 national banks have admitted these charges, how many, do you suppose, could be found in the 27,050 banks doing business in the United States?— many of them under no supervision whatever.

In short, under the present Banking and Currency System we have 27,050 cancers upon the body politics, absorbing the earnings and destroying the life and vitality of the people.

Now that this ''bank credits'' system has been explained and shown to be absolutely indefensible, the bankers will assume an awful responsibility if they do not accept this solution. The issue is squarely drawn, the banks on one side and the people on the other. When the ninety per cent. of the voters of this country, who are debtors, fully realize the fraudulent process by which the great burden of debts have been placed upon them and their children, nothing will be able to save this infamous system from the wrath of an outraged people.

There are many good men in the banking business who have never realized the great injustice and suffering this system has inflicted upon the people, they should now use their great influence on the side of the people to prevent an industrial revolution in the United States, the like of which the world has never known.

In considering the passage of a Money Bill through Congress in the interest of the people, I desire to call attention to the action of the Banking and Currency Committee of the Senate and House on the Bill that became the present Federal Reserve Act. This Bill was pushed through the House by a Democratic Caucus. The hearings on this Bill were commenced by the Banking and Currency Committee of the United States Senate, September 2nd, 1913.

On September 25th, 1913, I made a statement which is (see insertion) in opposition to this Bill, exposing the gold basis fallacy and the loaning of Bank Credits—false money—to the people by Banking Corporations. On Tuesday, October 24th, 1913, during the hearings on this Bill by the Banking and Currency Committee of the Senate, one of the witnesses appearing before the Committee was making a vigorous attack on the Bill and advocating the Government's control of the money system of the United States. At this time I was seated at the left of the acting chairman of the Committee and he leaned across me and said to another Senator, a member of the Committee, "Can't you cut this gentleman off? He is only taking up our time. *You know we cannot go outside this Bill.*"

I know these so-called public hearings were used to divert the attention of the people from the preconceived "Bankers' Asset Currency Schemes," as embodied in the Federal Reserve Act. After this statement of the acting Chairman of the Banking and Currency Committee of the Senate, it left no doubt that this Federal Reserve Act was all the result of a previous agreement between the Bankers and the President of the United States. Confirmation of this is found in the admission of the Chairman of this Committee on the floor of the Senate when he said: "I admit this (the Federal Reserve Act) is a Banker's Bill." The method of appointment and the personnel of the members of the Federal Reserve Board only verifies the facts above stated.

For over twenty years I have seen the inside of the "game" of politics played on "Capitol Hill" to deceive the people on money legislation. The representatives of farm and labor organizations will be throwing away their time and accomplish nothing by attending the so-called public hearings, given by the Banking and Currency Committees of Congress, or meeting members of these Committees in Conferences. A majority of these Committees are controlled by the Bankers, and the minority quickly submits, for reasons best known to themselves.

It was an open secret that President Wilson, under the domination of the Federal Reserve Board, representing the Banks, would have vetoed the Agricultural Bill sooner than let the Rural Credit amendment remain in the Bill, giving direct Government aid to the farmers.

IT IS PLAIN THERE IS NO HOPE FOR A COMPROMISE IN FAVOR OF THE FARMERS, EVEN IF IT WERE JUSTIFIABLE OR DESIRABLE, GOING THROUGH THIS CONGRESS AND BECOMING A LAW THAT WOULD EVER BE ENFORCED

It is not desirable for the following reasons:

1st. It would be an attempt to mend a system that is not subject to amendment, being fundamentally false.

2nd. It would be useless to amend it as it would give no relief to the borrowers as the banks could continue to loan false and non-existent money to the people and create perpetual interest-earning debts upon the real producers and honest workers of the United States.

From my knowledge of Congress I know a bill to grant a special money privilege to the farmers as a class would give them little worry or concern as Representatives in Congress have frequently used this kind of a bill as a stage play to fool their constituents while they keep on good terms with the bankers. Those who vote against these bills easily justify themselves in doing so by saying it is class legislation.

On the other hand those who are fighting for an honest money system in the interest of all the people could not justify themselves in fighting class legislation in favor of the banks and at the same time ask for class legislation for the farmers.

The same international bankers who fabricated the Federal Reserve Act now have their agents trying to deceive the people by hiding themselves, and having Senators and Representatives in Congress introduce their money bills under the guise of ''Rural Credits'' to help the farmers.

These bills if enacted into law will simply mean chartering more corporations to put debts upon the farmers by loaning them "bank credit." By this infamous subterfuge they hope to again deceive the people and protect and perpetuate their gold basis Federal Reserve System, which is responsible for present conditions.

To illustrate the power given banking corporations by Congress, the banks are allowed to put a mortgage upon the home of a farmer by loaning him fictitious money; control the amount of money in circulation in which the debt has to be paid, and fix the price of the farmer's products that he must sell in order to get the money to pay his debt.

The Capper Bill, backed by the agents of international bankers and lobbied by Eugene Meyer, Jr., and Aaron Sapiro, has for its object to put the farmers deeper in debt by loaning them a substitute for money, under the deceptive term of "Rural Credits," the object being to bring about a temporary prosperity among the farmers, in order to protect the fraudulent gold-basis Federal Reserve System, through which not less than 25 billion dollars in the value of agricultural products and farm lands have been destroyed.

I consider both the Capper Bill and the Lenroot-Anderson Bill bastard money bills, being used for the above purpose. It should be fully realized that any bill based on and controlled by the Federal Reserve Act is not in the interest of the people.

I notice in all these rural credit bills the use of the term "credits" is applied to this legislation, and nothing is said of loaning the farmers money that should be put in circulation in the agricultural sections of the country, that would increase and sustain the value of farm products, and be available to the farmers to pay off their debts.

Congress after enacting into law the gold basis Federal Reserve Act, which transfers the control of money and credit to banking corporations organized for private gain, subsequently, under the guise of rural credits to help the farmers, chartered the Federal Loan Banks and the Joint Stock Banks, and are now about to charter additional corporations to create debts upon the farmers by exchanging bank credits for loans secured on agricultural products.

The question now to be answered is: How can farmers be helped by being put deeper in debt by being loaned this false and fictitious money?

The fight should now be made on the direct issue of loaning legal tender money direct to the people at a low rate of interest by the Government as against the loaning of false money "bank credits" to the people at high rates of interest by Banking Corporations.

No charge of class legislation could be made against the following fundamental principles being incorporated in a bill. No Senator or Representative in Congress could successfully attack such a bill, but would realize for the first time in fifty years that he was confronted with the real issue and was on trial before the voters of the country if he opposed its passage and stood any longer on the bankers' side of this great issue.

I have made this full statement to impress upon the people's organizations the vital importance of endorsing a complete bill, thus taking it out of the manipulating control of the Banking and Currency Committees of Congress, and the doctoring processes of a conference committee of the two Houses.

The fight should be made in the open on the floor of the House and Senate and every Representative held responsible for his vote by the people.

All the local, State and National farm, labor and people's organizations should bring their influence to bear upon individual Representatives and Senators in every Congressional district. It should be made an aggressive fight against the present false "Corporations Bank Credit system" and to establish an honest money system in the interest of all the people.

CONTINENTAL CURRENCY, FRENCH ASSIGNATS AND
GERMAN MARKS

Anticipating the old arguments of the opposition about the depreciation of Continental currency and French Assignats I will answer them in advance. Continental currency and French Assignats are the ghosts which are conjured up by the bankers to frighten the public, the bankers wishing the right to furnish the circulating medium of exchange and loan their credit substitutes for money.

Continental currency was not issued as an act of sovereignty that could enforce its acceptance as a legal tender, and Congress had no power to levy and collect taxes. Whatsoever was done had to be done through the thirteen different states. Even after the adoption of the articles of Confederation in 1781 Congress possessed only the semblance of authority. Judge Story describes the situation at that time in the following language:

"In the first place there was an utter want of all coercive authority to carry into effect its own constitutional measures, it possessed no one solid attribute of power."

The population of the thirteen colonies was estimated in 1775 at 2,448,000 and the entire property of the country at less than $600,000,000. It is one of the most remarkable facts connected with the Revolution that this non-legal tender paper currency should have circulated at all. It was issued to an excessive amount by thirteen sparsely settled colonies, in a state of rebellion, under a revolutionary government possessing only a shadow of authority, fighting against the most powerful nation on earth.

The French Assignats were issued in France against the confiscated property of the church. They were in no sense legal tender money and the property so assigned was of questionable title.

Germany was on the gold standard, or the gold basis, and all other forms of money or currency were redeemable in gold.

At the beginning of the European war Germany realized that her gold-based money system could not stand the strain of carrying on the war, and allowed corporations to issue and loan their non-legal tender money. Upon this fraudulent gold basis, billions of debts were created upon the German people by the loaning of "money of account," a false and fictitious money, having no existence and represented only by credit and debit figures upon the books of banks.

These banking corporations were also granted the power to issue billions of marks in "bank notes" as a substitute for money. In this connection it should be clearly borne in mind that any form of money or currency in a money system that has to be redeemed in gold before it becomes a legal tender to pay debts is not real money, but a debt redeemable in gold.

The gold-basis money system upon which this gigantic issue of currency—German marks—is based has been absolutely destroyed by the war.

The validity and value of money depends upon its being full legal tender; upon the solvency of the country issuing it; upon the sovereign power of its Government to force its acceptance in payment of all debts public and private; and upon a proper regulation of its quantity. The German mark lacks these essential requirements to protect its value.

It is impossible to protect the value of the money of a country if the sovereignty of its government is in jeopardy, or its people bankrupt by debts. Germany is now bankrupt and in the hands of receivers (the Reparation Commission) representing the Allies, holding a mountain of debts against the German people, sufficient to keep them in debt slavery for over a hundred years. Destroy the sovereignty of a country and you destroy the validity of its money.

Any man or publication using the depreciation of the German mark as an argument against the United States issuing its legal tender notes is either suffering from arrested mental development on the subject of money, or controlled directly or indirectly by the present money power operating the fraudulent gold basis bank credit debt manufacturing system, through which the people are robbed of their earnings.

Such references by bankers only show the weakness of their position in opposing the issuing of legal tender money by the government, the only power that can issue real money.

BREAKDOWN AND EXPOSURE OF THE
BANKERS' FALSE GOLD STANDARD

The bankers' "gold standard" scheme broke down under the first strain put upon it by the European war; the whole bank credit scheme, being built upon this economic fallacy, its protection was a matter of first consideration to the group of International Bankers in Europe and the United States.

Sir George Paish, special adviser to the British Chancellor of the Exchequer (at this time Lloyd George), and B. B. Blackett, of the British Treasury, were sent to the United States in October, 1914, with this object in view, and at the same time to realize on American securities, railroad bonds, stocks, etc., underwritten by corporation on the resources and people of the United States which Europe had acquired under the operations of the British gold standard international banking scheme.

From an editorial in the *Washington Post* of October 21, 1914, are taken the following extracts:

"After some days of speculating as to the nature of the business which brought Sir George Paish and Basil Blackett to the United States, and after having reached the comfortable conclusion that their errand was to extend assistance, it is now made clear that their mission is to inquire why the United States does not pay its debts."

If the *Post* had stated the whole truth it would have said they came to do both, viz., to protect the gold standard scheme and at the same time to collect their debts. The article then says:

"So far as Europe is concerned the United States has declared a moratorium, if a moratorium means the suspension of debt paying. . . . The United States does not wish to part with its gold, even if it be true that it has four times as much as England possesses."

Again if the *Post* had stated the whole truth it should have said that the banks in the United States did not want to part with their gold because it enabled them to loan ten dollars of "bank credit" for every dollar of gold they had. In fact they had already used all their gold in creating a million dollars of debts upon the people for every one hundred thousand dollars of gold they could place in their reserves.

Therefore, in order to ship one hundred thousand dollars of gold to Europe—and keep their gold reserve intact—the banks would have had to call in a million dollars of loans they had made by the lending of "bank credits." This would have jeopardized the gold standard money scheme with its consequent embarrassment to Europe.

"LONDON, Dec. 1, 1914.—David Lloyd George, Chancellor of the Exchequer, told the House of Commons last Friday, 'America, I suppose, owes us nearly $5,000,000,000 in fixed and floating capital, but we could not buy. It was impossible to do any business. Why? The exchange had broken down. This paper machine had crumbled and somehow got out of order, and the result was that no business was possible.' "

This paper machine was a vast superstructure of debts created upon the people by loaning them what is called in Europe "money of account," that is, a bank substitute for money that has no existence, and represented only by debit and credit figures in the books of the banks. Therefore when real money was demanded the whole "bank credits" scheme based upon the false "gold standard" went to pieces and moratoriums were declared—in other words debts could not be paid in any kind of money. And the gold standard fraud, the infamous subterfuge by which England had mortgaged the people of the world with a false substitute for money had broken down and was about to be buried in its cradle on the Thames.

The money scheme of the United States tied to the same standard, resting upon the same false foundation would have gone down in the crash.

The great International Bankers of the world realized this had to be prevented at any cost, or the gold standard fallacy upon which the Plutocracy of the world depends to gather the earnings of the people through debts, would be destroyed forever.

The desperate methods resorted to in order to do this
will follow in their logical order.

The *Washington Post*, published within two squares of
the United States Treasury, with exceptional facilities for
gathering financial news—and in no way antagonistic to
the money power—in the following extracts taken from its
editorials and news columns at the different dates gives
valuable evidence, facts and admissions showing the utter
failure of this absolutely false "gold standard" world-
wide money scheme of Plutocracy.

WASHINGTON POST EDITORIAL, OCT. 15, 1914

"The approval by the Federal Reserve board of the
plan of the syndicate or pool to ship out of this country
$100,000,000 of gold needed by Europe was accepted by
the country as a measure of assistance to exchange bankers,
to importers, corporations owing moneys abroad, as a
measure helpful to the finances of this nation and also to
those abroad so distressed by the demands of their people
for gold."

WASHINGTON POST EDITORIAL, FRIDAY, OCT. 16, 1914

"FINANCIAL FACTS WORTHY OF CONSIDERATION

"It sounds well to tell of there being a gold dollar, during the next few years, in the United States Treasury, for
every legal tender note that is issued, but the benefit to the
people of that state of affairs is not apparent nor can it
be demonstrated.

"No one lacks confidence in the legal tender issues of
the United States.

"They are just as firmly based, have behind them fully
as great assets as have the national bank currency, or the
emergency currency, or as will have the Federal Reserve
currency when issued.

"Boasts of gold strength now by any nation are not in
order. Boasts of ability to pay gold may produce a test
of that ability.

"It is to avoid a test of that in this country that the
stock exchanges are closed.

"It is no time now for boasts as to the efficiency of the gold basis, of the soundness of the theory of gold payments, for the practice has demonstrated that the theory is unsound—when tested.

"The theory that the world's currency is redeemable in gold, that debts are payable in gold, was shattered years ago, and has been smashed to atoms in the practices of Europe.

"Sixty days ago the European countries abandoned all attempts to practice what their financiers have preached as to the gold basis.

"To-day eighteen countries in Europe, Asia, Africa, and South America have gold moratoriums, all debt paying suspended, and current business done on paper currency. If unable to hold on a gold basis 60 days ago what is their condition now, to-day, with $25,000,000 per day expenditures, paid mostly in paper issues and $25,000,000 each day of destruction of the wealth of the nations which issue these notes?

"The weekly window dressing of the statements of gold in the Bank of England, the Bank of France, the Bank of Germany, is accepted by many at its face value, but what relation does it all bear to the note issues of these countries? How far will these comparatively small accumulations—obtained by collecting gold and paying none out—how far will they go toward carrying the huge values of issues of paper and other debts heaped upon them?

"The *Post's* advice to gold basis advocates is that silence is golden when the whole world is demonstrating every hour the absurdity of their theory by inability to transact business in so many lines."

WASHINGTON POST EDITORIAL, OCT. 18, 1914

"MORE GOLD MUST GO TO EUROPE

"Sir George Paish was here but a few months ago, but at that time the gold basis system, though evidently tottering, had not collapsed; it was shaky then, it is in ruins now.

"His desire then was to facilitate gold shipments from

the United States to Europe to prevent the impending disaster, and his desire now is evidently to influence such shipments at this time to lessen the effects of the breakdown, to repair the damage done, and to *reëstablish a system that is proving unfitted to the needs of modern business; a system which has brought Great Britain itself to suspension of debt payments by her people and has closed all the leading exchanges of the world.*"

WASHINGTON POST EDITORIAL, OCT. 23, 1914

"To representatives of Great Britain's fiscal system, familiar as Sir George Paish and Mr. Blackett are with conditions throughout the world, hopeful as they are of building in the future more securely, the fact stands out plainly that Great Britain's misfortune and weakness in August was her inability to obtain sufficient gold to meet the demands of the fiscal system she maintains and strives to support. It is insufficient now.

"The chain snaps at the weakest link.

"Great Britain's chain broke through the inability of the government and her banks to obtain the amount of gold necessary to transact business under the British system, under that system which *Europe, with Great Britain leading, particularly insisted upon adoption of by the world.*

"All gilding and varnish, all decorations of financial speech and ornaments of explanatory diction disappear under this acid test of strength and security, and the moratoriums of Great Britain and France, more than the moratoriums of all the other nations, disclose the unsoundness of attempting to do the business of the world, of this twentieth century world, upon the single gold basis.

"The cause for government stoppage of business was the inadequate supply of gold at the disposal of Great Britain, the greatest of all creditor nations, the commander of the gold of all continents, as fully as it is the sovereign of all seas.

"Great Britain was forced to the moratorium by her lack of gold.

"Great Britain now, in her great desire to get gold, is stripping all the other continents of their gold holdings.

"To maintain the unsound basis, the insecure basis, the inefficient and inadequate basis for the twentieth century affairs, Europe, Asia, Africa and South America are placed in moratoriums, financial morgues, and North America is holding with a death grip upon the gold supply it has in hand.''

THE WASHINGTON POST, DEC. 3, 1914

''GOLD BASIS COLLAPSE

"Four months ago eighteen countries of the world acknowledged their inability to carry on current business by declaring moratoriums—in other words, suspending collections of debts.

"Great Britain and France, the two great capitalistic countries of the world, were among those who confessed their financial systems were inefficient, unsound, and insufficient.

"Is there any more testimony needed as to the insufficiency of the gold basis system?

"New York, Aug. 16, 1915.—The American dollar rules the financial world to-day with an iron grip. Pounds sterling, francs, lires, virtually all foreign exchanges, went down to new depths in a torrent of bills that poured into the exchange markets from American manufacturers seeking pay for the big war contracts of munitions and other supplies purchased here by the warring nations of Europe.

"London, Aug. 17, 1915.—Sir George Paish, editor of the *London Statist,* gave out to-day a statement concerning the present abnormal rate of exchange and the proposals for rectifying the situation by *establishing a large credit in the United States.* Sir George is a recognized *authority on international credit operations* and was sent to the United States last fall to adjust the *disturbed credit conditions then existing. . . .* He said American exports will be limited in the current year only by the ability of Europe and other nations to pay for goods first by shipment of their own products to the United States; second by shipment of gold; third by selling of securities, and fourth, by means of credits. If the American people are dubious about giving credit, then it is obvious the amount of goods they sell must be reduced to the amount foreign nations can pay for by other means.''

INTERNATIONAL BANKERS ENTANGLE THE PEOPLE OF THE UNITED STATES FINANCIALLY WITH BANKRUPT EUROPE

New York, Aug. 14, 1915.—''Conferences were being held in New York to-day by the American group of international bankers to arrange the details of an American credit system for the Allies.'' ''American manufacturers of munitions, filling contracts for the Allies, want to know where they are to look for their money.''

New York, Sept. 10, 1915.—''The Anglo-French commission, seeking to meet the huge bills of Great Britain and France for American munitions and other supplies, reached New York to-day, and were welcomed by J. P. Morgan, and met approximately a hundred prominent bankers, insurance heads, and leaders in other lines of finance late this afternoon at a reception in Mr. Morgan's library. To-night the commission were dinner guests at a party of New York financiers.

''The British delegates are the Right Hon. Lord Reading, Chief Justice of England; Sir Edward Holden, Bart; Sir Henry Babington Smith and Basil P. Brackett, of the British Treasury. The French delegates are M. Octave Homberg, representing the French Treasury, and M. Ernest Mallet, director of the Banque de France.''

New York, Sept. 11, 1915.—''Must Follow Europe's Lead. The United States should now follow what Europe has done for many generations for the United States, that is to say, the bank facilities of the United States should be used for the carrying of import and export transactions for foreign countries just as much as Europe up to now carried by its acceptances the import and export transactions of the United States.'' ''Formation of the syndicate was left to J. P. Morgan & Co. and a large group of American bankers and financial houses.''

New York, Sept. 28, 1915.—''The agreement between the Anglo-French financial commission and the American bankers with whom they have been conferring over the proposed credit loan to Great Britain and France has resulted in the formation of a definite plan, it was officially announced here to-night, for the establishment of a $500,-000,000 loan issue on five-year, 5 per cent. joint British and French bonds, payable jointly and severally by the two nations upon which the big loan will be a first lien.

"The bonds will be issued to the public at 98, thus yielding approximately 5½ per cent. to the investor, and to the nation-wide syndicate of bankers which will subscribe to the loan at 96.

"It is proposed by the commission that the proceeds of the loan be handled so as in no way to disturb our own money markets, and to that end the general plan will be to leave the cash realized from the bonds on deposit with banking institutions which become members of the syndicate throughout the United States."

In plain English this means that the whole financial transaction would be financed by the use of "bank credits," a false substitute for money, created and controlled by banking corporations organized for private gain and based upon debts put upon the people.

The fraudulent gold basis of the dishonest European money system having been exposed and destroyed, a last desperate call is made upon the International Bankers of the United States to save the false gold basis of the Banking and Currency System of the world.

GOLD STANDARD THREATENED BY FOREIGN INFLUX; GREAT
    BANKERS MEET TO DISCUSS MEANS OF AVERTING FI-
    NANCIAL CRISIS

(By the International News Service.)

Chicago, Nov. 3rd, 1916.—"One of the gravest financial problems that ever confronted the United States was discussed behind closed doors to-night at the Chicago Club, where gathered twelve men associated with the biggest financial houses of the nation.

"It is known that the conference had to do with the financial relations of the United States with Great Britain, France and Russia, and it was said that even the retention of the gold standard of money among the four nations might hang on the outcome of the meeting.

"MUST STOP GOLD IMPORTS

"Henry P. Davison, of J. P. Morgan & Co., financial agents of Great Britain, France, Russia, who had recently returned from Europe, stated:

'It is virtually impossible to prevent the building of credit on the gold we are receiving. The obvious problem is to stop gold imports, and the remedy is equally obvious. We must give generous credits to the allied governments. I believe the time has arrived for us to recognize it as a matter of safety for us to accept the bonds of a great nation, such as England or France, rather than demand collateral for our lendings.' The leading bankers present at the conference were Henry P. Davison of J. P. Morgan & Co.; Charles Sabin, president of Guarantee Trust Co. of New York; George M. Reynolds, president of the Continental and Commercial National Bank of Chicago; A. H. Burnham, of Lincoln, Nebraska; J. B. Forgan, Charles G. Dawes, Arthur Reynolds, E. B. Hurlbert, H. J. Rawson, L. A. Goddard, Samuel Insull, John A. Lynch, William A. Tilden, R. G. Dunham and J. E. Otis."

The article continued:

"MAY ASK $1,000,000,000 LOAN

"The report that Great Britain might be forced to demonetize gold was based on a telegram received to-night by one of the biggest houses in Chicago from New York. It read:

"Information from reliable sources states that the future of the gold standard depends upon the attitude of the bankers of the United States in regard to the next British loan, the amount needed will be $1,000,000,000. If the loan is not obtained without collateral England is prepared to form a new pool with Russia and France to send $1,000,000,-000 in gold. The latter countries have hesitated because their note circulation is based on gold reserve. It is now agreed to form a new pool for sending gold here if England will agree to demonetize gold. This is a serious situation for the United States demanding quick action.''

At this time, Nov. 3rd, 1916, the banks of the United States had been loaded down with about two billion of foreign bonds and other securities and had about reached their limit. Then came the death notice of the gold standard from England to their allied bankers of the United States—expressed in the following ultimatum: ''The future of the gold standard depends upon the attitude of the bankers of the United States in regard to the next British loan.''

For the people to fully realize the vital importance to the bankers of the world of sustaining this ''Gold Standard'' fallacy they must understand that by restricting the real money to gold and controlling this gold money in their reserves, the banks are able to create debts upon the resources and people of the world by loaning them a bank created substitute for money called in England ''Money of Account,'' and in the United States ''Bank Credits.''

This substitute for money having no existence is represented only by credit and debit figures on the books of the banks. As long as the banks could uphold this false ''gold standard,'' the banks could control the money and credit of a country and continue this process of creating debts by loaning a substitute for money and gather the earnings of the people.

The destruction of this ''gold standard'' fallacy would not only deprive the banks of the tremendous privilege of mortgaging the resources and people of the world in future, but it would reveal the infamy of the gigantic fraud by which the billions of debts had been already created upon the people.

This was the perilous situation:

First—The loss of this privilege of mortgaging the people of the world in future with a substitute for money.

Second—The exposure of the dishonest economic process by which they had already created the enormous debts that are now absorbing the earnings of labor.

Third—Restitution of property taken from the people without just and honest compensation. More than this the destruction of the false ''Gold Standard'' would restore to the government of the different countries of the world their sovereign control over their money systems and free the people from debt slavery.

The Bank of England was appointed by the Federal Reserve Board, in December, 1916, as its agent, through the influence of the Federal Reserve Bank of New York, the central bank of the system, of which Benjamin Strong was, and is now, the Governor.

On December 29, 1916, the writer addressed the following letter to the Federal Reserve Board:

"THE FEDERAL RESERVE BOARD, UNITED STATES TREASURY,
    "Washington, D. C.
    "DEAR SIRS: The Federal Reserve Act obligates the people of the United States to redeem in gold at the United States Treasury all the Federal Reserve notes issued. I notice your board has selected and appointed through the Federal Reserve Bank of New York the so-called 'Bank of England' as its agent, thus putting the credit of the United States back of this foreign corporation organized for private gain, which is no longer able to make gold payments and fails to give a statement of its true condition.

    "Kindly inform me under what Constitutional power the Federal Reserve Board is thus entering into these entangling money alliances with the bankrupt countries of Europe.
                "Very respectfully yours,
                    "(Signed) T. CUSHING DANIEL."

to which the following reply was made:

                                    December 30, 1916.
"MR. T. CUSHING DANIEL,
    "1416 F Street, Washington, D. C.
    "DEAR SIR: Your letter of December 29th relative to the permission given by the Federal Reserve Board to the Federal Reserve Bank of New York to open relations with the Bank of England is received.

    "Your letter will be called to the attention of the Federal Reserve Board and in the meantime I am enclosing herein a copy of the Federal Reserve Act for your information. Very truly yours,

"(Signed) H. PARKER WILLIS, Sec'y."

In this connection I call attention to the following "special cable" dispatch to *The World*, London, June 15, 1917.

The article begins as follows:

From Washington, D. C. "The imperialistic and capitalistic interests, which stake all their hopes on a victory for England, naturally are heart and soul in the war and will do everything to whip up the people and popularize the war. One should not underestimate their power. They rule the press and wield a gigantic influence at the capital. The President is himself whole-heartedly on their side."

Washington Post—"London, July 6, 1917. Lord Cunliffe, governor of the Bank of England, has recently returned from the United States whither he had gone as a member of Mr. Balfour's mission. . . .

"As regards the Bank of England more especially, Lord Cunliffe assured me that its volume of business is already now much larger than before the war. . . .

"Some financial authorities I had recently consulted affected to look upon the war as being in the main one of finance, the issues of which will be decided by the maneuvers of the money market. . . .

"Lord Cunliffe said, 'Shortly after the outbreak of the war, in the spring of 1915, Mr. Benjamin Strong, of the Federal Reserve Bank (an institution in the United States similar to those of the Bank of England) came to England and entered into definite arrangements with us, so as to bring banking matters between the two countries into closer touch. . . .'

"In reply to my question whether the war will be likely to affect London's position as the center of the money market of the world, a position which before the war it had been the ambition of Berlin to win, Lord Cunliffe replied: 'I hope that after the war New York, Paris and London will divide the financial business of the world between them. I do not ask for more than that [he added]. In any case there can be little doubt that we shall share between us whatever Berlin may lose.' "

Here the plan of Plutocracy is admitted by one of its principals, to establish a three-cornered "World Money Power" after this war to mortgage the earth and keep the people in financial slavery, by continuing to loan them their false substitute for money.

In confirmation of this partnership agreement for the United States to finance bankrupt Europe, I quote the following statement of England's financial authority, Mr. Hartly Withers, who succeeded Sir George Paish as editor of *The Economist.*

Special cable to the New York *Times,* February 24, 1917:

"America will back Britain to the end of the war, for America has cast the die against Germany, no matter whether the breach of relations goes on further than now. American financiers will see that Britain and her Allies lack nothing they need, and the war may go along on a credit basis indefinitely. And it is comforting to us to know that with America as her financial ally Britain's credit will never end, no matter what strain is put upon it."

It is here shown, and subsequent events verify the fact, that International Bankers controlling the money and credit of the United States, through the gold basis Federal Reserve System, in the spring of 1915, entered into a secret foreign entangling financial agreement with the Bank of England, carrying with it the power to bankrupt the people of the United States.

They admit Great Britain to be bankrupt in money and the absolute failure of their gold basis money scheme, and then decided thus to fight the war to its finish with "bank credits," a false and fictitious money, created by banking corporations, based upon bond issues and debts, the effect of which would be to enrich the bond-holding class and put the people deeper in debt slavery.

The result has demonstrated that to be a disastrous fact.

INTERNATIONAL BANKERS UNIFY THEIR INTERESTS

Not being able to deal with the United States upon a money basis, and in order to prevent the exposure and total destruction of the false ''Gold Standard,'' the fraud-ulent basis of this whole gold reserve banking scheme, the International Bankers unified their interests and fabricated the greatest ''bank credits'' money scheme the world has ever known, to create national debts upon the people to protect and perpetuate the control of Plutocracy over the ''money and credits'' of the different countries of the world now, and after the European war.

These associated banks holding these securities represent and control and receive the deposits of the largest Trust combinations in the United States. The greatest amount of these interest-earning debts of governments are appor-tioned to the Trusts by the banks in payment for war and other supplies, or taken as collateral security for ''bank credit loans'' held by the banks against the trusts. In the underwriting of these securities the associated banks take a large portion of these interest-earning debts as collateral for ''bank credit'' loans for the Allies to check upon to pay for war munitions bought from the said trust combinations, and to settle trade balances in the United States held against Europe.

The bonds and securities of these foreign governments are accepted as collateral security by the banks, as the basis of ''bank credit'' loans to American buyers of these securities. Thus, these interest-earning debts put upon the poverty-stricken taxpayers of Europe are again used to pyramid more interest-earning debts upon the borrowers of ''bank credits'' in the United States; while these inter-est-earning debts upon the people of Europe and of the United States are held and practically owned by the banks!

The Bank and Trust combinations controlled by the Banks, having become loaded down with the debts of the Allies for loans made them, and on open accounts, the question as to the ability of the Allies to pay these debts became a serious and vital question to the Banks and Trust combinations, as it was evident to them that these foreign countries, owing to the enormous expenses of carrying on the war, were heading for bankruptcy. It was then evi-dent that their only salvation was to get the United States Government involved, so as to support the exhausted credit of the Allies.

The only way this could be done was to force the United States to issue bonds which could be used in exchange for bonds of the Allies or accepted by the banks and Trust combinations, in payment of balances on open accounts or for future supplies of ammunitions, etc., sold to the Allies or the United States. To illustrate: The Allies owe large sums to the U. S. Steel Corporation and other corporations practically owned and controlled by the banks, the United States by an Act of Congress loans the Allies two billion dollars. The first installment is paid to England in Treasury certificates amounting to $200,000,000 which can be used as cash by the banks in payment for U. S. bonds bearing 3½ per cent. interest, principal and interest payable in gold by the tax-payers of the United States. These Treasury certificates, represented by a United States Treasury warrant payable to the order of the English Government, is immediately endorsed over to J. P. Morgan & Co. by the English Ambassador at Washington and the amount placed to the credit of England on the books of J. P. Morgan & Co. England then draws checks on this credit, payable to the United States Steel Corporation, et al.

The checks given these corporations by England are deposited in the associated banks and charged up against the amount to the credit of England to the sum of $200,000,000. To state it plainly: the bonds and Treasury certificates issued by Congress upon the tax-payers of the United States are being used to pay the debts of the Allies to the banks and Trust combinations of the United States—holding their obligations.

In the final analysis the interest-bearing bonds which are a first mortgage upon the tax-payers of the United States, are being used to pay the bills of the U. S. Steel Corporation and other Trust combinations, controlled by the banks, for war supplies, etc., including profits running as high as 600 per cent. Total profits as estimated in the report of the Finance Committee of the United States Senate to be from three to four billion dollars a year.

President Wilson and Mr. Bryan, when Secretary of State, opposed foreign loans being made by the banks of the United States and so informed Henry P. Davison of J. P. Morgan & Co.

The State Department was soon reorganized by Plutocracy.

Subsequently the Administration allowed the banks to make the first five hundred million dollar loan to the Allies under the provisions of the Federal Reserve Act, and the United States ceased to be a neutral in the European war. When the amount of these loans to the Allies reached two billion dollars, most of it held by the banks and trusts, does any one suppose this combination would remain quiet and see the Allies defeated? Or would they prefer to have these loans additionally protected by indemnities on the German people?

The proceeds from these foreign loans and securities, amounting to billions of dollars, were used to pay for war and other supplies furnished by the banks and trust combinations, who are the main profit takers of this war.

Plutocracy believes in militarism and wars, as it feeds fat upon the bonds of nations and the debts upon the people. The ill-gotten gains amassed by this dishonest scheme are now termed "vested rights," and a large military establishment is demanded for their protection all over the world.

Fully realizing the impending ruin of the people and this Republic, I had the following open letter, dated April 2nd, 1917, addressed to the President and leading members of the Senate and House of Representatives:

"WASHINGTON, D. C., April 2nd, 1917.
"DEAR SIR:—

"Before this country is railroaded into financing this European war by the capitalistic and military class, the voters and tax-payers would call the serious attention of their Representatives in Congress to the true conditions. In order that they may not be misled by the statement that the national debt of the United States is only about one billion dollars and therefore we can lend an indefinite amount to carry on this European war, for which the people of the United States are in no way responsible, we desire to marshal the following facts for your consideration.

"Congress has turned over that sovereign control of the

money system, exclusively given to it in the Constitution of the United States, to banking corporations organized for private gain, granting them the astounding privilege of loaning from 8 to 10 dollars of 'bank fabricated money' for every dollar of lawful money they have to loan.

"Banking corporations exercising this unlawfully delegated power to create debts upon the people by loaning them a 'bank-created false substitute for money,' have established a debt-manufacturing scheme through which about ninety-five billion dollars of debts have been put upon the people of the United States.

"Upon a 5 per cent. basis this is an annual charge of about $4,750,000,000.

"The *interest and dividends* on *this crushing burden of debts are now being added to the price of things people buy or use.*

"So far as our people are concerned this burden is greater than if it were a national debt.

"*As tested upon their own resources in financing this European war the belligerents have already become bankrupt.*

"Before being plunged blindfolded into financial bankruptcy along with the admittedly bankrupt countries of Europe as a result to them already of this war, the people of the United States demand to know the ultimate object that their Government has in view before obligating them to finance this gigantic undertaking, and the following questions should be first answered:

"First—Is it to indemnify the Allies by putting a bonded indebtedness or mortgage amounting, now, to over fifty billion dollars, upon the masses of the people of Germany who are really not responsible for this war (being but the victims of militarism), which would place them and their children under financial bondage for over a hundred years to come?

"Second—What will be the position of the United States at the end of this financing, after mortgaging the people of the United States to carry on this nation-wrecking war in Europe?

"Third—Is it the purpose of this Government to demand disarmament in return for joining the Allies in conquering Germany, that the burden of militarism and navalism be removed from the shoulders of the people for the future and to prevent a future conflict of these very powers with this country brought on by a trade war or by an attempt on the part of the United States to collect defaulted debts against those same powers by taking possession of their customs houses?

"The United States now being master of the situation, now is the time for its Representatives to have a clear and unmistakable understanding as to the *conditions* upon which the people of the United States are asked to assume these tremendous obligations.

"No one will now deny that the *people* of the belligerent governments of Europe are anxious to end this war and would hail with infinite gratitude the good offices of the United States, with this end in view.

"It should be fully realized that by the control of 'Money and Credits' an organized money power controls the policies of the United States and foreign governments. The executive heads of these governments are dominated by this 'Invisible Government of Money and Credits,' upon which they and their governments must depend under the present false banking system of the world.

"A new Declaration of Financial Freedom should now be declared by the people of the United States, before this great republic is drawn into the Hell of European Wars, by the entangling foreign alliances now being consummated by international bankers to protect and perpetuate this absolutely false 'bank credit money scheme' through which the financial despots and usurers of the world have absorbed the earnings of the people.

"Respectfully submitted,

"THE MONETARY EDUCATIONAL BUREAU,

"T. CUSHING DANIEL."

INTERNATIONAL BANKERS AND AGENTS OF "PLUTOCRACY" FORCING BOND ISSUES ON THE PEOPLE OF THE UNITED STATES

Banks prefer government bonds over all other forms of debts as they give a mortgage upon the government itself and the national taxing power collects the interest and guarantees the payment of the principal. More than this it destroys the *independence of that sovereignty of the government without which there can be no Democracy.*

Under the bond issuing scheme of Plutocracy the United States is losing its independent sovereignty and is being stripped of its power as a Democracy, *to represent the people,* and becomes a defenseless *debtor* in *issuing bonds* to carry on this war. The debtor is the servant of the lender, the wide world over. It applies to nations as to individuals.

The failure of our government to exercise its exclusive sovereign power to issue and loan its lawful money as a circulating medium of exchange, has put it in debt to its own creatures—the banks, and so has made *its creatures —the banks—the holders of its debts—superior to their creator—the government.*

Why should the government, having the *exclusive power under the Constitution to create money,* impair its credit by becoming *a borrower* of money? How can any credit be stronger than the credit of the government? By the issuing of *bonds to get money that it has the exclusive power to create, the government is prostituting its own credit.*

The Constitution of the United States provides that *taxation* shall originate in the *Lower House of Congress, directly representing the people.* This Republic was brought *into existence by resistance to taxation without representation. It is the basic principle of Democracy.* Here you have international bankers and the beneficiaries of a Plutocracy *originating and consummating a gigantic scheme to force bond issues of billions of dollars to be paid by taxing the people into bankruptcy, without representation.*

The scheme to force these bond issues was conceived in secret conferences and the representatives of the people kept in ignorance of the proceedings. Congress was then ordered to promptly pass the bill.

The organized money power back of the administration and controlling the public press brought to bear its powerful influences and all *representation of the people was destroyed* in Congress.

Plutocracy became supreme in our government taking absolute *control of the taxing power over the people.*

The members of the "Advisory Council," the members of the "Federal Reserve Board," the Secretary of the Treasury and the financial representatives of the bankers of Europe met in secret conference to discuss the plans for protecting this false "Gold Standard," but evidently reached the conclusion that it was necessary to have Congress authorize the issue of seven billion dollars of interest-earning debts upon the people of the United States in order that their comprehensive scheme to protect the "Gold Standard" in future should be legalized by Congress. This would eventuate in Plutocracy putting billions of dollars in mortgages on the Government to be used in future to control the money system and credit of the United States.

At these conferences the question arose: How can we put such an immense debt upon the people of the United States?

Plutocracy's logical answer would be: "It can be done only in time of war, it is now or never; nothing else can save our 'Gold Standard' scheme from exposure and absolute destruction."

In making the amount seven billions, its very magnitude will so daze the mind of the people that they will not comprehend what it means to them and will only feel their utter inability to prevent it. Now that Congress has been forced to declare war few Representatives will have the moral courage not to vote any amount of debts and taxes upon the people in order to carry on the war.

It is only necessary for us to take advantage of the war, and appeal to the patriotism of the people and our motive of mortgaging the Government and protecting our Gold Standard scheme will never be comprehended by the people. Why should not we be able to do this? The Anglo-American bankers took advantage of the Civil War and put three billion dollars of bonds upon the people of the United States. Now with our present hold on the

Government and the public press we can put seven billion dollars of debts on the people, and more, as long as the war fever can be kept up.

If a Representative did oppose this bond issue, the Public Press would denounce him as a traitor to his country and his opposition would be of no avail.

In these bankers' conferences the so-called "Liberty Bond Issues" were conceived. Calling them "Liberty Bonds" was a deceptive appeal to the patriotism of the people. Issuing bonds means bondage of the people, call it by any name you please.

The Government in issuing these bonds is putting Democracy further in debt to Plutocracy. If these bond issues are allowed to continue, Plutocracy will have so mortgaged the United States as to absolutely own it after this war is over. Calling it a part of a world Democracy will be of no value to the people.

The tax-payers who have to pay the interest and principal of these debts should realize the demand for money that is being put upon them, calling for billions of dollars in payment. To do this they should know what a billion dollars means. At $1.00 a minute, night and day, Sundays and week days, to create a fund of $1,000,000,000 would require 2,000 years! One billion dollars is more than the assessed value of the property of the state of North Carolina and seven billion dollars is equal very nearly to the entire assessed value of all the property in the New England states reported by the secretary of commerce to amount to $7,599,580,847. At 4 per cent. this amount doubles every 15 years. Think of this, Mr. Tax-payer, and then think of your children who will carry the burden to their graves. In order to make it appear to be popular subscription to these bonds, every device known to the ingenuity of man was resorted to, even implying that a man is a traitor to his country if he did not buy them.

Banks offered to loan a subscriber the first installment payments, and even the full amount if he would only give them his name as a subscriber.

Since the sale closed desperate efforts and misleading statements are being sent out to conceal the ugly fact that most of the bonds are really to be owned by Banks and

Trust combinations and millionaires, the American Plutocracy.

Plutocracy, in its selfish and inordinate greed for wealth and the power that goes with it, has never hesitated to sacrifice the interests of the people to protect the operation of the false money scheme through which it controls the "money and credit" of the different countries of the world, which means the control of the Governments.

Inconceivable to the people as it may seem, the facts prove that Plutocracy is taking advantage of the excitement and demoralization caused by this inhuman war, and in forcing billions of bonds upon the people of the United States is now carrying out the most ruinous and gigantic financial conspiracy ever put upon a Government calling itself a Democracy.

In floating these debts on "bank credits" it was arranged to issue two billion of Treasury certificates of indebtedness on the people bearing 3 per cent. This to be followed by five billion of U. S. bonds bearing 3½ per cent. interest, the certificates and bonds issued in installments to meet the requirements of the Federal Reserve Board in coöperation with the banks that it represents. April 21, 1917, the Secretary of the Treasury states, *"Treasury certificates purchased by the banks may be used in lieu of cash in paying for bonds when issued. Monies received from Treasury certificates will be promptly returned to the market so that there may be no derangement of the money market.*

"The proceeds will be paid out by the Government in business transactions, the money will again be deposited in the banks and *the banks will be in position of having both the money and the certificates with which to meet any withdrawals by depositors subscribing for the bond issue."*

Same date: "The fullest coöperation of the Federal Reserve Board will be given the Treasury Department in disposing of the certificates of indebtedness; letters so instructing the Federal Reserve Boards were sent out yesterday by the board after Mr. McAdoo had announced his program."

So-called Popular Subscriptions

Upon every dollar paid in cash by the subscriber for these bonds, the banks can convert into lawful or reserve money and loan from eight to ten dollars of ''bank credits'' to borrowers upon these bonds, which the bank holds until paid for. Result of this transaction is as follows: The banks charge the borrowers no more interest than the Government pays on its bonds, but as the banks can loan from eight to ten times the amount of the cash paid in by the purchaser of the bonds, in ''bank credits,'' the banks are earning from 28 to 35 per cent. on the actual cash paid in by purchase of the bonds.

Under this process of using credit and cash based upon the percentage of the Clearing House operations two billions of bonds could be handled by the associated banks of the United States with a payment of one hundred million cash; and the cash would be immediately returned to the banks under the plan in operation.

Among many inducements held out by the banks to patriotic subscribers was the speculative one that these 3½ per cent. bonds could be exchanged for 4 per cent. bonds to be issued later by the Government. This would not only insure a profit to the subscriber, but as these bonds were to be listed on the stock exchanges, would insure their sale and increase their speculative value.

This is indeed patriotism at a ruinous price to the taxpayers of the United States.

By contracting the currency and calling in loans, or causing a premium on gold, banks can depress the market value of these bonds and interest bearing Treasury certificates, exchangeable for bonds, and destroy the credit of the Government. This was done by the Anglo-American bankers after the Civil War when they drove down the price of United States bonds, bearing six per cent. interest, to $65 and then sold them as high as $120.

The history of the world shows that Plutocracy has never won a battle against the people under its own banner and is now using the word ''Liberty'' to establish more securely its system of debt slavery upon the people of the world.

To trace a conspiracy or fix a crime find those who

would have the motive in bringing it about, and if the goods are then found in their possession conviction follows.

In addition to circumstantial evidence sufficient to hang a man, the people have documentary and recorded facts to convict "Plutocracy" of the crime of destroying *Democracy in the United States* and trying to *financially enslave* and *ruin* the *people* of this Republic.

The increase in the value of the assets of the banks during the war period of five years amounted to $20,565,067,-121. The Comptroller of the Currency states: "The growth in the assets of the National Banks (private corporations) in the last five years has been greater than the increase which took place in the preceding twenty-five years." Report of Comptroller of the Currency, 1918.

PLUTOCRACY AGAIN FORCES CONGRESS TO PROSTITUTE ITS HIGHEST ACT OF SOVEREIGNTY TO FURTHER ENSLAVE THE PEOPLE WITH DEBTS

As soon as the European War started, International Bankers began to formulate their plans.

The Federal Reserve Act had been forced through Congress by their influences in 1914.

The Federal Reserve Act enlarges the Bank of England scheme of manufacturing debt without lending money, or putting money in circulation to be used by the people.

The larger banks of the United States, especially those owned and controlled by international bankers, were overloaded with debts that they owned and held as collateral security against the great industrial trusts, manufacturing corporations and business enterprises of the people of the United States. Fully 90 per cent. of these debts had been created by the banks loaning a false and fictitious substitute for money, known as "bank credits," that is money having no existence and represented only by credit and debit figures on the books of banks. As a logical result, when the demand for these debts was made, calling for payment in money, business depression set in.

In 1914 when the European war started tremendous war orders from the Allies in Europe were placed with these great trusts and corporations, showing profits running as high as 500 per cent. and as a result the stock of these trusts and corporations advanced in value to unprecedented high levels, which enabled them to obtain additional loans from banks to increase the capacity of their manufacturing plants to meet this growing demand for their output. This afforded the banks the opportunity of making unheard-of profits.

This was their situation when the alarm started that the Allies had exhausted their means of making payments on their debts, and could not purchase more in the United States unless they were given uncovered credits, in other words, they could put up no more collateral security for loans, or pay the debts then due the United States, amounting to billions of dollars. It was then forced upon the attention of these bankers that if the Allies were defeated, or Europe became bankrupt as a result of the war, they would face a total loss.

The resourcefulness of the international bankers in high finance was put in operation, and the plan put through to shift the obligations owed them by the Allies upon the tax-payers of the United States. This was done by getting Congress to authorize the exchange of United States bonds for the doubtful promises to pay of the bankrupt countries of Europe; which they the bankers would not accept, knowing that Europe with a war debt of over two hundred billion dollars, would have to repudiate them.

Plutocracy, believing from *past experiences that the gullibility of the people in the false gold basis scheme was unlimited,* framed up their combination scheme of "Certificates of Indebtedness and Bond Issues" to accomplish their double purpose, as follows: "Enable the banks to buy the bonds of the United States in exchange for 'Bank Credits' and at the same time prevent the Government from putting its lawful money in actual circulation to be used by the people."

The Government was then forced to use the sovereign power delegated to it by the people, to issue certificates of indebtedness—then deposited them with the banks and received a *"Credit on the books of the banks for the amount."*

And the certificates of indebtedness became the property

of the banks, and the Government was allowed to draw checks against the credits on the books of the banks.

These checks drawn by the Government are matched up and cleared through the Federal Reserve Banks and Clearing House Associations of the banks.

In this operation the banks pay for the certificates of indebtedness with "Bank Credits," a false, fictitious and non-existent money, then exchange these certificates of indebtedness for interest-earning bonds of the United States. The banks can then sell the bonds to the people for money or accept them as collateral security for more "Bank Credit" loans of the banks.

UNITED STATES BONDS FIRST UNDERWRITTEN BY THE BANKS

The operation of their banking and currency scheme, through which billions of watered securities had already been placed upon the railroads and industrial trusts of this country by the loaning of "Bank Credits," was to be applied to the underwriting of Government bonds, yet realizing that if the *Government deposited United States bonds direct to the banks in exchange for "Bank Credits" in the same way, it would be too flagrant an act to be tolerated or overlooked by the people even in time of war,* the banks, therefore, framed up and put through Congress the subterfuge of having the Government first issue to the banks its "Certificates of Indebtedness" with which they could buy the bonds.

The following reply from the Secretary of the United States Treasury, under date July 25, 1918, gives the amount of this special currency that has already been issued to the banks for this purpose:

"By direction of the Secretary and in reply to your letter of the 21st instant you are advised that prior to the series now being offered in anticipation of the Fourth Liberty Loan, a total of $9,165,187,000 certificates of indebtedness has been issued since the beginning of the war."

In order to provide for the underwriting of the Fourth Liberty Loan by the banks, $6,000,000,000 of certificates of indebtedness were issued by the Government to the banks. It is now provided that an additional $6,000,000,000 of certificates of indebtedness will be issued to the banks to underwrite the Fifth Bond Issue, exchangeable for United States bonds, making a total of this special currency issued to the banks by the Congress of the United States, exchangeable for interest-earning United States bonds, amounting to $21,165,187,000, principal and interest payable by the people in money.

By the banks substituting the use of their "Bank Credits" for money and matching incoming checks drawn against bank credits, one against the other by credit and debit figures upon the books of the banks, they thus exchanged bank credits for U. S. bonds.

The records of the Federal Reserve Banks and Clearing House Associations, owned and controlled by the banks, show that only 5.22 per cent. in cash or money is used in settling these balances. Here we have the most remarkable exhibition of high and frenzied finance the world has ever known, endorsed by the Representatives of the people of the United States in Congress assembled, the sovereign power of their Government being used to issue to the Banking Corporations, organized for private gain, over $21,000,000,000 of a *special currency* to be *exchanged by these banks for interest-earning bonds of the United States, at the same time denying the people the exercising of that sovereign and exclusive power delegated to it by the people to issue and loan into circulation for full value received the lawful money of the United States as the medium of exchange as provided in the Constitution of the United States.*

In order to deceive the people and divert their attention from the fact that the banks are exchanging "Bank Credits" for United States bonds and at the same time collect the cash required from the people, the banks are appealing to their patriotism and urging them to economize and save every dollar possible and put it in the bank in order to carry on this war.

WAR SHOULD HAVE BEEN FOUGHT WITH LAWFUL MONEY

If the United States Government had issued and loaned into actual circulation during this war additional money to make the total of legal tender money in active circulation about ten billion dollars—less than a per capita of $100—I do not hesitate to say it would have caused less inflation of prices than the borrowing of billions of "Bank Credits" by the issuing of bonds. And this ten billion of lawful money of the United States would have developed the great resources and activities of this country in every direction necessary to carry on this war.

Full legal tender money used as a medium of exchange is instantaneous in its convertibility into everything else, and when given its legitimate and lawful right of way as the *medium of exchange,* circulates throughout the entire body politic, nourishing all its parts as the blood circulates through the human body, and when unobstructed, as a medium of exchange, will develop all the resources of the country in time of peace or war.

Wars are not won with money, but by men and materials. If you have the men it only needs an adequate amount of money in actual circulation as a medium of exchange, to produce the materials to carry on war.

With an adequate amount of actual money in circulation, a war can be carried on as long as the resources of a country are not exhausted.

If a full legal tender money, issued by the Government, is used as the medium of exchange, wars could be fought without leaving the burdens of an interest-earning National Debt upon this and coming generations, that were absolutely innocent of the causes that led up to the war.

To refute this it would be necessary to assume the senseless position that no country could ever be rich enough to win wars without borrowing a false substitute for money to be used as a medium of exchange, when the Government has the exclusive Sovereign power to create *real money,* the only *honest medium of exchange* to carry on commerce or war.

It would have then only been necessary for Congress to pass a regular "War Revenue Bill," and tax all war profits into the United States Treasury to pay the expenses of this war. This legal tender money would remain in circulation to build up the country in the reconstruction period to follow the war.

When the extra money was no longer needed by the people as *a medium of exchange,* it would be returned to the Government by those who borrowed it in order to stop paying the interest; thus preventing any unnecessary increase of the circulating medium of exchange.

If wars are fought by issuing interest-earning bonds upon the people, Democracy will always lose by inheriting the war debts, and Plutocracy always win by owning the bonds and keeping the people in debt slavery.

Lawful money issued or loaned into circulation for value received by the Government, as a "medium of exchange" when it is *used* by its owner, *completes the transaction and leaves nothing else to be done,* and can be used indefinitely in transferring property and paying debts by those earning it or receiving it in exchange.

Not so with "Bank Credits" or "Money of Account." The use of this false and fictitious substitute for money when borrowed does not complete the transaction, but leaves the burden of an interest-earning debt behind it and no corresponding money in existence to pay the debt.

The war has been fought, but not paid for. The billions of debts now hang like a millstone around the neck of the people of the world, dragging them down into poverty and financial ruin. For what? To protect the fraudulent gold basis banking and currency system established by international bankers to create dishonest debts upon the resources and people of the world.

"LEAGUE OF NATIONS TO ENFORCE PEACE WITH ARMS"

An European idea being foisted upon the people of the United States. England, under the false money scheme of loaning "money of account," a dishonest substitute for real money, had so mortgaged the resources and people of her colonies that the burdens of interest-earning debts and taxation was driving the people into revolution.

England, before 1910, was planning to head off this unrest of Democracy, which was spreading over Europe.

In 1911 Dr. Timothy Ricards, a distinguished Englishman, outlined this English scheme of a "League of Nations to Enforce Peace with Arms" as follows: "*We are living in the days of anarchy. Unite the ten leading nations; let all their armaments be united into one to enforce the decrees of a Superior Court of the World. And since it will then be the refusal of recalcitrant nations to accept arbitration that will make necessary the maintenance of any very large armaments by these united nations, let them protect themselves by levying discriminating tariff duties against the country that would perpetuate present conditions."*

This "League of Nations to Enforce Peace" is a monarchical conception, born of the failure of European Governments, and is the last hope of Autocracy to control Democracy. "A League of Nations to Enforce Peace with Arms" is an inhuman and monstrous idea and absolutely at variance with and repugnant to every Democratic principle upon which this great Republic was established.

"Advocates a Common Force"

This was adopted by the Wilson administration, and the President openly aligned himself with the advocates of "some common" force behind international institutions by consenting to address the First Annual Assembly of the League to Enforce Peace in Washington on May 27, 1916. On that occasion he spoke for this country as follows:

"I say that the United States is willing to become a *partner* in any feasible association of nations formed in order to realize these objects and make them secure against violation.

"I feel the world is even now upon the eve of a great consummation, when some *common force* will be brought into existence which shall safeguard right as the first and most fundamental interest of the peoples and all governments, when coercion shall be summoned not to the service of political ambitions or selfish hostility, but to the service of common order, a common peace."

President Wilson, in his address to the United States Senate, January 22, 1917, made the following statement:

"There can be no sense of safety and equality among nations if great, preponderating armaments are henceforth to continue here and there to be built up and maintained.

"Mere agreements may not make peace secure. It will be absolutely necessary that a force be created as a guarantor of permanency of the settlement much greater than the force of any nation now engaged or any alliance here-after to be formed or projected that no nation, no probable combination of nations, could face or withstand it. If the peace presently to be made is to endure, it must be a peace made secure by the organized major force of mankind."

Realizing that our people were pledged by the Government to give up everything they had necessary to win this war; that our soldiers were sent to war to protect those at home; that thousands of them have been lost to their homes forever, and that billions of war debts were put upon the tax-payers—the question now to be answered is:

Shall the same Government that demanded the sacrifices of the people now protect the war profits made by corporations out of these misfortunes of a people?

In order to put this question squarely before the Congress of the United States, I sent the following letter to the Hon. Claude Kitchin, Chairman of the Ways and Means Committee of the House, and Senator F. M. Simmons, Chairman of the Finance Committee of the Senate in charge of the War Revenue Bill, and a similar letter to President Wilson:

"WRIGHTSVILLE BEACH, N. C., June 12, 1919.
"Hon. F. M. Simmons, Chairman, Finance Committee, U. S. Senate, Washington, D. C.

"DEAR SIR—President Wilson in his address to Congress on May 27, 1918, referring to profiteering, said: 'There is abundant fuel for the light in the records of the United States Treasury with regards to profits of every sort. The profiteering that can not be got at by the restraints of conscience and love of country, can be got at by taxation.

" 'There is such profiteering now and the information with regard to it is available and indisputable.' [1]

---

[1] Under the operation of the Federal Reserve Banking and Currency Scheme put through Congress in 1914, and covering the war period up to November 1, 1918, "The growth in the assets of the National Banks in the last five years has been greater than the

"It is now an open secret that the manufacturers and Trust combinations are hiding their excess war profits in interest-bearing, non-taxable bonds of the United States.

"The time for 'soft concealments' by the Representatives of the people has passed. The cold grim facts of this war are now being realized and felt by the voters of this country and are daily intensifying.

"As Chairman of the Finance Committee of the United States Senate, your attention is called to the last annual report of the Comptroller of the Currency, page 108, showing that the Banking Corporations of the country, organized for private gain, have increased their profits, represented by capital, surplus and other assets, about $6,000,000,000; an increase of about $5,000,000,000 over the pre-war year of 1915, showing an excess war profit of five hundred per cent.

"The voters now ask and will later require their Representatives to answer why these war profits of banking corporations are not taxed.

"In 1917, the figures of 48 manufacturing corporations showed that their excess war profits will be as high as $1,200,000,000. Based upon these figures the excess war profits of all the profiteering companies conservatively estimated will come to $3,600,000,000.

"It is thus shown that $8,600,000,000 of excess war profits have been made out of the people in the past year by these corporations.

"As stated by the President, the figures to verify these facts are available in the United States Treasury.

"In order that no Representative in Congress may be able to plead ignorance of the facts herein stated, when later held responsible for the failure to tax the war profits of these corporations, I request this letter be filed in the records of your Committee when considering this revenue Bill.

"Talking patriotism while conniving at profiteering at this time would be treason of the basest character.

"Very truly yours,
"T. CUSHING DANIEL."

increase which took place in the preceding twenty-five years." Annual Report, Comptroller of the Currency, December 2, 1918, page 6.

DEFLATION

From careful investigation and the recorded facts, the inevitable conclusion is reached that international bankers created the fraudulent gold basis money system, with the deliberate purpose to exploit the people of the different countries of the world, by using the dishonest "gold basis" for a money system.

A study of the International Conferences on bimetallism and monometallism, over a long period of years, will show that International Bankers fully appreciated the fact that if they could control money they could control prices of raw material and the wages of labor; in fact, the business affairs of the people.

At these International Conferences the subject was brought up, when about ten million people were starving in India, and the question was asked whether it would not be helpful to the people of India to increase the amount of money in circulation in that country, and give them a profit on agricultural products; the answer given was: yes, "to increase the amount of money in circulation would be a matter of infinite consolation to the people of the world, and our philanthropy would be a subject of admiration, but our business sagacity a subject of ridicule."

On another occasion an international banker stated their position in a more direct manner: "We own the money, India owns the wheat, it is to our interest that the same amount of money will buy double the amount of wheat, therefore, it is not to our advantage to increase the amount of money in circulation."

This does not only apply to India, but to every agricultural country in the world, including the United States. This fraudulent gold basis money system, created and controlled by international bankers, is the cause of the ruin of agriculture and the poverty and distress of farmers.

The greatest achievement of human government is to

get man properly related to the soil, in order that the great natural law of demand and supply shall operate on the necessities of life. International bankers, in absolute disregard and violation of this great law of nature and nature's God, formulated their plan to fix the price of raw materials and the wages of labor for the people of the different countries of the world.

Under this plan the agricultural products of the farmers of the United States were to be put in "a pool" in competition with the wheat, cotton and rice of India; the cattle, corn and wheat of Argentina, etc., and the executive committee of the Economic Section of the League of Nations, dominated by International Bankers, was to be given the power to fix the prices of the crops of the farmers of the world.

The stabilization of the wages of labor was to be accomplished in one of two ways, either by advancing wages in European countries, or reducing wages of labor in the United States. The logical result would be to reduce the price of labor and raw material in the United States.

This treasonable financial conspiracy to continue the control of the money systems of the world on a fraudulent gold basis, and fix the price of raw materials and the wages of labor, was defeated by the Senate of the United States in refusing to ratify the Versailles Treaty. Thereupon, these International Bankers and their emissaries determined to accomplish their infamous purpose by "Deflation" of farm products and wages, by their control of the fraudulent gold basis Federal Reserve system operating through their agencies, the Federal Advisory Council, and Federal Reserve Board.

The record shows that on May 17 and 18, 1920, the Federal Advisory Council of the Federal Reserve Board ordered "Deflation." On September 27, 1920, Bulletin No. 2, issued by the First Federal Foreign Banking Association, which is controlled by the leading banking associations of New York, states that the League of Nations is carrying on a world campaign "for drastic credit restrictions through existing banking institutions." It also says that measures have been taken in the United States, "to restrict the granting of credits and put up the cost of borrowing," and that "our restrictions of credit show far-reaching influences, bringing about reduced production and liquidation of commodities."

In November, 1920, one of the largest conventions of Representatives of the Farmers waited upon the Federal Reserve Board in the United States Treasury, and described the intolerable suffering and disaster brought upon the farmers by the deflation of the value of their products and property.

In response to this distressing appeal, Governor Harding of the Federal Reserve Board, with apparent indifference, pointed to a diagram on the wall of his office and coolly stated that he could do nothing to relieve the agricultural situation and the fall of prices of farm products as the gold reserve of the banks had gotten down to 40 per cent. and he had to protect the gold reserve of the banks as required by the Federal Reserve Act.

In view of the fact that the Federal Advisory Council and the Federal Reserve Board knew that this deflation plan had been conceived by international bankers, under whose domination they were acting, it is impossible to escape the conclusion that international bankers deliberately planned to destroy, by deflation, about eight billions of dollars in the value of farm products of this country; throw millions out of employment, and paralyze the legitimate business of the entire country, with its attendant losses and sufferings of our people—for what? To protect the gold basis Federal Reserve System.

At a meeting held May 17 and 18, 1920, in the United States Treasury the following questions were asked by the Federal Reserve Board, the answers being made by the Federal Advisory Council:

Q. "How can the gold reserve position of the Federal Reserve Banks be materially strengthened?"

A. "By urging upon member banks, through Federal Reserve Banks, the wisdom of showing borrowers the necessity of curtailment of general credits."

Q. "If steps cannot be taken at this time leading to a more normal proportion between the volume of credits and the volume of goods, when can they be taken?"

In their opinion the time was then, as shown by the

action taken by the Federal Reserve Board in their policy of deflation.

Q. "What are the objects to be obtained by the policy of credit control in the existing circumstances?"

A. "Taking the index numbers of the United States Bureau of Labor Statistics as the most comprehensive and most scientifically prepared of the index number covering the entire period 1913 to 1919, inclusive, we may say the wholesale price increased from 1913 to April, 1920, 165 per cent.; in other words, if one calls the dollar of 1913 a 100 per cent. dollar in its purchasing power over commodities at wholesale, the dollar of to-day is approximately a 38 per cent. dollar."

To accomplish this purpose, deflation of values was deliberately put in operation by the Federal Advisory Council and the Federal Reserve Board, under the domination of international bankers, which, according to the Manufacturers' Record, Feb. 1, 1923, "was at a conservative calculation the startling total of $32,000,000,000, as the aggregate of the decline in values of farm real estate and the crops of 1921, as compared with 1919, in the United States."

I quote the following: Reginald McKenna, ex-Chancellor of the Exchequer of Great Britain, referring to the disastrous effects of deflation in England, made the following admission: "No one has difficulty in understanding that any measure of deflation tends to lower prices, and we had an illustration of this process in 1920-1921 when the United States adopted deflationary methods in concurrence with British financial authorities."

The cold figures and the ugly facts now conclusively show that international bankers brought on inflation by creating debts, that became assets of the banks by loaning "bank credits," a false and fictitious substitute for money; and as soon as the war ended they consummated their plans to bring on deflation of value to reëstablish and perpetuate the fraudulent gold basis of their money system, through which they control the "money and credit" of the world. They knew full well that deflation would result in increasing the purchasing power of money, and the value of debts held against the people.

Abraham Lincoln said: "If a government contracted a debt with a certain amount of money in circulation and then contracted the money volume before the debt was paid, it is the most heinous crime a government could commit against the people."

NOMINATION OF WARREN G. HARDING

During and since the European War the record shows that Col. E. M. House, Paul M. Warburg, W. G. McAdoo, as Secretary of the United States Treasury, B. M. Baruch, Eugene Meyer, Jr., Henry P. Davison, Thos. W. Lamont et al., acting in the interest of the International Banking Power, have been the advisors of Presidents, Senators and Representatives in Congress, and have directed the financial policies of our Government to protect their fraudulent gold basis Federal Reserve System to strengthen the control of international bankers over the money and credit of the people of the United States.

Exercising this control, international bankers have put an unnecessary National Debt of $25,000,000,000 upon the tax-payers of this country.

Stripped of all financial hypocrisy the real purpose of these bankers is to reëstablish their gold basis debt manufacturing scheme by which they absorb through interest and dividends the earnings of the people, and to protect their war debts, and make them payable in gold.

Warren G. Harding, with only one state to his credit, was agreed upon by Senator Murray Crane and Col. Harvey (the same Col. Harvey who discovered Woodrow Wilson) and endorsed by Thomas W. Lamont, a partner in the international banking firm of J. P. Morgan & Co., at a meeting in a Chicago hotel on the day of the balloting in the Republican Convention in 1920.

In this connection it should be remembered that Thomas W. Lamont was the dominating figure in the group of men who attempted to amend the plank in the platform to be adopted by the Republican National Convention, preventing the United States from going into the League of Nations, so that it might approve the establishment of a World Court of International Jurisdiction. This group of men approved of the selection of Warren G. Harding and he was elected president of the United States.

With these facts in mind, I addressed an open letter to President Harding and the Representatives of the people, April 11, 1921.

"The question in which the people are most vitally concerned is, will the Harding Administration be controlled by the International Bankers who wrecked the Democratic party, and ruined Woodrow Wilson, President of the United States?

"The following extracts from letters addressed by the writer to President Wilson should be a timely warning to the Republican Administration.

" 'August 10, 1913.

" 'Do you propose to force the American people into partnership with a convicted money trust through a Democratic caucus?'

" 'November 25, 1913.

" 'In legislating on money you deal with the highest attribute of sovereignty of a great people. The Constitution provides that Congress shall coin (create) money and regulate the value (quantity) thereof. This means money and not asset currency or debts redeemable in gold, the quantity of which is measured only by the debts that the banks can manufacture against the people by rediscounting debts already held against them.'

" 'October 5, 1914.

" 'The mountain of debts manufactured by the use of non-existent, fictitious money created by banks, have become ruinous demands upon the borrowers for actual money. The 25,175 Banking Corporations have been calling on the people for payment of these debts to such an extent that they have exhausted the supply of money in the possession of the people, resulting in universal stagnation of business and a feeling of desperation among the people.

" 'Mr. President, yours was the opportunity to reverse this economic curse upon the people and live in history as the greatest statesman of this or any other age. It is evident you were not equal to this great economic emergency, for without giving one sound economic reason to justify it, you put through Congress this indefensible Federal Reserve Act, legalizing and perpetuating this false and ruinous money system, amplifying its powers, enabling the banking corporations to multiply more unpayable debts upon a people already overburdened with debts, created with "bank credits," a corporation substitute for money.'

"International bankers, striving to prepetuate this infamous and dishonest financial scheme for robbing the people of the world, are now engaged in a propaganda to deceive the people of the United States into believing that this great country with its boundless resources, producing everything the people really need, can not prosper independent of the bankrupt countries of Europe, that have already been ruined by the burden of debts similarly created upon them. And that prosperity cannot come to our people until we first put bankrupt Europe on its feet.

"I quote from the Manufacturers Record, March 3, 1921: 'The cable reports Sir George Paish, the British Economist, as saying: "The war created a European debt amounting to nearly $250,000,000,000. I have examined conditions in various Continental Countries and have reluctantly concluded that practically the whole of Europe will repudiate its debts." '

"The evidence is now accumulating to show that in their desperation international bankers are trying to use the Harding Administration to give a judicial turn to their 'League of Nations' and to create an 'International Judicial Court' to destroy the sovereign control of our Government over the money of the United States, by construing money to be an international question, and under this false construction, international bankers would control the money and credit of the world.

"This would be in direct violation of the Constitution of the United States, and nothing short of treason against our Government.

"No one having an intelligent appreciation of the facts can doubt the 'conclusion reluctantly reached' by Sir George Paish as to Europe.

"President Harding and the Representatives of the people in Congress without further delay should realize that

the world—including the United States—has been done
to death with debts, and at once abandon the false gold
basis bank credits debt manufacturing scheme embodied in
the Federal Reserve Act, and establish an honest money
system as provided in the Constitution of the United
States, in the interest of all the people. Unless this is done,
President Harding will soon be discredited, and Congress
reorganized by a disappointed, debt-ridden and indignant
people, who are now understanding that international
bankers are responsible for the creation of this infamous
debt manufacturing scheme, and that Congress is responsible for its being inflicted upon the people of this country,
and its present continuance.

"Respectfully submitted,

"T. CUSHING DANIEL."

It is now a well-known fact that the Harding administration was dominated in its financial policy by the same
international banking power that directed the financial
policy of the Wilson administration. President Harding
ignoring this warning, aligned himself with the International Bankers in their efforts to reëstablish the fraudulent
"gold standard," and committed himself as follows, on
May 24th, 1921:

"I could wish that the tendency of the world's gold
to gravitate to us might be checked. Beyond the point of
insuring security to our circulation, gold would be more
useful to us in vaults of the great banks abroad, where
it would be a better guarantee of the 'gold standard.' I
feel strongly that the protection of the 'gold standard' is
one of the great obligations which peculiarly appeal to
us."

Three days after this declaration, on May 27th, 1921,
the following announcement was made in the public press:

"The Gold Stock in United States Causes World Stagnation. Experts Believe American Wealth Must Again
Be Sent to Europe. President Harding has begun a series
of conferences with Kings of finance, the first being a
quietly arranged dinner at the White House Wednesday
night."

Those present at this private dinner were, J. P. Morgan,
of J. P. Morgan & Co.; Paul M. Warburg, of Kuhn, Loeb

& Co.; Benjamin Strong, Governor of the Federal Reserve Bank of New York; C. E. Mitchell, President of the National City Bank of New York; James A. Alexander, President of the National Bank of Commerce of New York; Charles Sabin, President Guaranty Trust Co., of New York; William Kent, President Bankers Trust Co., of New York; and H. C. McEldowney, President Pittsburgh Trust Co.

The following men, holding high and controlling positions in our Government, were present: Warren G. Harding, President of the United States; Andrew J. Mellon, Sec'y. United States Treasury, and Herbert Hoover, Sec'y. of the Department of Commerce of the United States.

The purpose of this meeting was to make the United States a party to this undertaking to reëstablish the socalled "gold standard." No senator, nor representative, nor governor of any state was there to represent the people, or listen in on this financial scheme of a super-government to get the people of the United States committed to the reëstablishment of the fraudulent "gold standard," and the creation of a world court to protect this, the most gigantic swindle ever conceived by the mind of man.

This plan of international bankers being agreed upon, President Harding was sent on a speaking tour to advocate the United States becoming a member of this world court; and J. P. Morgan, representing the international bankers, was sent to Europe and commissioned to arrange for the reëstablishment of the gold standard.

I quote the following statement from the Universal Service, London, Oct. 30, 1923, by Robert J. Prew: "I am enabled to reveal authoritatively why J. P. Morgan abruptly ended the labors of the Committee last year. It appears that Morgan personally spent three months investigating in Germany as to her capacity to pay, with the understanding that his recommendation would be received with serious consideration. Morgan's report was accepted by a committee of financiers, France dissenting, and was sent to the Premier Poincaré for approval. The report consisted of four principal recommendations.

"1. Germany's total debt to be reduced to approximately fifty billion gold marks.

"2. Germany to be granted a full moratorium for two years, with a partial moratorium for the three following years, with payments then gradually scaling upward, according to Germany's economic recovery.

"3. Troops of occupation to be reduced to a minimum.

"4. Given the above conditions, the bankers will be ready to consent to a large gold loan to Germany to be exclusively devoted to the rehabilitation of the German mark."

Premier Poincaré replied, refusing the first condition; accepting the second, and reserving decision on the third and fourth.

Morgan thereupon declared that it was useless to proceed, the conference broke up and he went home.

This was a direct attempt to reëstablish the gold standard in Europe, the United States becoming a party thereto and furnishing the gold for this purpose, with the approval of the President of the United States and the Secretary of the Treasury.

International bankers, with the endorsement of the British Government and the President and Secretary of State of the United States, were in control, and the ending of this conference by Morgan only meant that international bankers would wait until the debtors would eventually accept their terms.

The present move of international bankers for an economic council of experts to adjust German reparations and stabilize the mark, is an international subterfuge to entangle the United States financially with the bankrupt countries of Europe, to reëstablish the gold basis banking and currency scheme. The people of the United States should resist this at any cost, as it will inevitably rivet the chains of debt slavery upon ninety per cent. of our people.

This dinner at the White House was more than a meeting of bankers representing the money trust of the United States, the question to be decided was an international question of vital world-wide importance, not only affecting the sovereign control of the people of the United States over their money system, but committing them to the reëstablishment and perpetuation of the false gold standard money system of Europe, which has already bankrupted the people of Europe with debts.

International bankers were conspiring to permanently destroy the control of the people of the different countries of the world over their money systems, and thus consummate their fixed purpose to establish a world money power to govern the people of the world.

This sinister purpose of international bankers has been hidden from the people under the propaganda for a League of Nations and a World Judicial Court, their plan being to make the false gold standard of money an international question, thus taking it out of the control of the people by having it judicially determined by a World Judicial Court, organized and dominated by international bankers, whose record since the introduction of this dishonest currency principle based on gold, and the establishment of the fraudulent "gold standard" banking and currency system in Europe and its incorporation in the charters of the so-called national banks of the United States, down to the enactment into law by Congress of the fraudulent gold basis Federal Reserve Act, show that its creators and promoters were international banking and currency financial crooks of consummate ingenuity, and in their avarice and greed for wealth, and the power that goes with it, used this false gold standard of value as a pretext upon which to mortgage individuals, communities, colonies and states by the use of a fictitious money of account, based upon debts of borrowers, and represented only by credit and debit figures upon the books of banks.

The President of the United States is being asked to violate his oath of office to support the Constitution and enter into a financial conspiracy to wreck this Republic. When you attack the sovereign control of the people's Government over their money system, you violate the Constitution and attack the very vitals of our Government.

The international bankers are making a desperate effort to have gold considered and made an international question—as money of the world—to be decided by a World Court, thus taking it out of politics and beyond the control of the people of the different countries of the world.

"No Such Thing as a Money of the World"

Money is only money within the jurisdiction of the Sovereign power of the Government that creates it, and can enforce its acceptance in payment.

The value of the money of a country is in the agreement of the people to accept it in *payment for their property, services, and debts,* as decreed by the Sovereign act of their own Government. This puts the *value* in money.

QUESTIONS AND ANSWERS EXPLAINING THE FRAUDULENT GOLD BASIS BANKING AND CURRENCY SCHEME

The following direct questions and answers will clarify this financial mystery and expose the fraudulent gold basis reserve Banking and Currency scheme to the people of the world, through which they have been robbed of their earnings and property.

I will put an international banker, familiar with the operation of this gold basis debt manufacturing financial scheme, upon the witness stand.

Q. How did this debt manufacturing financial scheme originate?

A. Gold and silver were originally deposited with goldsmiths and its ownership transferred from one owner to another by written orders on the goldsmith. Most of the gold or silver remained always in the safe or strong box of the goldsmith. The receipt for same, given by the goldsmith, was the medium through which it was transferred in exchange to new owners. Banks, realizing how little gold or silver was taken out of the keeping of the goldsmith, invented the checking system of credit and debit figures on their books, as a good scheme to avoid having or paying out money having actual existence in making loans to borrowers.

Q. How was this currency scheme established?

A. By first making gold and silver the basis of the currency, then narrowing the basis to gold by demonetizing silver to increase the loaning of ''bank credit'' as a substitute, and more easily control the basis of the currency.

Q. What is the currency principle introduced by Sir Robert Peel at the suggestion of Mr. Jones Lloyd, a practical banker, into the money system of England?

A. It made gold the basis of the redemption of this currency. It killed the legal tender function of real money and converted it into currency redeemable in gold. In other words, converted money into debts redeemable in gold, and established an asset currency based on the debts of borrowers, backed by the impossible and fraudulent promise of its redemption in gold.

Q. What is the advantage to the banks of this gold basis, upon which the banking and currency system has been established?

A. It enables the banks to put gold in their "Reserves" and loan as much as ten times the amount in "bank credits," to create debts upon borrowers; and as banks live and prosper on debts it enables them to make tremendous profits, and by exchanging "bank credits," false money, for debts, acquire the property of people without giving them anything of equivalent value. In other words, as soon as the borrower is given a credit entry on the books of a bank, the debt of the borrower becomes the property and an asset of the bank.

Q. How does this differ from money loaned by an individual in exchange for the debt of a borrower?

A. The individual must have and own the money and give it to the borrower in exchange for the debt. And as an honest worker and producer he has given something of real value in exchange for the money. Furthermore, he who earns money by honest labor puts something of value in the storehouse of the world for what he takes out of it. In the case of the farmer or laborer it represents so much of his life and energy, and it has taken years of toil and endeavor to accumulate the money.

Q. But the bankers will say: We loaned the borrower the bank's capital, and the borrower can check on this bank and pay his debts with "bank credit," just the same as if it were real money.

A. That looks very plausible, but let us examine this statement. If a man borrows "bank credit" from a bank to pay a debt, he does not actually pay the debt, he only transfers the debt from the party to whom he owed it for value received, to the bank for something of no relative value, that is, money of account, represented only by debit and credit figures upon the books of the bank; but the borrower must eventually pay this bank credit in money or property.

Q. Yet the banks say these debts of the borrowers are liabilities of the banks?

A. I will answer this false statement by asking you two questions. First, who has to pay this debt and the interest on same to the banks? The borrowers, of course. Then it is a liability of the borrowers, is it not? Second, how can an individual or bank earn interest on their liabilities? The statement that debts of borrowers are liabilities of the banks is thus shown to be a banking deception and a fraud upon its face.

Q. Are not the 30,000 banks in the United States drawing interest on all the money they have put in the banking business?

A. Yes.

Q. Do the banks owe each other anything?

A. Yes, we have borrowed from each other $2,783,312,-258.

Q. Then when you make a loan to us, what do you lend us?

A. We lend you "bank credit," or "money of account" that you can draw your check against.

Q. What is this "bank credit" or "money of account" based upon?

A. Your obligation to pay the debt back in money.

Q. In other words, it is based upon my property or services?

A. Yes.

Q. Then it simply means I am furnishing you the means to lend me a substitute for money that does not exist, upon which you charge me interest and I have to pay back in actual money or my property is taken.

A. Yes.

Q. Do you know that money can only be created by a sovereign act of the Government representing all the people, and that this sovereign power has been delegated to the Government by the people to be exercised only in their interest?

A. Yes, money can only be created by the sovereign power of the Government.

Q. How can you then justify your scheme in thus violating the Constitution of the United States in putting debts upon the people by loaning them fictitious or false money? Do you not know that the Constitution of the United States prohibits even a *sovereign state from creating money or issuing bills of credit?*

A. We cannot justify it and can only say, the Congress of the United States has granted us the privilege and we use it to make all we can out of the people, and this act of Congress protects us in doing it.

Q. It is a known fact that an organized "Money Power," controlling and operating this gigantic scheme, absolutely controls the money and credit of the United States and dictates to the one hundred million people of this country how much or how little money and credit they shall have to carry on their business. Do you not know this to be a fact?

A. Yes.

Q. It has been ascertained that the interest and dividend earning debts, created upon the resources and people of the United States, amount to about one hundred and forty billion dollars. I would like to ask you how these debts were mostly created.

A. By the loaning of "bank credits" or "money of account" as a substitute for the lawful money of the United States, *but having no actual existence and represented only by credit and debit figures on the books of the banks.*

Q. It has been ascertained that the interest and dividends on these debts have practically absorbed all the net earnings of the real producers and laborers of the United States. According to statistics the great wealth of this country is in the hands of a Plutocracy, composed of only about one per cent. of the population; while the real producers and honest laborers who have created this wealth and have it not, are in debt, without homes, in want of the necessities of life and without hope of independence in the future.

Cannot this unequal distribution of property be traced to the creation of debts with a bank created substitute for money that has no existence and through the gathering of interest and dividends on these debts have absorbed the earnings of the people, and by foreclosure of mortgages, trusts, etc., taken from them their property?

A. It can be accounted for in no other way.

Q. After calling your attention to the following: Irwin Fisher, professor of Political Economy at Yale University, after teaching and advocating the economic absurdity that 25.8 grains of gold fixed the value of other things now makes the following admission:

"In fact, I am very strongly of the opinion, based on considerable study, that the present high cost of living is largely ascribed to this check inflation which is going on all over the world. They are increasing daily all over the world. I believe the rise in price is about half due to that alone."

This being admitted, how is this inflation by "bank credits" limited?

A. Only by the amount of debts created against borrowers that the banks can discount, and rediscount at the Federal Reserve banks.

Q. Then you must admit that the issuing and loaning by the Government of its lawful money, for a valuable consideration direct to the people on security satisfactory to the Government as provided in the sections of a bill, p. 330, would cause less inflation of the currency and prices than the present reserve scheme of banks creating billions of dollars of interest earning debts upon the people by loaning them "bank credits," a false and fictitious money?

A. I do not think there is any doubt about that.

Q. Do you admit that under the operation of the gold standard banking and currency system over 90 per cent. of the debts put upon the people of the world have been created by banking corporations loaning "bank credits," false and fictitious money?

A. Yes, this is no doubt true.

Q. As the use of bank credits necessitates the creation of more debts upon the people, and is now used to carry on over 90 per cent. of the business of this country, and the interest and dividend bearing debts amount to more than $140,000,000,000 in the United States, how long do you think this process can go on without causing the repudiation of debts?

A. We cannot see how it can go on much longer as we

realize that the interest and dividend earning power of these debts are absorbing all the profits of labor.

Q. Do you not also realize that the European War left not less than $250,000,000,000 of debts upon the people of Europe; this being the situation, why do not bankers stop pyramiding debts upon the people by the loaning of this false and fictitious money called "bank credits"?

A. They would like to do so, but as over 90 per cent. of the business of this country is now carried on by the use of bank credits, the business of the whole country would break down if we stopped creating debts by the loaning of bank credits; and our gold basis banking and currency system would go down in ruin, followed by great loss to the capitalistic debt holding class.

Q. The Federal Reserve Act also gives banks the privilege of impounding the lawful money into their "Reserves" and loaning as much as ten times the amount in "bank credits," does it not?

A. Yes.

Q. Does it also give the member banks of the Federal Reserve System the privilege of rediscounting the debts of borrowers and having the proceeds of their notes credited to the "Reserve" of the bank, the same as gold, and loan as much as ten times the amount in "bank credits"?

A. Yes. To illustrate its operation we will consider a debt created upon a borrower by a member bank loaning him $10,000 of bank credit, and taking his note for same. The bank endorses this note and then rediscounts it at a Federal Reserve Bank and has the amount $10,000 placed to its "Reserve" account. Upon this reserve, so created, the member bank can loan as much as $100,000 of "bank credit," which at 6 per cent. would earn 60 per cent. on the original debt of $10,000.

Q. Have not many sovereign states passed laws limiting the rate of interest to 6 per cent. to protect the people from usury?

A. Yes.

Q. Have not the banks been paying from 10 per cent. to 200 per cent. upon their capital stock, representing the money invested?

A. Yes.

Q. Have not the banks increased their "surplus," accumulated from interest, etc., charged the people, hundreds of millions of dollars annually?

A. That is so.

Q. Is not this wholesale usury of the most ruinous character?

A. Yes.

Q. Is it not infinitely more injurious to all the people for banks to create over 90 per cent. of the debts held against borrowers, running into billions of dollars annually, by loaning "bank credits," with the fact staring them in the face that the accumulation of these debts is now driving the people into bankruptcy?

A. I admit this is the situation.

Q. What advantage has Congress given banking corporations, organized for private gain, over the individual in the use of its lawful money of the United States?

A. Congress has given a lawful dollar of the United States ten times the earning power in the reserve of the banks that it would have when loaned by the individual.

Q. Is it not necessary for the banks to have this reserve to meet the demands for money at any time by its depositors?

A. No, for two reasons. First, the banks never have in their reserves but a small per cent. of money, with which to meet their outstanding demands; and secondly, in case of a run on the bank in the Federal Reserve System, the bank can rediscount notes of its borrowers and get Federal Reserve notes to meet the run.

Q. Who established gold as the basis of the money system?

A. International Bankers, in order to control the basis of the money system, upon which to loan "bank credits" as a substitute for money.

Q. Does not this gold basis bank reserve system give those in control of the gold reserve of banks the power to say how much or how little money or credit the people shall have?

A. Yes; that was demonstrated in the position taken by the Advisory Council and the Federal Reserve Board in the answer given by Gov. W. P. G. Harding to the appeal for relief from "Deflation," by the farmers. He said he could do nothing to relieve the agricultural interests by granting them any more loans, as he had to protect the "gold reserve" of the banks, as required by the Federal Reserve Act, as the "gold reserve" had gotten down to 40 per cent.

Q. Do you admit that this power to say how much or how little money or credit the people shall have, carries with it the power to fix prices by "inflation" or "deflation" of money and bank credits?

A. There is no doubt about that.

Q. Does this not result in the fact that those who control the gold reserves in the banks, control the business, the value of property of the people, and the value of debts?

A. I see no escape from this conclusion.

As International Bankers originated this fraudulent and dishonest gold basis bank reserve financial scheme, questions and answers bearing on its international effect upon the people of other countries, should carefully be considered; and as an international banker I would like you to answer the following questions.

Q. Do not the foregoing questions in regard to gold apply with equal force to every country where the gold basis, or so-called "Gold Standard," banking and currency system operates?

A. Yes.

Q. What is the advantage of the gold basis, or so-called "Gold Standard," banking and currency system to international bankers and dealers in debts of the different countries of the world?

A. It gives them the control of the money systems of these countries, with the power to fix the value of their products, and the debts they hold against the people of these countries.

Q. In other words, by manipulating the gold basis can they put up or down the value of the property of the people of any country, and the value of the debts held against the people of that country?

A. Yes.

Q. I would like you to illustrate the process.

A. The Bank of England, situated at the crossroads of

the trade of Europe, was the clearing house whereby the use of bills of exchange, matching of drafts and checks, the use of real money was reduced to the minimum, as it is now done by clearing houses in the United States.

Q. What was the result of this operation on the people?

A. It enabled the banks to exploit the people of other countries, by creating debts upon them with a bank created and bank controlled false and fictitious money, represented only on the books of banks, and by collecting in payment of these debts, the agricultural products and raw material, have absorbed the property and earnings of the people of these countries. This system of financial robbery is the underlying cause of the World War, and wars will continue until this dishonest financial system is destroyed.

Q. Does the establishment of this gold basis bank reserve system in Europe, as in the United States, give international bankers the control of the money systems of the different countries of the world?

A. Yes.

Q. How is this done?

A. By coöperating, the international bankers can withdraw gold from the reserves of the banks of any country, restricting credit, calling loans, thus causing a fall in prices in that country, and a business depression, bringing about untold losses to the people. The process can be reversed by shipping the gold back to the country from which it was taken.

Q. Does not the control of this gold basis absolutely destroy the power of Congress to regulate the value of money in the United States?

A. Yes.

Q. Does not this destroy the power of the government to protect the people of the United States from financial ruin?

A. Yes.

Q. How do international bankers and dealers in gold and foreign exchange bring about this withdrawal of gold from the United States.

A. For every dollar of gold in the reserve of the banks, they have loaned as much as ten times the amount in bank credits, for which they hold debts of borrowers; and for every dollar of gold withdrawn from the reserves of banks, ten times the amount in loans will have to be called in to protect the gold reserve of the banks. If Europe withdraws $50,000,000 in gold from the United States, $500,-000,000 will have to be paid by borrowers into the banks, and if large amounts are withdrawn it will result in contraction of money and credits, and a fall in prices followed by business depression in the United States.

Q. Is there any such thing as a gold standard of value?

A. No; the standard or value, that is purchasing power of money, is regulated by the amount of money used as a circulating medium of exchange in the monetary system of the country issuing it.

Q. Do you admit there is no intrinsic value in gold?

A. I do; all value is relative, the value of the dollar is not in the gold, but in what the dollar will buy.

Q. How can a standard of value for money—its purchasing power—be established?

A. Only in one way: by ascertaining its purchasing power.

Q. How can this be done?

A. By index numbers showing the average price level of the necessities of life, and regulating the amount of money in the monetary system accordingly.

Q. Suppose the Government had exercised its sovereign power and issued into our money system, for value received, an adequate amount of lawful money as a medium of exchange, to sustain the average price level of the necessities of life in the United States, and labor had received its just reward, what would have been the result?

A. It would have established a debt paying money system in place of the present debt manufacturing scheme. As the profits made by the workers would have enabled them to build homes, would have reduced the cost of living and not more than ten per cent. of the present debts would exist to burden this and coming generations.

Q. What proportion of debts are created by the loaning of bank credit or money of account?

A. The records of banking will show that not less than 90 per cent. of the debts are so created.

Q. I notice from government statistics the national

wealth of the United States has increased billions of dollars annually, yet it is harder for the people to meet their living expenses and they are more heavily in debt than ever before.

A. Investigation will show that it has been mortgaged with about one hundred and forty billions of paper tokens created by the banks and calling for interest and dividends which have to be paid by the people.

Q. Would it not have been impossible to have developed the resources of our country, built its railroads, etc., without the use of bank credit?

A. No, with an adequate amount of lawful money in actual circulation as the medium of exchange, it could have been done without leaving a burden of unpayable debts upon our people, the interest and dividends upon which are now absorbing the net earnings of labor, and if continued, can only end in bankruptcy of the people.

Q. Why is it that notwithstanding the tremendous development of the great natural resources of this country by the labor of our people, debts have steadily increased upon the people until the burden has become unbearable?

A. It has been brought about by the false principle in our banking and currency system, which enables banking corporations to create debts upon the people by loaning false and fictitious money.

Q. Explain this more fully.

A. It should be borne in mind that every debt created by the loaning of bank credits is a new demand for money that does not exist, and the banks by keeping lawful money scarce, or out of circulation, will increase the demand for its only substitute, "bank credits," the inevitable result being an ever increasing amount of debts upon the resources and people of a country.

Q. The more the people get out of debt the less demand there will be for money or credit, will there not?

A. Yes; for the reason that debts have now become so numerous that the greatest demand for money is to pay debts.

Q. What are frozen credits?

A. Inability of borrowers to pay in money the debts created by the banks in loaning them this false and fictitious money, having no existence, and represented only by credit and debit figures on the books of banks.

Q. What causes business depressions?

A. Banking corporations creating debts by loaning bank credits, non-existent money, and demanding of borrowers payment of these debts in money. And if the payment cannot be made in money the property of the borrowers is taken.

All these answers should be tested by the following provision of the Constitution of the United States, which declares, "The Congress shall have power to coin money, and regulate the value thereof." Confirmed by the following decision of the Supreme Court of the United States, U. S. S. Court, Vol. 110, pg. 447: "Congress is *exclusively authorized to establish a national currency* either in coin or in paper and to make the currency a lawful money for all purposes as regards the national Government or private individuals." U. S. S. Court 12 Wallace: "*Whatever power there is over the currency is vested in Congress.*"

It should be clearly borne in mind that no other power can create money and make it a legal tender for debts, and any acts passed by Congress authorizing banking corporations to directly or indirectly create money, or any substitute for money, is in vital violation of the Constitution of the United States.

It should be realized that a bill put through Congress and signed by the President cannot legalize the robbery of the people under the Constitution of the United States, it matters not how long it has been in operation. No statute of limitation runs against a fraud committed against the Government and people of the United States.

I call attention to the definition of the gold standard of value of what is known as the famous Bank Charter Act of England: In 1844 Sir Robert Peel, the author of the Peel Act, clearly explained what was meant by the "gold standard" of value, as follows: "Now the whole foundation of the proposal I am about to make rests upon the *assumption that according to practice, according to law, according to ancient monetary policy of this country,* that which is implied by the word 'pound' is a certain definite quantity of gold with a mark upon it to determine its weight and fineness, and the engagement to pay a 'pound' *means nothing, and can mean nothing else than the promise to pay the holder,* when he demands that definite quantity of gold. That is the meaning of the 'pound' according to the ancient monetary policy of this country.''

Now apply this ''gold standard'' of payment to the people of the United States; there is not less than $75,-000,000,000 of debts in the United States specifically payable in gold, and the gold in the reserves of the banks to protect the gold basis, or so-called ''gold-standard,'' is not available to the people with which to pay these debts. The free gold owned by the Government amounts to less than $20,000,000 (1923). Will you tell me how the people can pay these debts in gold, or protect this so-called gold standard of value in the United States?

A. We see no way in which it could be done.

Q. It has been ascertained that the World War has left a debt of $250,000,000,000 upon the people of Europe, and there is little or no gold in Europe available to pay these debts. This being the situation how do you bankers justify this attempt to reëstablish the ''gold standard'' in Europe, which has already wrecked the people with debts, and caused untold suffering, poverty and crime?

A. We must admit it is unjustifiable.

Q. Do you consider that those who established the gold basis for our banking and currency system made a mistake?

A. It is worse than a mistake. I consider it a gigantic financial fraud that has bankrupted the people of the world.

Q. Who do you think has been most guilty in perpetrating this fraud upon the people of the world?

A. The International Bankers who conceived this dishonest debt creating scheme based on gold, whereby debts could be created upon the people without loaning money, and thus by indirection rob the people of their earnings.

Study the works operating a watch, and say whether the result is an accident. Apply the same reasoning to the operation of this banking and currency scheme, based on gold, and say from the result achieved whether it was conceived and operated in the interest of the people or the debt owning class.

Q. What should the people now do to right this wrong?

A. Notify their Representatives in Congress that if they do not destroy the power of international bankers and substitute an honest money system in place of the dishonest gold basis banking and currency scheme, they will be branded as traitors to the best interest of the people, retired to private life, and no longer be qualified to hold a public office in the United States.

Q. Are you in favor of a full legal tender money, issued and controlled in quantity by the Sovereign Power of the Government, based upon the imperishable wealth of the United States and redeemable in all the assets and the services of all the people; or are you in favor of the use of ''bank credits,'' a false substitute for money, used and controlled by banking corporations, organized for private gain?

Let each answer this question for himself.

THE REMEDY

In organizing human society, individuals gave up their power to impose upon each other for the general protection of all. Laws were then enacted to protect the weak against the strong, for the manifest reason that the strong need no protection.

This being the justification of the very existence of a government, the first duty and responsibility of a Representative in Congress is to protect the people against exploitation by any class or corporation.

The creating of interest and dividend earning debts upon the natural resources and people of the world by the loaning of "bank credits," has given a favored class the means of absorbing the wealth of the country without paying for it in anything of real value. This creating of debts by the loaning of a fictitious money has aggregated the wealth of this country in a few hands in direct violation of the Constitution, the laws of common honesty, and the great moral law of the commandment: "Thou shalt not steal."

This debt-manufacturing financial scheme has brought about the present unequal distribution of wealth, and engendered in the hearts of the people a feeling of injustice, discontent, and resentment against their fellow men, expressing itself in strikes and industrial revolutions which will eventuate in civil wars unless this system of debt-slavery is abolished.

With the farmers going into bankruptcy, millions out of employment, and the destruction of billions of dollars in the value of the property of the people, does any one desire greater demonstration of the ugly fact that the prosperity of banks, built upon the fraudulent gold basis Federal Reserve Act, means the ruin of the people.

On the night of November first, 1923, I heard the farewell address of Lloyd George, delivered in the Metropolitan Opera House, New York. He stated his admiration for the boundless resources of the United States, illustrating his feeling by the exclamation of the poor farmer from the interior when he first beheld the ocean: ''Thank God there is plenty of something.'' He made a strong appeal to the people to help Europe and save civilization.

In this long speech, showing ability and versatility, he suggested no practical way in which the United States could help Europe. Although he had been Chancellor of the Exchequer and had been urged to take over the Bank of England to finance the war, and thus avoid bankrupting the people with debts, he failed to do so.

Although the war left a debt of $250,000,000,000, and the people and civilization of Europe are now sinking under the burden of debts, Lloyd George studiously avoided mentioning the word DEBTS in his entire speech.

No real peace followed the World War; an armistice was declared, but the war over debts, dishonestly created, still goes on.

The present situation in Europe is the result of the false currency principle legalized by the governments of Europe, allowing banks to create debts upon the people of the world by the loaning of a fictitious and dishonest substitute for money. Every one of these governments, including that of the United States, has been dominated by an international money power, and the people, or democracy, have in no way been responsible for the failure of these governments and the bankruptcy of the people.

Out of the failure of European Governments, and from every home and hamlet in the United States comes the despairing questions: What is the matter with the world? What is the matter with civilization? What is the matter with the United States, the greatest Republic on earth?

The answer comes back from the four corners of the earth, in unmistakable tones: The world is sick unto death with debts.

The remedy advocated by international bankers is to have the United States coöperate by sending a sufficient amount of gold to reëstablish the false gold standard currency system of Europe.

The same international banking power that was back of the World War, the Treaty of Versailles, and the World

Court is still in control of Governments. This world Money Power has won by capturing the leaders of the people; it is now time to make a direct attack on the international bankers and their fraudulent gold standard currency system.

It is true that the international bankers created the false gold basis Federal Reserve scheme, but the Representatives of the people in Congress are responsible for its enactment into law and for its continuance. It has been to the everlasting disgrace of the American Congress that the money system of the United States has been left for nearly sixty years in the control of banking corporations, organized for private gain.

The duty of our Government is to save the people of the United States from bankruptcy by the establishment of an honest money system, and let the governments of Europe follow our example. Civilization can be saved and a new birth of freedom will come to the people of a suffering and debt-ridden world.

The remedy for the diseased condition of our money system is found in the Constitution itself: Equal rights to all, special privileges to none. Take from banking corporations the monstrous privilege of issuing "bank credits," and let the Government give equal rights to all by issuing a full legal tender money, as a medium of exchange, with which to carry on the business of all the people.

The Constitution is a written agreement between the people and their government and it stipulates "the Congress shall create and regulate the value of money."

The United States Supreme Court has decided that: Congress is exclusively authorized to establish a national currency (not an international currency) either in coin or in paper, and make the currency a lawful money for all purposes as regards the National Government or private individuals. And: "Whatever power there is over the currency is vested in Congress."

Therefore, it is the absolute duty of every Representative in Congress to right this great economic wrong that has been done the people.

A representative in Congress was asked what answer

could he give his constituents to justify his having voted for the Federal Reserve Act. He replied: I will tell them that the Democratic party on the way down to Jericho fell among thieves. No more truthful and honest answer can be given. But any Senator or Representative who now defends or fails to repudiate this fraudulent gold basis Federal Reserve Act, under the provisions of which a National Debt of $25,000,000,000 was unjustifiably put upon the tax-payers of this country, and $8,000,000,000 in the value of the farm products of the people was destroyed by "Deflation," should be retired by the voters and placed in legislative history of Congress as one of "the many crafty and insidious animals called politicians," who receive pay from the people while giving aid and comfort to their financial enemies, who have wrecked this Republic.

Heretofore, the people have always lost out before an organized banking power that knew exactly what they wanted and went after it. To achieve real results the people must unite on A MONEY BILL, insist on that bill and see that it is passed without having been doctored in the Committees of Congress. For this purpose a bill has been drawn up, economically sound, which will give equal benefits to all classes, and lift the burden of debts and taxation from the suffering people of the world. This bill, S. 134 (printed at the end of this book), has been introduced by Senator Ladd of North Dakota. It is now the duty, and will be for the greatest benefit of the people, to do all they can to have this bill enacted into law.

What can you do?

Write your Senators and Representatives and insist that they help and vote for this bill.

Mr. Voter, remember you do not owe your Congressman anything. He owes you for the job he holds. He is your legislative agent. See that he carries out your wishes, not those of Plutocracy.

This bill S. 134: Provides that the Government shall exercise its sovereign function, as provided in the Constitution, and issue and loan, into actual circulation, for value received, an adequate volume of legal tender money, as a medium of exchange, with which to do the business of this country and develop its boundless resources.

This bill provides that as the value of the dollar is not in the dollar itself, but in what the dollar will buy, the quantity of dollars shall be regulated by the average price level of the necessities of life in the United States.

This bill provides for a loan bureau in Washington and other necessary machinery for making loans; for the issuing by the Secretary of the Treasury of legal tender currency in sufficient quantity to meet the demands of legitimate business; for short or long time loans or personal endorsement, warehouse receipts, certain stocks and bonds, and real estate in country and town, and for a maximum rate of interest not to exceed four per cent. per annum.

Under this bill the Government will receive full value for every dollar issued into the currency system of the United States, and receive the interest on loans made direct to the people instead of transferring this right, as under the present system of banking corporations, and allowing them to create false money—"bank credits"—and loan it to the people as money, thus taking the profit from the Government to whom it belongs.

The expenses, or overhead charges alone on this present banking system, would more than pay the legitimate expenses of running the Government, thus reducing the taxes upon the people.

It does away with the pernicious bank reserve system and keeps the money in circulation in the communities where it belongs.

It should be clearly borne in mind that there is far less risk to the Government in making loans, as provided in this Money Bill, which establishes a debt-paying system of real money, than under the present debt making system of loaning "bank credits."

This bill will establish property as the thing of value, money as the medium of exchange, make man the master above the dollar, and free the people from financial bondage.

PLUTOCRACY MUST BE DESTROYED

As exposed, no honest man will defend this false money scheme, to rob the people of their earnings; and no self-respecting man, who loves his country and believes in democracy, will submit to it. Ninety per cent. of the voters are in debt and financial bondage under this infamous scheme, and are heart weary longing for some sign of relief from debt slavery, and will vote accordingly at the first opportunity.

The Farm and Labor organizations alone by uniting the votes of their members can win this great economic victory in the interest of the people.

The American Federation of Labor has endorsed the following:

"We favor a system of finance whereby money shall be issued exclusively by the Government, with such regulations and restrictions as will protect it from manipulation by the banking interests for their own private gain."

The National Farmers' Union of America have stated:

THEREFORE, BE IT RESOLVED, By the Committee appointed by the National Farmers' Union of America to draw up a money bill in accordance with the Constitution of the United States; and believing the time has come to proclaim a new declaration of "Financial Freedom" for the people, they do now embody these principles in the following "Money Bill," to establish an honest money system where the medium of exchange will give equal benefits to every American citizen, and wherein the credit of the Government shall be used for the benefit of all the people instead of banking corporations organized for private gain.

But the people should now realize that they who would be free "themselves must strike the blow." This is a direct individual responsibility, every voter in the United States should now assume it and so inform his Representative in Congress.

How can the Representatives of the people right this wrong?

By enacting into law an honest constitutional money bill containing the following provisions:

SIXTY-EIGHTH CONGRESS, FIRST SESSION

S. 134

IN THE SENATE OF THE UNITED STATES

DECEMBER 6, 1923

Mr. Ladd introduced the following bill, which was read twice and referred to the Committee on Banking and Currency.

A BILL

To establish an honest money system where the medium of exchange will give equal benefits to every American citizen and wherein the lawful money of the Government shall be used for the benefit of all the people instead of banking corporations for private gain; to reduce the rate of interest of loans, encourage agriculture, the ownership of homes, and for other purposes.

Be it enacted by the Senate and House of Representatives of the United States of America in Congress assembled, That the Government now exercise its sovereign function and perform its sovereign duty to issue or loan into circulation for value received an adequate volume of lawful money with which to do the business of this country and develop the great resources in the interest of all the people. That there is hereby established in the United States Treasury a bureau to be known as the Loan Bureau, and a branch of said bureau shall be established in every postal savings bank in the United States and the District of Columbia, and the rate of interest shall be uniform and shall not exceed 4 per centum per annum on all loans meeting the requirements of the Government.

SEC. 2. BUREAU; HOW CONDUCTED.—That said Loan Bureau shall be in charge of a commissioner to be appointed by the President of the United States, by and with the consent of the Senate.

SEC. 3. SALARY OF COMMISSIONER.—Said commissioner shall receive a salary of $12,000 a year and hold office for a term of eight years, and shall be eligible to reappointment. During his term of office he shall not be interested, directly or indirectly, in any banking corporation. He may be removed from office during such term for cause, but only after a public hearing on charges duly made, of which he shall have reasonable notice, and then only upon a finding in writing by the President of the United States.

SEC. 4. OTHER EMPLOYEES.—There shall be in said Loan Bureau an assistant commissioner, a chief examiner, chief clerk, and such other clerks, agents, and employees as Congress may provide from time to time. The said commissioner shall appoint said assistant commissioner, chief examiner, and chief clerk. All other employees of the bureau or its branches shall be subject to the provisions of the civil service laws.

SEC. 5. In the absence or disability of the commissioner, the assistant commissioner shall perform the duties of the said commissioner.

SEC. 6. BOARD OF SUPERVISION.—Said commissioner, together with the Secretary of the Treasury, the Comptroller of the Currency, the Secretary of Agriculture, and the Secretary of Labor, shall constitute the board of supervision of the Loan Bureau. The said commissioner shall be ex officio chairman of the board of supervision. Within thirty days after the approval of this Act by the President of the United States the members of said board shall meet in the city of Washington, District of Columbia, and prepare and promulgate proper rules and regulations for the government of said Loan Bureau and for the making of the loans as herein provided for.

SEC. 7. LEGAL TENDER; HOW ISSUED.—The Secretary of the United States Treasury shall issue on the terms and for the purposes herein mentioned full legal tender notes from time to time to meet the business requirements of the country. As the value of the dollar is not in the dollar but what the dollar will buy the volume of money as issued by the Secretary of the Treasury shall be regulated by the average price level of the necessities of life in the United States as shown by registered and recorded index numbers attested by the signatures of the members of the Board of Supervisors of the Loan Bureau and regularly reported to the Congress of the United States and given to the public press.

All notes as herein provided for shall be a legal tender and payable for all debts, public and private, and shall be a first lien upon all the assets and services of the people of the United States for their redemption.

SEC. 8. RETURN LOANS; HOW HELD.—Upon payment to the Government of any loan the amount of money so received shall be held in the Bureau of Loans in the United States Treasury, and shall be either canceled or used in making new loans to meet the business requirements of the country as herein provided for. Preference shall first be given those sections of the United States where the rates of interest are the highest.

SEC. 9. No banking or other corporation or association of men or individuals shall be allowed to issue any kind of money or currency, or loan any bank credit substitute for money.

SEC. 10. EARNINGS; HOW USED.—The earnings of the Government Loan Bureau from all sources, after paying the conservative and legitimate expenses of the Loan Bureau and its branches, shall be applied to the payment of the general expenses of the Government, thus reducing the taxation upon the people of the United States.

SEC. 11. CORPORATION LOANS RESTRICTED.—The Loan Bureau and its branches shall be restricted in loans to corporations on collateral as follows: Approved State, county, and municipal bonds, approved first mortgage, railroad, telegraph, and telephone bonds upon which interest has been regularly paid out of its earnings for a period of not less than five years, and a sworn statement showing the physical valuation of the property upon which these are issued shall be filed with the Loan Bureau. A margin of not less than 50 per centum shall be required on all such securities upon which the Government is authorized to loan.

SEC. 12. PERSONAL CREDIT.—The Loan Bureau and its branches shall discount for individuals notes and bills of exchange arising out of agricultural, industrial, and commercial transactions, having three signatures, those of the drawer, drawee, and indorser: *Provided,* That in place of one of these signatures there may be deposited as security stocks and bonds upon which interest or dividends have been paid consecutively for a period of not less than five years and a statement of the physical valuation of the property upon which they are issued has been filed with the Government Loan Bureau. This shall apply to all notes and bills of exchange issued or drawn for commercial, agricultural, or industrial purposes, and under no circumstances for carrying stocks or bonds or other securities for speculative investment. Warehouse receipts meeting the requirements of the Loan Bureau shall be eligible to discount.

PARAGRAPH 1. FARM LOANS.—The term "farmer" for the purpose of this Act shall be construed as meaning any person engaged in the business of tilling the soil and raising farm products, or that shall hereafter engage in the said business. The bureau shall make loans to farmers on farm lands located in any of the States of the Union or in the District of Columbia, under rules and regulations made by the board of supervision as hereinbefore provided. Said loans shall be made payable to the bureau and shall bear interest at the rate of not more than 4 per centum, payable annually. It shall be the policy of the board in making loans to discourage speculation in lands, and the assessed valuation of the property to be taken as a factor in determining the amount of the loan.

SUBPAR. 1. AMORTIZATION PREMIUMS.—The terms of every loan extending for more than five years shall contain a provision for its amortization or reduction by annual payments of 1 per centum on account of the principal. The terms of every loan shall provide that at any interest date the borrower shall have the right to pay the entire loan or to make payment of $50 or any multiple thereof on the principal thereof, and upon such payment being made the interest on the amount so paid shall thereon cease.

SUBPAR. 2. LOAN TIME LIMIT.—No loan shall be made for more than thirty-five years.

SUBPAR. 3. APPLICATION FOR LOANS.—No person shall be entitled to a loan until he has made application therefor under oath upon blanks to be furnished by the Loan Bureau. Such application can be sworn to before any person authorized to administer an oath, and all postmasters and their deputies in the United States are hereby authorized to administer oaths to applicants making application for loans under this Act, and to administer oaths to such applicants or other persons in connection with the preparation of other affidavits made necessary by the rules and regulations of the board of supervision. Whenever any oath is administered by a postmaster or deputy postmaster no charge shall be made therefor.

Subpar. 4. To whom loans shall be made.—No loan shall be made to any person who is not an actual resident on the land and engaged in the cultivation of land offered as security: *Provided,* That where the applicant for the loan is endeavoring to secure money for the purpose of building a house upon the land, or for the purpose of making part payment upon the purchase thereof, the bureau may waive the stipulation if convinced that it is the intention of the applicant to reside upon the land as soon as possible and to cultivate the same.

Subpar. 5. Amount of loans limited.—No loans shall be made for more than 60 per centum of the value of the land offered as security and 40 per centum of the value of the improvements attached to the land. Whenever the improvements are a part of the security for any loan, such buildings or destructible property shall be insured by the borrower to the satisfaction of the bureau.

Subpar. 6. Tenant farmers' loans.—If a tenant farmer desires to purchase a farm for a home and said farmer is found to be reliable and of good character, the Loan Bureau, or its branches, are authorized to loan said farmer 75 per centum of the value of said farm.

Subpar. 7. Town tenants.—The provisions contained in this section shall apply to farm or town tenant desiring to purchase a homestead.

Subpar. 8. Total loan on single mortgage.—Loan shall not be made upon a single mortgage for more than $20,000, and no loan shall be made for less than $200, and loans upon single mortgages for less than $10,000 shall receive preference.

Subpar. 9. Confidential reports; how made.—That it shall be the duty of every postmaster, deputy postmaster, or other employee or official of the United States Government, without fee or pay therefor, to make confidential reports to said bureau upon anything pertaining to any loan and upon the character or standing of any applicant or witness whenever such information is requested by the Commissioner of the Farm Loan Bureau through the head of the department in which the employee is engaged.

SUBPAR. 10. REPORTS; HOW MADE.—That the Commissioner of the Bureau of Loans shall receive applications for loans, supervise collections, keep a correct registry of all securities, and by his direction all disbursements from the funds of the bureau necessary to carry out this Act shall be made. He shall keep correct account of the loans, sales, investments, receipts, expenditures, profit, and loss, and make a report of this and other work of the bureau to Congress at the end of the fiscal year.

SEC. 13. BOARD OF LOANS.—That the commissioner, chief examiner, and the Treasurer of the United States shall constitute the board of loans of said bureau, and all applications for loans shall be submitted to said board for such action as it may see fit to take.

PARAGRAPH 1. LEGAL PROCEDURE.—The commissioner of the bureau by himself, or his agent duly appointed for such purpose, for and on behalf of the Government of the United States, is hereby authorized and empowered to appear in any United States court, or State, Territory, or district court in the United States in any legal procedure on any question arising from the making or collecting of loans, sales, or purchases made under the provisions of this Act.

SUBPAR. 1. POSTAL SAVINGS AND LOAN BUREAU CORPORATION.—That the trustees of the Postal Savings System are hereby authorized and directed to coöperate with the Commissioner of the Loan Bureau in order that the money deposited in the postal savings bank of the United States may be used for loans as herein provided.

SUBPAR. 2. POSTAL SAVINGS ENCOURAGED.—In order that the deposits in the postal savings bank may be increased all limitations upon the amounts that such bank may receive on deposit are hereby removed.

SUBPAR. 3. TRANSFER OF SAVINGS FUNDS.—The deposits in the various postal savings banks shall be turned into the United States Treasury and placed in the loan fund, and the Commissioner of the Bureau of Loans is hereby authorized to draw warrants, which shall be countersigned by the Commissioner of the Loan Bureau, against the said loan fund, and the same shall be signed by the Treasurer of the United States. The treasurer of said bureau shall keep account of such moneys in the manner prescribed by the bureau, and all accounts of the bureau shall be audited by the Auditor for the Department of Agriculture in the Department of the Treasury.

SEC. 14. UNITED STATES DISTRICT ATTORNEYS; DUTIES.— That it shall be the duty of every United States district attorney or deputy district attorney, upon request from said Loan Bureau, to examine the abstract of title to any land offered as security under this Act, and to make return thereof to the said bureau. It shall likewise be the duty of any district attorney or deputy district attorney, when requested by the said bureau, to foreclose any mortgage taken as security for a loan under this Act and to prosecute the same to final judgment. All such services so rendered by an attorney connected with the Department of Justice shall be rendered without pay, but said bureau shall pay in all cases the actual expenses of any such attorney in connection with such litigation.

SEC. 15. INTEREST AND PRINCIPAL; HOW PAID.—That in making any payment of interest or principal or part payment of either principal or interest upon any loan made under this Act, the person making such payment may pay the same to any postmaster designated by said Commissioner of the Loan Bureau, and such postmaster shall immediately notify the bureau of such payment and the transmission of the money so paid, and thereupon credit shall be given for the payment of such money as of the date the same was paid to the postmaster. The said bureau shall notify each person to whom a loan has been made as to the post office where the payment upon said loan may be made. The bureau may make such designation by general circular or by specific notice in writing, and may designate by such notice a post office within a county or other district to which all payments within such district may be made. Loans may be made upon approved city real estate at the same rate of interest as farm loans, but for not more than 50 per centum of its value.

PARAGRAPH 1. POWER TO SUE AND BE SUED.—That the bureau shall have the power to sue and to be sued, to complain and defend in any court of law or equity having jurisdiction of the subject matter of litigation. To protect any loan it may pay the taxes or pay any other prior lien due and unpaid against the land securing said loan, and in such case the amount paid in liquidation of such taxes or lien shall be added to and become a part of its mortgage on said real estate, and from the date of such payment shall bear interest at the rate of 6 per centum per annum.

It shall have the right and authority to purchase at sale under judgment or decrees of court rendered in foreclosure proceedings of any mortgage it owns on the lands so mortgaged, but in such case it shall not bid a greater amount for such land at such sale than the amount due in such proceedings, together with costs and expenses expended in relation to said loan. In case the bureau obtains title as set forth in this section to any real estate, it shall have authority to sell the same at such price as may be for the best interests of said bureau in the judgment of the commissioner, and to convey title to the purchaser thereof by deed signed and acknowledged by the commission.

SUBPARAGRAPH 1. In making such sale it shall be authorized to accept a return mortgage from the purchaser for part of the purchase price thereof in accordance with the provisions of this Act.

SUBPAR. 2. LAWFUL MONEY.—Any discrimination in favor of gold against the lawful money of the United States, or any combination in restraint of the free and unobstructed circulation of the lawful money of the United States shall be a criminal conspiracy against the Government and punished by imprisonment for not less than ten years, and for its further protection as a circulating medium of exchange and a debt-paying money available to the people, it shall not be used as bank reserves upon which to loan "bank credits" and without a special Act of Congress the amount of money in actual circulation shall not exceed $75 per capita in the United States.

SEC. 16. APPROPRIATION.—That there is hereby appro-

REAL MONEY VERSUS FALSE MONEY

priated from any unexpended balance in the Treasury of the United States the sum of $200,000 for the purpose of carrying out the provisions of this Act and organization.

SEC. 17. That all Acts and parts of acts inconsistent herewith are hereby repealed.

www.ingramcontent.com/pod-product-compliance
Lightning Source LLC
Chambersburg PA
CBHW011301210326
41599CB00035B/7083